THE
SOCIOLOGICAL
METHOD

THE SOCIOLOGICAL METHOD

SECOND EDITION

STEPHEN COLE
State University of New York
at Stony Brook

Rand McNally College Publishing Company / Chicago

76 77 78   10 9 8 7 6 5 4 3 2 1

For Paul F. Lazarsfeld and Robert K. Merton

Preface

This book is the product of ten years of experimentation with the teaching of introductory sociology and research methods. In the course of these years I have come to believe that introductory courses in sociology should have two main goals: to teach the students what is distinctive about the sociological interpretation of human behavior and to teach them the methods sociologists use to determine whether their ideas are right or wrong. For this reason, an introduction to sociology would not be complete without an introduction to research methods.

The approach employed in this text differs from that used in most methods texts. This book is *not* aimed at teaching the student how to do research. I believe that this can only be learned by actually doing research under the supervision of an experienced researcher. Rather, the purpose of this book is to give the students a conceptual understanding of the logic of doing research and of the types of problems researchers encounter when they interpret their data.

Thus, although reading this book will not enable students to be able to do research on their own, they will be better equipped to read and understand research reports.

In order to conceptually explain complex topics (for example, linear regression analysis) to beginning students, I have avoided the use of mathematical formulas, complex terminology, and precise statistical definitions and, instead, have focused on methodological procedures in terms of their underlying logic. Unfortunately, to gain pedagogical clarity it is sometimes necessary to give up statistical precision.

In writing this book I owe a large intellectual debt to my teachers in graduate school, Robert K. Merton and Paul F. Lazarsfeld. Merton taught me how to apply the sociological perspective to a wide range of empirical problems. Paul Lazarsfeld taught me the logic of data analysis and, more importantly, that doing quantitative analysis could be fun. In recent years I have learned a good deal of methodology from my colleagues Hanan C. Selvin, Judith M. Tanur, and Eugene A. Weinstein. Judith Tanur advised me on the section on sampling and Chapter 4. Eugene Weinstein is a coauthor of the section on analysis of variance. Gerald D. Suttles offered many useful suggestions for the chapter on qualitative methods. Ann H. Cole and Lorraine Dietrich criticized an earlier draft. Appreciation is also due the many users of the first edition who offered me suggestions that have been very useful in preparing this edition. Any inadequacies that remain are, of course, my responsibility.

I would also like to thank John Applegath for suggesting that the first edition of this book be written; Lorraine Wolf for an extremely competent editorial job; and Larry Malley for his support of this project.

Stephen Cole
Old Field, New York
December 1975

Contents

Preface   vii

1. **The Sociological Perspective**   1

The Sociological Study of Suicide   **2**

The Sociological Study of Happiness   **10**

The Sociological Study of Fear   **13**

The Great Man and Blunder Theories of History   **15**

Great Men and Women, and the Growth of Culture   **20**

Sociology of Illness   **23**

The Sociological Perspective and Research Methods   **27**

2. **The Logic of Proof**   29

Descriptive Research   **29**

Explanatory Research   **31**

Use of Tables in Explanatory Analysis **35**

Arranging Data in Tables **35**

Using Tables to Test Hypotheses **42**

Causal Analysis **46**

Three Conditions of Causality **47**

Elaborating Two-Variable
Relationships **51**

Interpretation and Explanation **52**

Specification **66**

Review of Elaboration **69**

Exercises **71**

3. **Quantitative Methods: Types of
Data 77**

Surveys **77**

Sampling **78**

Measurement **84**

Indexes **91**

Indirect Indicators **94**

Problems in Measuring Variables **96**

Precollected Data **99**

Experiments **106**

Summary **117**

Exercises **118**

4. **Quantitative Methods: Types of
Analysis 121**

Tabular Analysis **121**

Contextual Analysis **121**

Studies of Social Change   **129**

Trend Studies   **130**

Panel Analysis   **133**

Linear Regression Analysis   **137**

Path Analysis   **144**

Analysis of Variance   **147**

Summary   **155**

Exercises   **157**

5.   **Qualitative Research**   **160**

Purposes of Using Qualitative
Research   **163**

Description   **163**

Formulation of Hypotheses   **164**

Understanding Causal Processes   **165**

Types of Qualitative Research   **166**

Participant Observation of Urban
Communities   **166**

Street Corner Society   **166**

The Urban Villagers   **176**

The Social Order of the Slum   **180**

Managed Integration   **185**

Tally's Corner   **189**

In-Depth Interviewing   **193**

The Unionization of Teachers   **195**

Crucible of Identity: The Negro
Lower-Class Family   **200**

The Poor Pay More **207**

Community Studies **210**

Qualitative Experiments **216**

6. **The Role of the Sociologist and the Uses of Sociology** **220**

The Role of the Sociologist **221**

Value-Free Sociology? **221**

Sociologist as Technician or Reformer? **222**

The Uses of Sociology **225**

Descriptive Research To Determine Facts **227**

Explanatory Research To Discover Causes **227**

Consumer Practices of Low-Income People **228**

Compensatory Education Programs **234**

Black Family Structure **245**

Summary **254**

THE
SOCIOLOGICAL
METHOD

Chapter 1 The Sociological Perspective

Many people believe that sociology and the other social "sciences" are unnecessary. Sociological explanations of human behavior are considered merely complex ways of saying what any observant and sensitive person would know anyway. Sociologists are accused of using jargon to disguise these commonsense explanations. Charges like these are never made against natural scientists, such as physicists and biologists. Why is sociology more often condemned as being trivial than biology, for example? This could lead to a discussion of whether sociology and its sister social sciences are in fact sciences. Such a discussion is generally semantic and boils down to what is meant by *science*, a subject best left to philosophers of science. In any case, whether sociology is or is not a science probably has very little to do with the low regard in which the subject is held by some people.

The reason why sociology is often said to be unnecessary probably has to do with the nature of the phenomena that sociologists study. Obviously, the natural sciences are more developed and have been more successful in understanding phenomena in their realm than have the social sciences. The structure of matter such as atoms and genes is invisible to the naked eye, and most of us feel that great expertise and wisdom are needed to understand them. But human behavior, far from being invisible, is something we all engage in and observe every day. Many people feel they do not need psychologists and sociologists to tell them why they behave as they do, because the reasons for human behavior are obvious. What such skeptics fail to realize, however, is that many aspects of human behavior are invisible to the untrained eye. Understanding sociology makes the invisible visible and thereby enhances our comprehension of our own behavior. Sociology is particularly difficult for us to understand because we live in a society in which people tend to explain behavior in individualistic ways. We see people as influenced by the particular circumstances of their lives rather than by their membership in social groups and in a society.

If this book is about research methods, why do we need a chapter on the sociological perspective? In order to understand sociological research, you must have some idea of how sociologists decide what topics to do research on. There are literally an unlimited number of problems concerning human behavior. Yet sociologists study only some of these problems and study them in a distinctive way. Sociological theory, which in its most general sense is called the "sociological perspective" or the "sociological orientation," serves as a guide for what to study and how to study it. It is, of course, impossible to give a thorough introduction to this topic in one chapter. We will concentrate on the differences between the sociological and individualistic explanations of human behavior. We believe that these differences point out what is most distinctive about the sociological perspective. Suicide is a good example of a type of human behavior that is thought to be exclusively the result of an individual's life circumstances and state of mind. How would a sociologist study suicide?

THE SOCIOLOGICAL STUDY OF SUICIDE Suppose one of your friends were to call you this evening to tell you that one of your mutual friends committed suicide. You would probably be shocked and upset. Later, however, you might wonder why your friend committed suicide. In fact, why would anybody commit suicide? At this point you can conduct a small experiment. Put aside this book and jot down on a piece of paper some of the reasons why you think people commit suicide. Then, after you read this section, look at your list and see if you have a different view of suicide. When nonsociologically trained persons think of the reasons why people commit suicide, they usually point out circumstances that create intense unhappiness or personal dissatisfaction with life. A woman commits suicide when she learns her child has leukemia. A man commits suicide when his business goes bankrupt. A girl commits suicide when she flunks out of college and her boyfriend breaks off with her at the same time. Personal tragedy is seen as creating a state of despondency and unhappiness. Such emotional states undoubtedly play a significant role in generating suicidal impulses. However, state-of-mind explanations fail to explain some interesting facts about suicide.

If we examine suicide rates (the number of suicides per 100,000 people in a particular category), we find that not all people are equally apt to commit suicide. For example, men are much more likely to commit suicide than women, Protestants more likely than Catholics, single men more likely than married men, people with a substantial amount of education more likely than people with little education, and soldiers more likely than civilians. Why? Do you suppose that men are less happy than women or highly educated people less happy than those with less education or Protestants less happy than Catholics? This is quite unlikely. In fact in this chapter we will cite a study which shows that there is no difference in the happiness of men and women and that people with a substantial amount of education are, on the average, actually happier than those with little education. We must conclude that differences in rates of suicide among various groups probably cannot be explained by different degrees of unhappiness in each group. The reason why Protestants are more likely to commit suicide than Catholics must have something to do with the *social* meaning of being a Catholic or a Protestant.

In a book entitled *Suicide* the French sociologist Emile Durkheim tried to explain the differences in rates of suicide among various groups.[1] Durkheim's theory of why people commit suicide is a prime example of the sociological perspective at work. In order to demonstrate the value of the sociological perspective, Durkheim wanted to prove that rates of suicide in social groups could not be explained by individual unhappiness. He found that people were more likely to commit suicide during periods of economic depression. This seemed to supply evidence in support of the unhappiness explanation. If people suffer economically, they will be unhappy and, therefore, more likely to commit suicide. Durkheim also noticed, however, that suicide rates went up during periods of great economic prosperity. How could the unhappiness theory explain this? Or how could the unhappiness theory explain the fact that middle-class people are more likely to commit suicide than lower-class people? We will present data below that show middle-class people actually consider themselves to be happier than lower-class people.

After studying much data on suicide, Durkheim concluded that there are really several types of suicide. The first two types, *egoistic* suicide and *altruistic* suicide, depend on the extent to which the individual is integrated into meaningful and cohesive social groups. The individual who is not integrated into meaningful groups will not have any goals and will not receive support in times of stress. The person who commits suicide because his or her self-perception is that of an isolated individual is called the "egoistic suicide." On the other hand, it is possible to be overly integrated into groups. When the group becomes all important, individual life becomes less important. An individual who commits suicide because his or her self-perception is that of an insignificant individual is what Durkheim called the "altruistic suicide." Too much or too little social integration creates conditions conducive to suicide.

At this point, let us be more explicit about how sociological theory determined the types of data Durkheim looked for in his research. Durkheim had the theory that over or under integration into social groups influenced the suicide rate. Therefore, he needed suicide statistics for groups that had a very high or a very low level of solidarity or cohesion. As you can see, a social theory is really nothing more than an informed hypothesis about the causes of

---

[1] Emile Durkheim, *Suicide* (1897; reprint ed., Glencoe, Ill.: The Free Press, 1951).

social phenomena. This hypothesis serves as a guide to the kinds of data we should look for.

Let us first look closely at the reasoning and data Durkheim used to develop his theory of altruistic suicide. In one type of altruistic suicide, the individual is required by rules or norms of the group to commit suicide. For example, in some Indian castes a widow was expected to burn herself to death on her husband's funeral pyre. The women were not forced to commit suicide; they wanted to and would have been anguished if prevented from doing so. They believed that this was the proper behavior for persons in their position. Similarly, during World War II, Japanese pilots who flew on kamikaze missions considered it an honor to commit suicide for the glory of their country. (Durkheim, writing in 1897, of course, did not use these Japanese pilots as an example.) For the Indian widows and the Japanese kamikaze, then, membership in a group led them to commit suicide. But in both these cases, suicide was in a sense obligatory; it was required by the norms of the group. The individuals involved were so committed to the group that they were willing to give up their lives in order to live up to group expectations.

Durkheim's theory suggested he look for a situation in which commitment to a group was excessively strong but suicide was not obligatory. If the theory were correct, Durkheim would find a high suicide rate for people in such a situation. One example can be found in the military, an organization in which the importance of the individual is downgraded and the importance of the collectivity stressed. In every European country, Durkheim found the suicide rate among the armed forces higher than among the civilian population. This fact, in and of itself, is not conclusive proof of the theory of altruistic suicide because it also could be used to support the unhappiness theory. Certainly men in the armed forces suffer many more hardships than civilians and thus might be considered to be less happy than civilians. However, if military life leads to suicide because of hardship, we would expect enlisted men to be more likely to commit suicide than officers. Certainly officers suffer less hardship in the army than enlisted men. It turns out, however, that the suicide rate among officers is *higher* than it is among enlisted men. This finding contradicts the unhappiness theory and supports the altruistic-suicide theory, for officers are generally more committed to the army than are enlisted men. Similarly, Durkheim found that the longer a man had been in the army, the more likely he was to commit suicide; volunteers were more likely than draftees; and men who reenlisted were more likely than men who enlisted for the first time. In every case, those who were more attached to the army were more apt to commit suicide.

Durkheim's general point is that when you belong to a group in which the importance of the group and the insignificance of the individual is stressed, the significance of life declines. Individuals who belong to such groups will not value their own lives as strongly as those who belong to less cohesive groups and will commit suicide because of provocations that would not motivate others to commit suicide. It is difficult for us to comprehend why a soldier in combat would throw himself on a grenade to protect his buddies. How many of us would do such a thing? Yet if you had lived for a while in a tight group in which loyalty to the group was an important value, you may better understand the willingness of individuals to sacrifice their lives to protect the group. Altruistic suicide, then, occurs as a result of belonging to groups in which the group is all important and the value of the individual is not emphasized.

Egoistic suicide is the opposite of altruistic suicide. When individuals do not belong to any cohesive groups, they do not receive group support during difficult periods. Also, most of the goals we have and the things we value are attained through our memberships in groups—whether the group is a family, an occupational group, an academic group, or a religious group. The less integrated an individual is into such groups, the less significance life will have and the more often life will seem meaningless.

If Durkheim's theory is correct, we would expect that married people would be less likely to commit suicide than single people. And this is indeed true. Furthermore, married people with children are less likely to commit suicide than those who are childless. Children tend to provide meaning in life for their parents, especially in their parents' later years.

Durkheim was also able to use this theory of egoistic suicide to explain the different rates of suicide among people of various religions. Both western religions that Durkheim analyzed have explicit taboos against suicide; therefore, differences in suicide rates between these religious groups must be explained by the way in which membership influences life. In Protestantism, great emphasis is placed on the self-reliance of the individual. The individual is supposed to have a direct relationship to God. In Catholicism, on the other hand, the church mediates the relationship between the individual and God. The rituals of the Catholic religion make it a more supportive, socially cohesive group. Catholics believe that if they sin, their guilt can be expiated through adherence to the rituals of the church. Protestants who sin cannot depend on the church for redemption. Also, the Catholic church offers the individual far more support in times of crisis than does the Protestant church, and it is for this reason that Catholics are less likely than Protestants to commit suicide.

Would you guess that Jews have a high or low suicide rate? They have a low suicide rate. This is largely because they have long been a persecuted minority and have been forced to band together in a tightly knit group. Durkheim was able to back up this interpretation by showing that Protestants were less likely to commit suicide when they were in a minority, as in France, than when they were in a majority, as in Germany. When Protestants were in a minority they were forced to stick together, and this cohesion countered the Protestant emphasis on the individual. The data on suicide rates for various religious groups lend support to Durkheim's theory of egoistic suicide.

One other major type of suicide that Durkheim discusses is *anomic* suicide. According to Durkheim, individuals are most satisfied with their lives when their day-to-day behavior is oriented toward a set of meaningful goals and is regulated by a set of rules or norms. When goals lose their meaning, the individual becomes disoriented, life seems aimless, and the probability of suicide increases. Feelings of aimlessness increase when there are no norms that tell us what we should do and how we should behave. A rapid change in society or in an individual's social position can destroy goals and norms and create a condition of *anomie* (normlessness). Durkheim posited that rapid change either in the society as a whole or in an individual's social situation would create anomie and increase the probability of committing suicide. The theory of anomic suicide can explain the increase in suicide during periods of economic instability—whether it is boom or bust. It is easy for us to comprehend why a person may commit suicide after losing a fortune, because this fits in with our commonsense view of the world. But it may be difficult for us to understand why a person may commit suicide after making a fortune. Consider, however, the following hypothetical case:

Jim Peters, the son of an immigrant, grew up in a New York City slum. To escape poverty, he worked very hard as a foreman in a small factory and earned $15,000 a year. His goal was to earn $20,000. He believed that if he could do this, his family would be able to have a comfortable life. Then he met an elderly man who owned a factory similar to the one in which Jim worked. The man was looking for someone to become his partner and run the factory. Within three years Jim was earning $100,000 a year. To his great surprise, he found that he was not happy. At first, having all that money was great; Jim moved his family into a lavish home in the suburbs, bought his wife expensive jewelry, and traded his Chevrolet for a Cadillac. But after this he didn't really know what to do with his money. He seemed to be losing interest in his job and was sorry he had never gone to college so that he might have been able to do something more "interesting." Work just did not seem to make any sense. Jim's wife began to see a psychiatrist and discovered that she really was dissatisfied with their marriage. Both Jim and his wife felt out of place in their new community—people seemed to look down on them. Jim figured it really must be true that money did not necessarily bring contentment.

What happened to this man? A sudden change in his life circumstances destroyed the meaning of all the goals that had guided him in his everyday life. When he was earning $15,000 a year, it seemed important to him to work hard to get raises. But when he earned $100,000 a year, money seemed to lose its meaning. All his life he had wanted to drive a big car, but when he suddenly had one he found it really was not all that much better than his old car. In other words, all his old goals rapidly lost their meaning. He became disoriented and was unable to develop meaningful goals. He suffers from anomie.

Durkheim's theory of anomic suicide explains increases in suicide rates in societies that experience rapid change. It also explains increases in suicide rates for groups of individuals who suddenly find themselves in changed social circumstances. An example would be divorced and widowed people, who, it is found, commit suicide more than either married or single people. Marriage puts limits on sexual aspirations and regulates wide areas of behavior. A married person has only one *legitimate* sex partner; for an unmarried person there are many people who can be legitimate sex partners. Marriage increases responsibilities and thus guides and limits behavior. For example, married people are expected to come home to dinner after work; unmarried people can do whatever they want to do. When marriage is ended, the field of legitimate sex partners becomes unlimited and responsibilities decrease; a regulated form of life is suddenly replaced by one with many more possibilities. This normlessness is conducive to suicide.

Durkheim was able to elaborate his analysis of the effect of marital status on suicide in a very interesting way. He found that the difference between the suicide rates of single and married people varied from country to country. In some countries there was a great difference between the two rates, and in others the difference was relatively small. Why did marriage serve to "protect" people from suicide more in some countries than in others? He found that the explanation lay in the type of divorce laws existing in the country. In those countries in which it was easy to obtain a divorce, the difference between the suicide rates of married and single people was less than in those countries in which divorce was difficult or impossible to obtain. In countries like Italy, in which divorce was impossible, marriage seemed to offer the most protection against suicide. From these data, Durkheim concluded that the possibility of easy attainment of divorce served to destroy the regulating nature of marriage. When it is easy to obtain a divorce, married people always have the idea in the back of their minds that the marriage could be dissolved. If divorce is difficult or impossible to obtain, married people are forced to accept the restrictions of marriage and must try to work out their marital problems. The more regulating marriage is, the more it protects against suicide. As you can see, Durkheim's study led him to believe that societies offering too much individual freedom were not beneficial for humanity.

Does Durkheim's theory mean that individual unhappiness has nothing to do with suicide? Of course not. Obviously, almost by definition, people who commit suicide are intensely unhappy. The sociological and individualistic perspectives are not mutually exclusive views of human behavior; they are complementary. The sociologist can tell us what social conditions raise or lower the probability of committing suicide. Thus, the sociologist could tell us that a Catholic is less likely to commit suicide than a Protestant. But the sociologist could not tell you exactly which Protestants will commit suicide. Here the psychologists, with their study of the individual's personality and unique situation, are useful. Sociologists do not attempt to explain unique individual behavior; rather they want to explain the behavior of groups of people and how the behavior of the individual is influenced by membership in social groups.

The unhappiness theory of suicide could be called a "state-of-mind explanation." It explains behavior in terms of the thoughts or sentiments of individuals. Sociologists do not deny that such sentiments play a significant role in motivating people. The sociological perspective, however, tells us to look beyond sentiments for the causes of human behavior. Thus, we will want to know how location in a particular type of society or part of society influences the development of specific sentiments. To further illustrate how sociologists view states of mind, we will discuss studies in which sociologists analyze emotional states, such as happiness and fear.

THE SOCIOLOGICAL STUDY OF HAPPINESS In criticizing the unhappiness theory of suicide, Durkheim made many assumptions about which groups were likely to be more happy than others. When Durkheim said that middle-class people were happier than lower-class people, he meant that the former group faced easier life conditions. Durkheim believed that happiness is a subjective state of mind. What influences this state of mind is a question that philosophers have debated for centuries. How would a sociologist go about studying happiness?

If you want to find out what social conditions are associated with happiness, you must be able to determine which individuals are happy and which are not. Since happiness is a state of mind, we have to ask people if they feel happy. Two sociologists, Norman Bradburn and David Caplovitz, conducted a study in which they asked people: "Taking all things together, how would you say things are these days—would you say you are very happy, pretty happy, or not too happy?"[2] They then examined how people with different social characteristics responded to this question.

Earlier in this chapter we said that women had lower suicide rates than men. Is this because women are happier than men? The Bradburn-Caplovitz study provides us with evidence that this is not so. Twenty-five percent of the men and 23 percent of the women said they were very happy. Basically, there is no difference in the self-perceived happiness of men and women.

Of all the social categories studied, income had the greatest influence on happiness. Whereas 38 percent of those people who earned $10,000 or more a year said they were very happy, only 14 percent of those who earned $3,000 or less said they were very happy.[3] These data suggest that although money may not necessarily make people happy, a minimum subsistence is necessary for people to consider themselves happy.

The more education people have the more likely they are to consider themselves very happy. Twenty-nine percent of those who were college graduates and 19 percent of those with only an elementary school education said they were very happy. Does education make people happy? Again, this is a question philosophers have debated for a long time. Is the professor happier than the parking-lot attendant? Does greater awareness of the world make people more or less content? The Bradburn-Caplovitz data might suggest that it does. Further analysis, however, revealed that people with higher education were happier than those with less education because the former group earned more money. The happiness of people with higher education was not so much a result of the education itself but of what the education brought with it. Likewise, the fact that older people were less happy than younger people seems to be a result of the fact that younger people had more

[2]Norman M. Bradburn and David Caplovitz, *Reports on Happiness* (Chicago: Aldine, 1965).

[3]In considering these sums of money, keep in mind that the study was conducted in 1962, when people in general earned less money. The important point to remember is not the absolute amount of money people earned but the relative amount.

money. Although 30 percent of people under thirty years of age and 18 percent of people seventy and over said that they were very happy, young people were no more likely to be happy than old people when both groups had incomes of $5,000 or more a year.

Are married people happier than single people? The Bradburn-Caplovitz study shows that they are. The data on marital status and happiness also cause us to question the commonly held view that marriage is more important for women than for men. Eleven percent of married women and 15 percent of single women say that they are not too happy. Thus, for women, marriage brings only a slight increase in happiness. But for men, we get a more considerable difference. Fourteen percent of married men and fully 31 percent of single men say that they are not too happy. Being married seems to be a much more important ingredient in the happiness of men than women. Data such as these illustrate how sociological research can show commonly held views to be mistaken. They are also suggestive of many interesting ideas about what it means to be a man or a woman in our society.

Why should marriage make a greater difference in the self-perceived happiness of men than in that of women? The Bradburn-Caplovitz data do not provide us with an answer. One possible explanation, however, could be that men are expected to suppress their emotions at work and thus come to depend heavily on their marriage for an emotional outlet. This and other hypotheses suggested by the finding require further research.

There is one final question we can ask of the Bradburn-Caplovitz data. Which is more important in making a man happy—his job or his marriage? The questionnaire included items that measured both marital satisfaction and job satisfaction. The men who were most likely to be happy were those who were highly satisfied with both their jobs and their marriages. Seventy-two percent of these men said they were very happy. Of the two conditions, a man's job turned out to be more important an influence on his happiness than his marriage. Of men who liked their jobs but were dissatisfied with their marriages, 48 percent said they were very happy; of men who did not like their jobs but were satisfied with their marriages, only 8 percent said they were very happy.

The Bradburn-Caplovitz study is instructive for two reasons.

First, it shows us how sociologists study states of mind. They are interested in how social attributes, such as education, income, age, sex, marital status, and job, influence a state of mind. Notice that the sociologists did not look to personality disturbances or neuroses as correlates of happiness. These may be important but they are not the specific concern of the sociologist. Second, the happiness study is a good example of how a relatively simple sociological study can cast light on philosophical questions that people have speculated on for years.

THE SOCIOLOGICAL STUDY OF FEAR The second example of how sociologists treat psychological states will be taken from a study of a teachers' strike in New York City.[4] We are concerned with the influence of fear on whether or not teachers supported the strike. There had been very few teachers' strikes when the strike took place in 1962, and many of the teachers who thought that the strike was justified were afraid to picket. They thought they would either be fired or the principal would make things difficult for them after the strike was over. Why were some teachers afraid while others were not? Sociologists would not seek to explain differences in fear by the presence of neurotic personality traits or by past idiosyncratic life experiences. Rather the sociological perspective calls for an understanding of how a particular location in society will create a sentiment, such as fear.

It turned out that elementary school teachers were more likely to be afraid to strike than secondary school teachers. We know that elementary school teachers are predominantly women. Perhaps women, being "naturally more timid," were more likely to be afraid. This would be a nonsociological explanation, since it would explain fear by a supposedly "natural" inclination rather than by location in the society. In fact, the data showed that women were slightly *less* likely to be afraid than men. Whereas most women were married to men who worked, most men were either the primary or sole supporters of their families. Thus, for most men the consequences of being fired were more serious than they were for most women.

---

[4]Stephen Cole, *The Unionization of Teachers: A Case Study of the UFT* (New York: Praeger, 1969).

Another interesting finding was that women working in elementary schools were much more likely to be afraid than women working in secondary schools. If teachers with the same individual characteristics behave differently in different types of schools, this is a clue that their behavior can be explained by the structure of the schools. In elementary schools, there is a much more direct relationship between school authorities and the teacher than in secondary schools. The elementary schools are relatively small, and contact between the principal and teachers is frequent. In high schools, it is easier to remain anonymous. If an elementary school teacher went out on strike, her behavior would have been clearly visible to the principal. Also, in elementary schools, the teacher's immediate supervisor is usually the principal, whereas in the high schools the teacher's immediate supervisor is a department chairperson. The chairpersons served as mediators between the principal and the teachers. Some of these chairpersons were members of the union and actively supported the strike. The president of the union was the chairperson of a social studies department. Thus, we concluded that the threat of reprisal was closer and more menacing in the elementary schools than it was in the secondary schools. Fear could be traced to the authority structure of the schools in which the teachers were working.

Another reason why elementary school teachers were more likely to be afraid to strike than secondary school teachers had to do with the sheer amount of social support for the strike in the two types of schools. Probably every teacher was afraid to some extent. But since the general level of support for the strike was greater in the high schools, it was easier for the high school teachers to overcome their fear. It is much easier to overcome fear if you are one among many; if you are alone, it is difficult.

In conclusion, then, we have traced a psychic state, fear, to social location and to the type of interaction experienced by the individual in different social locations. Throughout the analysis, we were interested in how social conditions were likely to give rise to individual emotions. Fear was a determinant of whether or not teachers supported the strike. But sociologists seeking an explanation of a phenomenon do not stop with a sentiment, a psychological state. They go further and try to specify what social conditions influence the development of a particular psychological state.

social structure————→state of mind————→behavior

THE GREAT MAN AND BLUNDER THEORIES OF HISTORY Thus far, we have been considering the sociological determinants of the behavior or states of mind of individuals. We have shown how suicide and subjective feelings of happiness and fear are influenced by the social location of individuals. But sociology does not, of course, deal exclusively with the behavior and attitudes of individuals. Sociologists also attempt to explain what happens to groups and whole societies. A sociologist may do a study of the social factors influencing the development of social movements, like the civil rights movement or the women's liberation movement; a historical sociologist may be interested in understanding why revolutions occur. Just as those of us who have not studied sociology tend to interpret individual behavior in terms of psychological factors, we also tend to view social movements and historical development as being the result of the work of great men and women. Indeed some well-known historians employ "great men" explanations of history. Social movements succeed or fail because of the genius or stupidity of individuals. There are two types of such explanations: the great man theory and the blunder theory.

Great men and women, whether good or bad, influence social change. Thus, it will be maintained that the civil rights movement began because of the charisma and leadership abilities of a handful of men, one of which would be Martin Luther King, Jr.; Fidel Castro almost single-handedly brought about the Cuban Revolution; Franklin D. Roosevelt saved the country from the Great Depression; and the insanity of Adolf Hitler caused World War II.

The blunder theory holds that social movements occur because of the blundering of key individuals. Thus, it is held that the American Civil War took place because President Buchanan stupidly refused to accept the principle of popular sovereignty; student demonstrations on college campuses in the late sixties took place because the university administrators acted unwisely; and the

French Revolution of 1789 would never have taken place if Louis XVI had had a slightly higher IQ.

Sociologists do not deny that strong or weak individuals exert a significant influence on historical development. However, the sociological perspective alerts us to the possibility that great men and women may owe at least part of their greatness to conducive social settings and that sometimes social conditions may cause normal people to behave in ways that appear "stupid" in historical retrospect. In other words, historical development is a result of the interaction of social conditions and individuals. It is often difficult for us to see the importance of the social conditions.

A good example may be found in analyzing the influence of the president on American society. In 1976 a presidential election in which many of us will be deeply involved will take place. Some of us will be strong partisans of the Democratic candidate, and others will be equally avid supporters of the Republican candidate. Although we all want our candidate to win, we must ask what difference it makes who is president. Will the society be substantially different if the Democrat or the Republican is elected? It often seems to us that the president has almost unlimited power to do what he wants and to propel the country in the direction that he wishes it to go. When Franklin D. Roosevelt took office in 1933, there were certain expectations of what a president could do and how far the executive branch of government could go in controlling the government. Roosevelt, being a strong and charismatic figure, was able to substantially moderate these expectations. But he was not left unchecked. The structure of the American political system actually prevented Roosevelt from initiating many changes at the time that he wanted to implement them. There is no clearer example of this than FDR's attempt to "pack" the Supreme Court. When the Supreme Court declared some of FDR's New Deal legislation to be unconstitutional, Roosevelt proposed, on February 5, 1937, the enlarging of the Court from nine to fifteen members. His clear intent was to place on the Court judges who would be more sympathetic to his legislative program. Congress refused to do this (although during the debate on the bill a conservative judge retired, which changed the political composition of the Court).

Economists and historians have often pointed out that despite all

Roosevelt's New Deal programs, the country did not really pull out of the depression until the start of World War II changed some basic economic conditions. If we examine the statistics on unemployment presented in Table 1.1, we can see that although by 1939 unemployment rates were lower than at the peak of the depression, they remained quite high until 1941, when we began to prepare for war.

Table 1.1.	Percent of Labor Force Unemployed, 1929-43

Year	Percent unemployed
1929	3.1
1930	8.7
1931	15.8
1932	23.5
1933	24.7
1934	21.6
1935	20.0
1936	16.8
1937	14.2
1938	18.9
1939	17.1
1940	14.5
1941	9.7
1942	4.4
1943	1.7

Even if Roosevelt's program was unable to end the depression, his dynamic presidency did change the range of acceptable presidential behavior. When Roosevelt died, the role of the executive branch of government was considerably wider than when he assumed office. Even presidents who believed the executive branch should not take so active a role could do nothing about it. This was made abundantly clear during the presidency of Dwight D. Eisenhower. Ike was committed ideologically to reducing the role of government—especially of the executive branch—in society. Yet despite his sincere attempt to act in accord with his beliefs, he was unable to reduce the governmental role. And, in fact, the historical trend for the government to intervene in all aspects of the society continued.

This was also true of the presidency of Richard M. Nixon. Despite Nixon's public statements that he was opposed to wage and price controls—a move that would substantially increase the role of the government in the economy—social conditions "forced" Nixon to initiate such a program. The general point is that an individual leader's own goals are limited by the social structure that he or she faces. On the other hand, we should note that strong individuals can influence change in the social structure. Roosevelt succeeded in broadening the role of the president. When Eisenhower became president, he could no longer act as Herbert Hoover had even if he had wanted to.

The political scientist Richard E. Neustadt made this point in his book *Presidential Power*. The president works within a complex administrative structure, and there is not an automatic connection between a decision and action:

> In the early summer of 1952, before the heat of the campaign, President Truman used to contemplate the problems of the General-become-President should Eisenhower win the forthcoming election. "He'll sit here," Truman would remark (tapping his desk for emphasis), "and he'll say 'Do this! Do that!' *and nothing will happen*. Poor Ike—it won't be a bit like the army. He'll find it very frustrating."[5]

In conclusion, let us return to the question with which we began this section. Does it make a difference who the president is? The sociologist's answer is affirmative—it makes some difference but not as much as we may think.

How social conditions limit the behavior of individuals can be further understood by looking at the reaction of authorities to rebellions and social-change movements. When we examine the history of most social-change movements, we see that there is usually some group that has a vested interest in maintaining the status quo or in putting down the social-change movement. Thus, the French king and aristocracy had a stake in stopping the French Revolution of 1789; college administrators, during the sixties, had a

---

[5]Richard E. Neustadt, *Presidential Power* (New York: John Wiley, 1960), p. 9.

stake in preventing student sit-ins; and boards of education have a stake in preventing teacher unions from acquiring too much power. When a social-change movement or rebellion succeeds, it often appears as if the authorities have let it succeed. We can usually look back and say if only they had done this or stopped it at that point, the whole movement would have collapsed. Adherents of the blunder theory of history see social-change movements as succeeding because of the stupidity of authorities. However, the sociological perspective leads us to believe that individual stupidity is rarely the prime cause of social change. There have always been unintelligent people in important positions. The sociologist must specify the conditions that create "stupidity," that make ordinary people commit acts that in retrospect seem to be blunders.

Let us look at one example in detail. On November 7, 1960, the United Federation of Teachers called a strike of New York City public school teachers. At the time, the union had only about 2,500 members and was very weak. Only about one-tenth, or 4,500, of New York's 40,000 teachers supported the strike. This strike lasted one day and resulted in the mayor appointing a three-member committee to look into the demands of the teachers. In retrospect, it is clear that if the board of education was ever to stop the growth in size and power of the union, the 1960 strike was the place to have done it. Union leaders agreed that if the board had severely punished the 4,500 striking teachers, the union might have been stopped cold. Why did the board not take advantage of the power at its disposal? It would be an error to see the board's inaction in terms of individual incompetence, although some board members may not have been the most capable officials. The board failed to act only in part because of the personal shortcomings of its members. More central to its inertia were the prevailing social conditions, a social atmosphere in which it would have been difficult for any board to have taken decisive action.

Perhaps the most important social condition was the political context in which the board operated. The board of education was appointed by the mayor. Mayor Robert F. Wagner was a well-known ally of the labor movement. In fact, Wagner's primary supporters were labor leaders. When the UFT went on strike in 1960, the leaders of organized labor pressured the mayor to be lenient on the fledgling union. Because the mayor was generally prolabor and depended heavily on organized labor for political support, it would have been difficult for a board of education appointed by the mayor to have taken a hard line with the union.

Three other social conditions made it difficult for the board to act. (1) Practically everyone recognized the legitimacy of the union's stated goal: the improvement of the quality of education. The board often stated that they felt the union's demands were justified but that funds were not available to meet them. It is difficult to suppress a movement that has stated goals with which everyone sympathizes. Even the supervisory personnel in the schools—chairpersons, assistant principals, and principals—supported the striking teachers. The sympathy and, in some cases, the active support of the personnel who were in the positions to carry out orders and administer sanctions reduced the effectiveness of those attempts that the board did make to stop the union. (2) A primary reason the board of education was not more effective in preventing the union's growth was that it had inadequate knowledge of the actual attitudes and intentions of the teachers and their leaders. Because channels of communication were so poor between the teachers and the board, the board never actually believed the teachers were serious when they said that they were going out on strike. Therefore, the board was completely unprepared for the strike when it occurred. (3) Finally, the fact that the law called for extreme sanctions, including the firing of the striking teachers, made it difficult to enforce the law. This is what happens when existing laws diverge from the real attitudes of the people.

The board of education may have had some inept members and administrators; it also had some efficient and intelligent ones. These people made "errors" because the social system in which they worked made it difficult for them to act otherwise. Similar analyses could be conducted of all rebellions, which in retrospect seem to succeed because of the poor judgment of authorities.

GREAT MEN AND WOMEN, AND THE GROWTH OF CULTURE

Just as many of us are inclined to think of the course of political history being determined by a few great men and women, we are also apt to think of the growth of culture, the arts and sciences, as the work of a handful of geniuses. For example, the growth of science is often seen as the product of individual geniuses, like Newton, Lavoisier, Darwin, Madame Curie, and Einstein. Although sociologists do not deny the significance of individual genius, they view science and other forms of culture as a social activity influenced by the internal social organization of science and by the society in which the scientists live. The sociologist asks the question: What would science be like today if Newton, Lavoisier, Darwin, Madame Curie, and Einstein had never lived?

We have data that enable us to argue that science probably would not be much different, even if many of the geniuses of the past had not lived. The main source of evidence for this belief is the existence of independent multiple discoveries.[6] Historians have shown that most of the discoveries made by famous scientists were independently made by other scientists. For example, Newton and Leibniz independently discovered calculus; Darwin and Wallace independently discovered the theory of evolution; and Mendel's laws of genetics were independently discovered by *three other* scientists at the beginning of the twentieth century.

The fact that there have been so many multiple discoveries does not seem strange when we recognize that new ideas are not originated in a vacuum. They emerge out of the work of a community of interacting scholars. Thus, if a particular discovery is not made by one person, it is likely to be made by another. This point was well illustrated by the molecular biologist James Watson, who, in his book *The Double Helix*, described how he and Francis Crick discovered the structure of DNA.[7] Watson and Crick were in a race with Linus Pauling to make the discovery. The winner was virtually assured a Nobel prize. Watson made it very clear that if he and Crick had not made the discovery, it would almost certainly have been made by Pauling. Which of two scientists or groups of scientists gets the credit for a particular discovery is frequently a matter of weeks and sometimes days.

How do sociologists explain the fact that science tends to flourish more in some places and times than in others? For example,

---

[6]Robert K. Merton, "Singletons and Multiples in Scientific Discoveries," *Proceedings of the American Philosophical Society* 105 (1961): 471–86.
[7]James Watson, *The Double Helix* (New York: Atheneum, 1968).

during the nineteenth century Germany was the hub of scientific activity. After World War II the United States has been the leading producer of scientific knowledge. Did nineteenth-century Germany have more geniuses than other countries at that time? Are post-World War II Americans smarter than their contemporaries in other countries? Sociologists believe that the level of native talent tends to remain roughly constant from place to place and time to time. What does differ are the social circumstances in which science is practiced and the social organization of science itself.

Robert K. Merton has analyzed the role of Protestantism as a contributing factor to the scientific renaissance in seventeenth-century England.[8] Protestant theology made science a respectable activity. Prior to the rise of Protestantism, many of the people who had scientific ability probably went into other more highly respected fields. Since talented people are likely to engage in activities that are socially valued, science is likely to prosper most in those countries in which it is viewed as a prestigious vocation.

The Israeli sociologists Joseph Ben-David and Awraham Zloczower have shown how the social organization of science itself exerts an influence on the rate of scientific advance.[9] They were interested in explaining why Germany became the center of scientific progress in the middle of the nineteenth century. Using physiology as the subject of their study, they tabulated the nationality of the prominent discoverers listed in histories. After showing that during this period more physiological discoveries were made in Germany than in any other country, they traced the prosperity of German science to the structure of the German university system. In Germany there were about twenty universities competing for prestige. This situation was very unlike that in France, where there was only one important university, or in England, where there were only two. Competition among the twenty universities in Germany facilitated innovation. When one university hired a professor in an emerging discipline, like physiology, the other nineteen would quickly follow suit. Thus, competition among the decentralized universities created

---

[8]Robert K. Merton, "Science, Technology and Society in Seventeenth Century England," *Osiris*, vol. 4, part 2 (1938; reprint ed., New York: Howard Fertig, 1970).
[9]Joseph Ben-David and Awraham Zloczower, "Universities and Academic Systems in Modern Societies," *European Journal of Sociology* 3 (1962): 45–84.

an expanding opportunity structure in new scientific specialties. Bright young science students would enter the fields with the most opportunities. Central to the Ben-David and Zloczower thesis is the hypothesis that in modern societies the prosperity of science depends on the number and type of scientific jobs available, which is in turn dependent on the social organization of science itself.

SOCIOLOGY OF ILLNESS   Illness is generally viewed as a physiologically determined state. A person catches a virus and becomes ill, eats the wrong food and develops a heart condition, or smokes too many cigarettes and gets lung cancer. Sometimes we view illness as resulting from psychological conditions as with nervous disorders. Very rarely, however, are sociological conditions or the individual's location in society viewed as contributing factors to illness. The research I shall discuss in this section is an example of the sociological perspective applied to the study of illness.

When is a person ill? A doctor would answer the question on the basis of a physiological examination. A psychologist might look for the display of neurotic symptoms. The sociologist has a very simple way of classifying individuals as ill. Individuals are ill when they act ill or when they use their poor state of health as a reason for failure to fulfill normal social obligations. Usually we think that individuals become ill for physiological reasons and then they are unable to fulfill normal social obligations. Some recent research suggests that the direction of causality between illness and the inability to fulfill social obligations is not as simple as it first appears.[10] The research suggested that sometimes rather than illness preventing persons from fulfilling social obligations, inability to fulfill such obligations may motivate individuals to define themselves as ill, to act ill, and indeed to become ill.

Normal Causal Order
physiological condition———→illness———→ failure to fulfill obligations

Hypothesized Causal Order
failure to fulfill obligations———→illness

---

[10]Stephen Cole and Robert Lejeune, "Illness and the Legitimation of Failure," *American Sociological Review* 37 (June 1972): 347–56.

This hypothesis should be immediately qualified. We are, of course, not suggesting that inability to fulfill social obligations will cause a person to get cancer or tuberculosis. Rather our hypothesis is concerned with most of the medical conditions that most of us have; that is, with conditions that are much less serious. The hypothesis is based on the fact that there is a great deal of variation in how different people respond to a whole range of nonfatal medical conditions. People with the very same physiological conditions will act quite differently. Some will magnify aches and pains, and others will ignore them. We are therefore interested in the type of social conditions that will influence a person who has a noncritical medical condition to act ill. Many studies have shown that people who define themselves as ill act ill. In the research summarized here the sociologists tried to discover the social conditions that will influence a person to define or think of herself as being ill. The working hypothesis was that those people who have failed to live up to their own expectations, who are self-defined failures, will be the most likely to think of themselves as ill as a means of legitimating their failure to themselves and others.

The first set of data used to test this hypothesis were two surveys of mothers on welfare. In New York City about 2,000 mothers on welfare had been interviewed and in Camden, New Jersey, about 400. Before we can directly examine the illness hypothesis, we must consider the meaning of being on welfare in the United States. Why do some people end up on welfare? There are many different answers that people would give to this question. Some may say that people on welfare have been discriminated against and cannot get decent jobs; others may say that they are lazy and just do not want to work. In general we can divide the answers to this question into two types: social failure and personal failure.

1 Social Failures	2 Personal Failures
discrimination	lazy
unemployment	stupid
poor education systems	immoral

People who would give the answers listed in column 1 tend to see poverty and welfare as resulting from flaws in the society. If society were reorganized, welfare could be eliminated. People who would give the answers listed in column 2 see poverty and welfare as resulting from individual shortcomings. (In general, most Americans have usually seen poverty or economic failure as resulting from personal shortcomings. This is a major reason why there has never been a strong socialist movement in the United States.)

Most important for our study was how the welfare mothers themselves would answer the question. If welfare recipients see their plight as a result of inequities and inadequacies in the organization of society, their discontent and hostility will be directed against the society and they will be strongly motivated to participate in a social-change movement. If, however, the welfare recipients see their plight as a result of personal shortcomings, then any anger or hostility will be directed inward.

The two surveys that were conducted indicated that most welfare mothers viewed welfare as an illegitimate status and accepted the stigma that the general society puts on welfare recipients. For example, 71 percent agreed that "a lot of people getting money from welfare don't deserve it." Eighty-seven percent agreed that "people should be grateful for the money they get from welfare," and 55 percent agreed that "getting money from welfare makes a person feel ashamed." It was concluded that many people on welfare considered themselves to be failures.

How do people who occupy a social position that they themselves define as illegitimate cope with this situation? One way is to believe that the situation is only temporary. Many welfare mothers believed that they would get off welfare in the near future. What about the mothers who more realistically saw that their chances of getting off welfare were not good? How do they cope with the situation? Now we can return to the illness hypothesis. The hypothesis was that welfare mothers who no longer thought of welfare as a temporary condition would be the most likely to define themselves as ill and to use illness as a means of legitimating their self-defined failure to themselves and others.

The data from the two surveys offered support for this hypothesis. Women who expected to be on welfare in the future were more likely to define their health as poor. Furthermore, those mothers who did not expect to get off welfare *and* defined being on welfare as failure were the most likely to define their health as poor. We are not saying that the mothers who defined their health as poor were lying; most of them probably really believed they were ill, felt ill, acted ill, and in many cases became ill. What we are saying is that a social condition precipitated this pattern.

The analysis was extended by looking at how the types of families the women had influenced their definition of health. There are many mechanisms that people can use to legitimate self-defined failure to themselves and others. Most welfare mothers had preschool children and said that they could not work because they had to stay home to take care of their children. If a woman had preschool children, she had a legitimate reason for being on welfare and had no need of another reason. Women who had school-aged children, however, could not use child care as a means of legitimating their dependency. Therefore, it was hypothesized that mothers of school-aged children would be more likely to define their health as poor than those who had preschool children. The data offered strong support for this hypothesis. Of those mothers whose youngest child was five or less, only 9 percent gave poor health as a reason for preferring not to work. But of those whose youngest child was eleven or older, fully 53 percent gave poor health as a reason not to work. It might be argued that those women with older children were themselves older and perhaps actually more ill. This turned out not to be the case. Even when we looked only at data concerning women who were over forty, the age of the youngest child had a strong influence on using health as a reason not to work. The relationship even held up when we looked only at data concerning women who had not gone to a doctor once during the preceding year. It was concluded that the family life cycle had an important influence on how the welfare mothers defined their health.

The sociologists were able to make one last test of the illness hypothesis. They interviewed a sample of working-class mothers who lived in a middle-income housing project in New York City. These mothers were asked a series of questions about how they felt they were doing as wives and mothers. For example, they were asked: "How often do you feel that you are not as good a mother as you would like to be—frequently, sometimes, rarely, or never?" and "Compared with your friends, would you say that you and your husband get along very well, about average, or not so well?" It turned out that those women who thought they were not succeeding as wives and mothers were also more likely to define themselves as being in poor health. This relationship held up even among women who reported no symptoms of physiological illness. Again, it was concluded that self-defined failure motivates people to define themselves as ill and to act ill. We find that behavior normally thought of as biologically or physiologically determined can be influenced by social conditions.

THE SOCIOLOGICAL PERSPECTIVE AND RESEARCH METHODS
In this brief chapter, we have only been able to touch on a few central aspects of the sociological perspective. We have tried to show that sociologists study the behavior and sentiments of individuals by showing how social location affects individuals. Even when sociologists study illness, they look for aspects of behavior that are socially conditioned. When sociologists study historical change or social movements, they attempt to show how the individuals involved were influenced by prevailing social conditions. When they study cultural development, they try to show how social conditions influence the particular parts of culture that attract human attention and how the social organization of culture itself influences its growth.

The sociologists' perspective, or view of the world, is what guides them in their decision as to what to study. You have seen that if sociologists study a behavior like suicide, they will not be concerned with why Jim but not Bill committed suicide. Rather, they will want to know why rates of suicide are higher in certain social groups than in others. If sociologists study social change, they will not concentrate their energies on the role of particular individuals but rather will be concerned with how social conditions influenced individuals. The sociological perspective acts as a broad guide to what sociologists should study.

Practically all sociologists adhere to the sociological perspective. As we pointed out, however, the sociological perspective is the most general type of theoretical orientation. Within this general orientation there are several different theoretical perspectives that you will learn about in a theory course. Among these are Marxism, structural-functional analysis, and symbolic interaction. Each one of these theoretical orientations provides researchers with more specific guides as to what questions to do research on. The more you know about these theories, the less arbitrary will the sociologist's choice of topics and approach seem.

The major purposes of this book are twofold: to show you the value of doing sociological research and to introduce you to the logic that sociologists employ when doing research. I believe sociological research is valuable for two reasons. First, the findings of sociological research can give us a greater understanding of the behavior of others and of developments in the society at large. Second, sociological research can play a crucial role in helping us solve some of our social problems. The latter will be discussed extensively in Chapter 6.

In Chapter 2, we will look at some of the basic concepts and tools of logic used in doing sociological research. We will examine, in Chapter 3, the different types of quantitative research done by sociologists; and, in Chapter 4, the various techniques of analysis used in quantitative research. In Chapter 5, we will look at the types of qualitative research done by sociologists.

Chapter 2   The Logic of Proof

DESCRIPTIVE RESEARCH   There are two basic types of sociological research: *descriptive* research and *explanatory* research. A sociologist does a descriptive study to discover facts, to describe social reality. How do people really behave? What is society really like? A sociologist, for example, might want to find out how many college students really use drugs. Newspapers or television news programs may give the impression that almost all college students are "heads," but is this really true? Or a sociologist might want to find out if the economic condition of blacks has improved in the last twenty years or if college students today are really more likely to have premarital sex relations than were college students in the past.

All these studies would have the same goal—the discovery of social facts. Sometimes descriptive studies get very complicated and deal with some way-out topics; for example, one sociologist had the idea that dying is influenced by social conditions.[1] When you die is

---

[1]David Phillips, "Death Takes a Holiday," in *Statistics: A Guide to the Unknown*, eds. Judith M. Tanur et al. (San Francisco: Holden-Day, 1972).

not solely determined by the physiological condition of your body. The sociologist wanted to find out if people would be less likely to die during important social events, such as holidays or their own birthdays. After studying many different groups of people, he discovered an effect that he called the "death dip." It was, in fact, true that people were less likely to die on certain important occasions. If dying were not socially influenced, then people would be just as likely to die in the month in which their birthdays fall, for example, as in any other month. But this is not what happens. People are less likely to die in the month of their birthday. To fully prove that the death dip did, in fact, occur was quite complicated. It took a great deal of ingenuity and the knowledge of how to use some simple statistical tools.

Although in this particular case, few people would say the discovery of the death dip was an obvious finding, people often accuse sociologists who do descriptive studies of making a big deal over the obvious, of saying in a complicated way what everybody knows to be true anyway. Sociologists become accustomed to hearing skeptical people ask, "Why do you need all those numbers and long words to tell me that? I knew that myself."

The claim that descriptive research deals with the obvious is not completely false. Take, as an example, an exhaustive study done during World War II. This study was eventually published in four volumes entitled *The American Soldier*.[2] The goal of the research team, headed by the Harvard sociologist Samuel Stouffer, was to study the morale of soldiers. Included among the results of this study were four rather obvious findings:

1. Better-educated men showed more psychoneurotic symptoms than those men with less education. (It is well known that intellectuals tend to be nervous, high-strung, and generally less stable than the average individual.)
2. Men from rural backgrounds were usually in better spirits during their army life than were soldiers from city backgrounds. (This was to be expected, since men growing up in

[2]Samuel Stouffer et al., *The American Soldier, Studies in Social Psychology in World War II*, 4 vols. (Princeton: Princeton University Press, 1949).

the country generally do more physical labor and are more accustomed to physical hardship.)

3. White privates were more eager to become noncommissioned officers than were black privates. (Because of the social conditions under which blacks grow up, blacks tend to be less ambitious than whites. Also, many blacks would have felt insecure giving orders to white men.)
4. Soldiers from the South were better able to stand the climate in the hot South Sea Islands than were soldiers from the North. (What could be more obvious than this? Southerners are, of course, accustomed to hot weather.)

Why did so many sociologists have to spend a lot of time and money to find out the obvious? The only thing wrong with all these obvious findings is that Stouffer and his colleagues found exactly the opposite to be true in every case. Better-educated men showed *fewer* psychoneurotic symptoms than those with less education. Men from rural backgrounds were *not* in any better spirits during their army life than soldiers from the city. Blacks were actually *more* eager to become noncommissioned officers than were whites. And even the most "obvious" statement of all was wrong: Soldiers from the South were *not* better able to stand the South Sea Islands climate than were soldiers from the North.[3]

The moral of this piece of deception is that very little is really obvious about human behavior until it is found to be true. Because all forms of human behavior are conceivable, many readers respond to a study that reports a prevailing regularity by thinking: "Of course, that's the way things are." However, since every kind of human behavior is conceivable, it is of great importance to know which reactions actually occur most frequently and under what conditions. It is the job of the descriptive sociological study to discover which of two obvious and conflicting beliefs is the correct one.

EXPLANATORY RESEARCH   Descriptive studies, as has been illustrated, only describe social reality; they fail to explain *why* things are

---

[3]This example of how sociological findings are far from obvious was first used by Paul F. Lazarsfeld in a review of Stouffer et al., *The American Soldier*, in *Public Opinion Quarterly* 13 (Fall 1949): 377–404.

as they are. What causes people to behave in the ways they do? When sociologists attempt to answer this question they are taking the next step; they engage in *explanatory research*. The best way to understand explanatory research is to look at an example.

In 1972 the attention of Americans was focused on one of the most serious political crises we have faced in the twentieth century. The Watergate break-in, its cover-up, and related matters caused Americans to ask for the first time in over one hundred years whether the president should be impeached. Serious discussion of impeachment began in late 1973 and grew hotter through 1974 until President Richard Nixon resigned on August 9, 1974. During 1974, as the debate over impeachment raged, a group of sociologists at the State University of New York at Stony Brook conducted a series of surveys aimed at discovering how Long Island residents felt about impeachment and why they felt as they did.

Long Island voters had heavily favored Nixon in the 1972 presidential election. Two-thirds of them had voted for Nixon and only one-third for his Democratic rival, George McGovern. But in the spring and summer of 1974, about one-half of the people we interviewed said that they favored impeachment of Nixon and one-half said they were opposed. Why were some in favor of impeachment while others opposed it? Data collected from several surveys were used to explain or understand the attitude of Long Island residents toward impeachment.[4] Among the results of the surveys were the following:

1. Jews were more likely than Christians to be in favor of impeachment.
2. People who had graduated from college were more likely to favor impeachment than those who had not graduated from college.
3. Registered Republicans were much less likely to favor impeachment than were registered Democrats or independents.

At this level we have only description—a reporting of the facts of who did what. The next question we want to ask is "Why?" Why were

[4]Some of the results were published in *Newsday*, a Long Island newspaper. All the surveys were conducted by telephone and paid for by the newspaper.

Jews more likely to favor impeachment than Christians; college graduates more likely than nongraduates; and registered Democrats and independents more likely than registered Republicans? The answers to these questions are examples of elementary explanatory analysis.

Before we proceed to the answers, we must first define a few important concepts. Explanatory analysis always involves a minimum of three elements. The first element is a behavior or an attitude that we want to understand. In this case it is the attitude toward impeachment. We want to understand why some citizens were more likely to favor impeachment than others. The second element is a posited cause, or determinant, of the behavior or attitude. In this case, posited causes of attitudes toward impeachment are religion (Jewish, Christian); education (college graduates, nongraduates); and political party affiliation (Republican, Democrat, independent). The third element is the reason why the causal element influences the behavior or attitude. One example is the reason why Jews were more likely to favor impeachment than Christians.

In all sciences, the phenomenon being studied is the *dependent variable*. In sociology, the dependent variable is usually a behavior or an attitude. A *variable* is any classification of people for which there are two or more categories. (A *category* is a class or division in a scheme of classification.) The categories should be mutually exclusive and exhaustive. Thus, for a particular variable, no individual will fall into more than one category, and every individual will fall into one of the categories. There is literally an infinite number of variables. Some of the most common ones considered in sociology are social class (working class, middle class); political affiliation (Democrat, Republican); sex (male, female); and the like. The phenomenon being studied is called the "dependent variable" because it depends on, or is determined by, other variables. For example, attitudes toward impeachment (the dependent variable) are determined by religion.

In all sciences, the variable that causes the dependent variable is the *independent variable*. Religion is one of the independent variables in the example we have been using. Religion determines the likelihood of a person favoring impeachment. Could attitude toward impeachment determine a person's religion? In the overwhelming majority of cases, the answer would be no. People had their religious affiliation before the issue of impeachment came up and were not likely to change their religion as a result of their feelings toward impeachment. Because attitude toward impeachment does not cause religion, we say that religion is independent of this attitude. Thus, the causal variable is called the "independent variable."

You will notice that a clear time relationship exists between the independent and dependent variable. The independent variable must precede the dependent variable in time. Your behavior today cannot be caused by an *unknown* event that will happen tomorrow. What people thought or did after Nixon resigned could not possibly have been a cause of their attitudes during the debate on impeachment. And the attitudes that people had toward impeachment during the debate could not possibly have been a cause of their age, religion, sex, social class, or political affiliation.

The third element in an explanatory analysis is the reason why the independent variable influences the dependent variable. This element does not have a uniform name. Sometimes sociologists use the term *explanatory variable* or *test factor*. We will call this element the "test factor," but this is merely a convention. In fact, the test factor is really another independent variable.

Since the test factor is very difficult to explain, we can better understand its meaning by studying some examples. Let us again ask why religion influenced (caused) attitude toward impeachment. Why should Jews be more predisposed to favor impeachment than Christians? Is there anything in the Jewish religion itself that would influence people to favor impeachment? Probably not. The answer must lie in some characteristic that goes along with being Jewish. The attitude of Jews may be formed by the fact that Jews have been a persecuted minority for centuries and have come to identify with the underprivileged and to take generally liberal political positions. Sociological studies of political behavior have consistently shown that Jews are more likely to be Democrats, to favor welfare state measures, and to support civil rights—in short, to be more "liberal" than any other religious or ethnic group. The sociologist Gerhard Lenski, in his book on religion, reports statistics showing that Jews are more likely to support nationalization of large industries.[5]

[5]Gerhard Lenski, *The Religious Factor* (Garden City, N.Y.: Anchor Books, 1963), pp. 137, 140.

Another study shows that one of the most important sources of opinion for New York City's immigrant Jews was the socialist trade unions.[6] This survey also found that election districts that were mainly comprised of Jews consistently gave more votes to leftist third-party candidates than other districts. Thus, it is possible that Jews were more likely to favor impeachment than Christians because of general political beliefs.

Liberalism, then, is the proposed test factor—the reason why religion (independent variable) influences attitude toward impeachment (dependent variable). This theory could be stated like this: Jews were more likely to favor impeachment than Christians because Jews are more likely to be liberals, and liberals are more likely to favor impeachment. Most people would accept this analysis at this point. The social researcher, however, will not accept any explanation unless there is some data to support it. We would want to make sure that this particular explanation is correct. Surely there are several other logical-sounding, possible explanations of the relationship between religion and attitude toward impeachment.

For example, it is a fact that Jews are more likely than Christians to have graduated from college. Above we pointed out that one of the findings of the survey was that college graduates were more likely than nongraduates to favor impeachment. Perhaps the reason why Jews were more in favor of impeachment than Christians simply had to do with their higher level of education. The second theory, then: Jews may have been more likely to favor impeachment than Christians because Jews have higher education, and people with higher education were more likely to favor impeachment.

One of the great things about social research is that we do not have to argue over which one of these two theories is correct. We can look at the data and prove one or the other or both theories to be right or wrong.

USE OF TABLES IN EXPLANATORY ANALYSIS

Arranging Data in Tables To prove a theory right or wrong, we must look at the data arranged in a table. In order to interpret data to answer our question of why Jews were more likely to favor impeach-

[6]Lawrence Fuchs, *The Political Behavior of American Jews* (Glencoe, Ill.: The Free Press, 1956), chap. 10.

ment than Christians, we need to learn how to read some simple tables. The simplest type of table is a one-variable distribution and is termed a *marginal*. (It is called a "marginal" because it usually appears in the margins of more complex tables.) If 1,000 people were interviewed, we would want to know how many were Jewish and how many were Christian.[7] The data might appear as in Table 2.1. We would usually find some people who were of other religions or who did not answer the question, but for simplicity of presentation, we will assume that everybody answered the question and that every person was either a Jew or a Christian. The table tells us that 500, or 50 percent, of the people interviewed were Jewish, and 500, or 50 percent, were Christian.

Table 2.1.

Religion		
Jews	500	50%
Christians	500	50%
Total	1,000	100%

We can now move on to two-variable tables—those in which we simultaneously classify people on two variables. We have already classified the people interviewed by their religion. Now we want to know how many of the 500 Jews and 500 Christians favored impeachment. This information would appear as in Table 2.2. Of the 500 Jews, 350 favored impeachment and 150 did not; of the 500 Christians, 250 favored impeachment and 250 did not. (Note that in the total column, we find the marginal of Table 2.1). In the two-

Table 2.2.

	Favor impeachment		
	Yes	*No*	*Total*
Religion			
Jews	350	150	500
Christians	250	250	500
Total	600	400	1,000

[7]Although the substantive conclusions of the impeachment survey were essentially similar to those reported here, we have altered the actual figures for didactic purposes.

variable table, every person is simultaneously classified on two dimensions. In order to understand this, picture a room with four corners. All the Jews will be asked to stand in front of the room; all the Christians in the rear. All people who favor impeachment will be asked to stand on the left side of the room and all opposed on the right. You will classify each person as he or she walks into the room. You ask the first person what his or her religion is—let us say the person is Jewish. You then ask whether he or she favors impeachment. If the answer is yes, you tell the person to stand in the front left corner of the room; if the answer is no, you tell the person to stand in the front right corner. If the next person is a Christian who favors impeachment, he or she will be asked to stand in the back left corner of the room. Thus, each cell of the table would correspond to a corner of the room. In the same way, you could classify any group of people on any two variables.

Usually, a two-variable table is percentaged, and the information we have collected would appear as in Table 2.3. Table 2.3 gives us all the information that is in Table 2.2. Of the 500 Jews, 350 favored impeachment; 350 is 70 percent of 500. One hundred and fifty Jews (30 percent of 500) opposed impeachment. The table also tells us that 50 percent of the Christians (250 out of 500) favored impeachment and 50 percent (250 out of 500) opposed impeachment. The numbers in parentheses always indicate the number of people in a particular category.

Table 2.3.

	Favor impeachment	Oppose impeachment	Total	Number of people
Religion				
Jews	70%	30%	100%	(500)
Christians	50%	50%	100%	(500)

When we look down a set of numbers in a table, we are looking at the columns; when we look across a set of numbers, we are looking at the rows. In Table 2.3, the categories of the independent variable appear in the rows, and the categories of the dependent variable appear in columns. Frequently, this procedure is reversed, and the data would be presented as in Table 2.4.

Table 2.4.

	Religion	
	Jews	Christians
Favor impeachment	70%	50%
Oppose impeachment	30%	50%
Total	100%	100%
Number of people	(500)	(500)

It should be clear that the data in Tables 2.3 and 2.4 are exactly the same. As long as you know which is the dependent variable and which is the independent variable, you should not be confused if the dependent variable appears in the rows rather than in the columns.

Frequently, a two-variable table, such as Table 2.3, will be presented with only one-half of the data (see Table 2.5). Table 2.5 tells us the exact same thing as Table 2.3. We know that if 70 percent of the Jews favored impeachment, then 30 percent must have opposed it. Likewise, if 50 percent of the Christians favored impeachment, then 50 percent must have opposed it. Thus, if we see a table that tells us the percentage favoring impeachment, for example, and we want to know the percentage opposing impeachment, we simply subtract the given number from 100 percent. The reason only one-half of the numbers are presented is to make the table as simple as possible. The other one-half of the numbers are merely redundant.

Table 2.5.

	Percent favoring impeachment	
Religion		
Jews	70%	(500)
Christians	50%	(500)

Looking at Table 2.5, we would want to know to what extent Jews are more likely to favor impeachment than Christians. We would compute the *percentage difference*. The percentage difference in this case would be 70 percent minus 50 percent, which is 20 percent. Thus, 20 percent more Jews than Christians favored impeachment.

Looking back at Table 2.2, we can see that the table could have been percentaged in two different ways. Instead of asking what percentage of Jews favored impeachment, we could have asked what percentage of people favoring impeachment were Jews. If we had done this, we would have constructed Table 2.6. How do we know whether we should percentage Table 2.2 as we did in Table 2.5 or 2.6? A simple convention to follow when doing explanatory research is to always percentage tables in the direction of the independent variable. Thus, we should always ask what percentage of *a category in the independent variable is a category in the dependent variable*. In Table 2.2 we would ask what percentage of Jews (a category in the independent variable) support impeachment (a category in the dependent variable). If we can tell which is the dependent variable and which is the independent variable, our tables will always be percentaged correctly.

Table 2.6.

	Percent Jews	
Favor impeachment		
Yes	58%	(600)
No	38%	(400)

You now should be able to correctly percentage any two-variable table. Suppose we were presented with the figures in Table 2.7. How would we percentage this table? The first thing is to determine which of the two variables is the dependent variable. Clearly, attitude toward impeachment did not influence educational level. Now we want to percentage in the direction of the independent variable. We

Table 2.7.

	Favor impeachment		
	Yes	No	Total
Education			
College graduates	350	100	450
Nongraduates	250	300	550
Total	600	400	1,000

want to know what percentage of college graduates (a category in the independent variable) favored impeachment (a category in the dependent variable). Table 2.8 is the correctly percentaged table. The percentage difference for Table 2.8 is 33 percentage points.

Table 2.8.

	Percent favoring impeachment	
Education		
College graduates	78%	(450)
Nongraduates	45%	(550)

Sometimes you will read a statistical report and will see an incorrectly percentaged table. Since an incorrectly percentaged table will not give us the information we want, we need to know how to convert it into a correctly percentaged table. What would we do with Table 2.9? The table is percentaged in the wrong direction.

Table 2.9.

	Percent Democrats	
Favor impeachment		
Yes	80%	(600)
No	40%	(400)

Instead of telling us what proportion of Democrats supported impeachment, it tells us what proportion of people supporting impeachment were Democrats. To convert the table, we must go back to the raw figures (the same principle as in Table 2.2). To do this, we would set up the table and fill in the information we have from Table 2.9. The table would be set up like Table 2.10.

Table 2.10.

	Favor impeachment	
	Yes	No
Political affiliation		
Democrats		
Republicans		

We know from Table 2.9 that 80 percent of the 600 people who favored impeachment were Democrats (80 percent of 600 is 480). Forty percent of the 400 people who did not favor impeachment were Democrats (40 percent of 400 is 160). Therefore, we would put the 160 in the first cell and the 480 in the second cell, as in Table 2.11.

Table 2.11.

| | Favor impeachment | |
	Yes	No
Political affiliation		
Democrats	480	160
Republicans		
Total	600	400

Now by subtracting 480 from 600, we find that 120 Republicans favored impeachment. We enter the 120 in the third cell, as shown in Table 2.12. In the same way, we figure out the number of Republicans who did not favor impeachment (400 minus 160 is 240). After entering the 240 in the fourth cell, we have all the raw figures in Table 2.12.

Table 2.12.

| | Favor impeachment | | |
	Yes	No	Total
Political affiliation			
Democrats	480	160	640
Republicans	120	240	360
Total	600	400	1,000

It is now a simple matter to percentage the table correctly, as shown in Table 2.13.

Table 2.13.

	Percent favoring impeachment	
Political affiliation		
Democrats	75%	(640)
Republicans	33%	(360)

Problems in Percentaging
Even more significant than age at divorce is how old the divorced were when they first got married. In 1965, the median age at marriage for all American males was 22.8 years; for females it was 20.6 years. We may then ask, how likely is it that persons who marry below the national median will become divorced? For females the chances are extremely high—almost 1 in 2—because in 1965, 48 percent of all wives involved in divorce had been married below age 20. While for men that relationship is more ambiguous, it is clear that when a woman marries before age 20 (still in her teens) or below the average age at which most women marry, she is running an extraordinarily high risk of separation and eventual divorce.*

The author is concerned with the effect of age at marriage (independent variable) on divorce (dependent variable). What he should be telling us is what proportion of people getting married at a young age eventually get divorced and what proportion of people getting married at an older age eventually get divorced. Instead he tells us what proportion of divorced women had been married below age twenty. He is reporting results based on an incorrectly percentaged table. Indeed if we were to take the data presented seriously we would have to reject the hypothesis that getting married at a young age leads to divorce, for we are told that half the women get married before the age of 20.6 years and that 48 percent of the women getting divorced were married under the age of 20. Thus, it would appear that women who are married young would have no higher probability of divorce than those who marry at an older age.

In fact, when the data are properly analyzed it becomes quite clear that women who get married at a young age are substantially more likely to get divorced than those who marry at an older age. For example, among white women whose first marriage took place at least twenty years ago, 25 percent of those marrying in their teens as opposed to about 12 percent of those marrying after the age of twenty have been divorced.†

*John Scanzoni, *Sexual Bargaining* (Englewood Cliffs, N.J.: Prentice-Hall, 1972), p. 17.
†Paul Glick and Arthur Norton, "Frequency, Duration and Probability of Marriage and Divorce," *Journal of Marriage and the Family* 33 (May 1971): 309.

Using Tables To Test Hypotheses Now that you have had some experience in reading tables, we can return to a test of our theory of why Jews were more likely to favor impeachment than Christians. We had hypothesized that Jews were more likely to support impeachment than Christians because Jews are more likely to be liberals, and liberals would be more likely to favor impeachment. This theory can be broken down into the following four statements:

1. Jews are more likely to favor impeachment than Christians.

2. Jews are more likely than Christians to be liberals.
3. Liberals are more likely to favor impeachment than conservatives.
4. Jews are more likely to favor impeachment *because* they are liberals.

To test the validity of each of the first three statements, we need three different two-variable tables. The validity of the first statement was established by Table 2.5, in which we saw that 70 percent of Jews and 50 percent of Christians favored impeachment. The data for the second statement are presented in Table 2.14. In Table 2.14 liberalism is the dependent variable and religion is the independent variable. Religion influences liberalism and not vice versa. Table 2.14 shows us that Jews are much more likely to be liberals than Christians; 80 percent of the Jews and 40 percent of the Christians are liberals. The percentage difference is 40 points.[8]

Table 2.14.

	Percent liberals	
Religion		
Jews	80%	(500)
Christians	40%	(500)

The data to test the validity of the third statement are presented in Table 2.15. What is the dependent variable in Table 2.15? We are interested in knowing which variables caused people to favor impeachment; thus, attitude toward impeachment would be the

Table 2.15.

	Percent favoring impeachment	
Political beliefs		
Liberals	80%	(600)
Conservatives	30%	(400)

[8]Not all Jews are liberals and not all Christians are conservatives due to the differing social conditions under which they live. Some Jews grew up in wealthy families with conservative Republican parents; some Christians grew up in families in which their parents were liberal Democrats.

dependent variable. Generally, the people we interviewed had their political beliefs before the impeachment issue came up. The data showed that liberals were much more likely to support impeachment than conservatives. The percentage difference is 50 points.

Now we come to the last statement in our theory: Jews were more likely to support impeachment *because* they are liberals. This theory is based on the following reasoning: No inherent characteristic of Judaism would lead Jews to favor impeachment. However, Jews are more likely than Christians to be liberals. There is something inherent in being a liberal that would increase the propensity to favor impeachment. There are several reasons why liberals would be inherently more likely to favor impeachment than conservatives. The most obvious would be that Richard Nixon was a conservative Republican, who, for more than twenty years, had been viewed by liberals as a political "enemy." Perhaps just as important, conservatives are more committed to the status quo. The impeachment of a president would have been a drastic departure from tradition and thus abhorrent to conservatives. If liberalism is the crucial variable influencing Jews to favor impeachment, then liberal Christians should be just as likely to favor impeachment as liberal Jews, and conservative Jews should be no more likely to favor impeachment than conservative Christians. We can tell whether or not this is true by looking at a three-variable table like Table 2.16.

Table 2.16.

| Religion | Percent favoring impeachment | | | |
	Liberals		Conservatives	
Jews	80%	(400)	30%	(100)
Christians	80%	(200)	30%	(300)

The numbers in parentheses in Table 2.16 represent the number of people in each category. Four hundred Jews were liberal. We can also see this in Table 2.14 (80 percent of 500 is 400). There are 300 people who are Christians and conservatives. There are 200 people who are Christian liberals and 100 who are Jewish conservatives. Here, as in Table 2.14, we can see that although Jews are more likely to be liberal, a substantial minority are conservative. There is also a substantial minority of Christians who are liberal. The percentages in the table represent the proportion of people in each category who favor impeachment. Thus, 80 percent of Jews who were liberals favored impeachment. The complement of Table 2.16 would be percent *not* favoring impeachment. Thus, 20 percent of Jewish liberals did *not* favor impeachment, and 70 percent of Jewish conservatives did *not* favor impeachment.

In Table 2.16, is there any difference in the attitudes of Jews and Christians? By comparing Jews and Christians who are liberals and comparing Jews and Christians who are conservatives, we can see that when people are "made alike" on liberalism, there is no difference in the attitudes of people of different religions. Eighty percent of liberal Jews and 80 percent of liberal Christians favored impeachment. Thirty percent of conservative Jews and 30 percent of conservative Christians supported impeachment. If we were to find results like those in Table 2.16, we would conclude that our theory about why Jews were more likely to favor impeachment than Christians was correct. However, suppose that we found results like those in Table 2.17. According to Table 2.17, a substantial difference still exists between the behavior of Jews and Christians. Jewish conservatives are just as likely to favor impeachment as Jewish liberals, and both Jewish liberals and conservatives are more likely to favor impeachment than Christian liberals and conservatives. If we found this, we would conclude our theory is wrong: Although Jews are more likely to be liberals than are Christians, this is not the reason why they were more likely to favor impeachment.

Table 2.17.

| | Percent favoring impeachment | |
	Liberals	Conservatives
Religion		
Jews	70%	70%
Christians	50%	50%

Note: Numbers in parentheses have been omitted because it would have been impossible to get these percentages and be consistent with the results obtained in Tables 2.14 and 2.15.

If we found data like those in Table 2.17 we would look for another explanation of the propensity of Jews to support impeachment. We might, for example, test our education theory: Jews are more likely to favor impeachment than Christians because Jews are more likely to be college graduates, and people who are college graduates are more likely to favor impeachment.

In general, an explanatory analysis involves the following procedure: We find an independent variable that is associated with the dependent variable; we then find a test factor that might explain the relationship between the dependent and independent variables. To see if we have found the correct test factor, we examine the relationship between the independent and dependent variables, which remain constant throughout one analysis, separately within each category of the test factor. If the test factor is the right one, the percentage difference should be less in each category of the test factor than it was in the original two-variable table. For example, in Table 2.5 the percentage difference between Jews and Christians is 20 points; in Table 2.16 the percentage difference between Jews and Christians in each category of the test factor is zero. The logic we have discussed in this chapter is the basic principle behind most social research—even that which uses very sophisticated quantitative analysis.

CAUSAL ANALYSIS Suppose that the following fact was reported to us: In those areas in Europe with many storks the birth rate is high, whereas in areas with few storks the birth rate is low. If someone were to argue that the storks brought the babies, what would we say? We know that storks do not bring babies, but how could we explain the "fact"? Undeniably, the two variables involved would be associated. Or take another example: The amount of damage resulting from a fire increases with the number of fire engines that come to the fire. Could we then conclude that the fire fighters, using their equipment, cause most of the damage and we should not call the fire department when we have a fire? A third example might be that the death rate among hospitalized people is much higher than among nonhospitalized people. Should we then conclude that when we are sick we should not go to the hospital because being in the hospital causes death?

All three examples illustrate the same point: Correlation, or association, between two variables is not enough to assume that one of the variables is a cause of the other. When a relationship actually *is* causal has been debated by philosophers of science and some sociologists for a long time. In practice, however, sociologists generally treat a relationship between two variables as causal if the relationship meets three conditions.[9]

Three Conditions of Causality *The first condition of causality is that the two variables be associated.* Religious status could not be a cause of suicide if there were no differences in the suicide rates of the different religious groups. If an independent variable is a cause of a dependent variable, a change in the first must bring about a change in the second.

The second condition is that the posited causal variable (independent variable) must precede in time the phenomenon it causes (dependent variable). Thus, socioeconomic status cannot be a cause of a person's race, although race can be a cause of socioeconomic status. We pointed out in this chapter that attitude toward impeachment could not be a determinant of a person's religion but that religion could be a cause of attitude toward impeachment.

The third condition is that there be no third variable that antecedes in time the independent variable and that, when held constant, will make the relationship between the independent and dependent variable "disappear." At the beginning of this section, we were presented with a fact that suggested the presence of storks influenced the birth rate. The relationship between the number of storks (independent variable) and the birth rate (dependent variable) will be a causal one if it meets all three conditions of causality. It does meet the first condition. As we pointed out, there is an association between the number of storks and the birth rate. The two-variable table might look like Table 2.18.

Table 2.18. Percent Counties with High Birth Rates by Number of Storks Present

	Percent high birth rate
Number of storks	
Few	30%
Many	80%

[9]See Travis Hirschi and Hanan C. Selvin, *Delinquency Research* (New York: The Free Press of Glencoe, 1967), chap. 3.

Does the relationship meet the second condition of causality? Since in any year the storks were present prior to the birth of the babies, the independent variable precedes in time the dependent variable and, thus, the relationship meets the second condition. If the relationship meets the third condition, we must conclude that it is a causal relationship and that storks bring babies. Therefore, we must determine whether there is some third variable that might influence both the number of storks and the number of babies and that, when held constant, will eliminate the influence of number of storks on the birth rate. (Holding a variable constant means we are examining the effect of the independent variable on the dependent variable separately within each category of the variable being held constant.)

In this example, a third variable may easily be found. Whether or not an area is rural or urban influences both the number of storks present and the birth rate. Urban areas have few storks and the birth rates are relatively low. Rural areas have more storks and the birth rates are relatively high. Table 2.19 has data that reflects what would probably happen to the relationship between number of storks and birth rate when the urban-rural character of the area is controlled, or held constant. In this three-variable table, "high" indicates a high number or percentage and "low," a low number or percentage. First, we see there is a high number of urban areas with few storks (the "high" in parentheses in the first cell) and a low number of urban areas with many storks (the "low" in parentheses in the third cell). The opposite is true for the rural areas. The table indicates that regardless of the number of storks in urban areas the birth rate is low and in rural areas the birth rate is high. In other words, within urban areas there is no relationship between the number of storks and the birth

Table 2.19.   Percent Counties with High Birth Rates by Number of Storks and Urban-Rural Character of the County

	Percent high birth rates			
	Urban areas		Rural areas	
Number of storks				
Few	Low	(High)	High	(Low)
Many	Low	(Low)	High	(High)

rate; the same is true in rural areas. If storks cause high birth rates, why is the birth rate low in those urban areas in which there are many storks? Clearly, the relationship between the number of storks and birth rate is noncausal because it does not meet the third condition of causality. There is a variable (urban-rural) antecedent in time to the independent variable (storks) that, when held constant, will make the relationship between the independent variable (storks) and the dependent variable (birth rate) "disappear."

When a relationship meets the first two conditions of causality but does not meet the last, we call the interpretation of the relationship as causal a "spurious interpretation." Since both the number of storks and the birth rate are influenced by the urban-rural character of the area, they are associated with one another. But their association is noncausal and an interpretation of this association as being causal would be spurious. Similarly, we could prove the interpretations that fire fighters and fire engines cause damage and that hospitals cause death are spurious interpretations. The size of the fire influences both how many fire engines are called and how much damage is done. The seriousness of the illness influences both whether or not the patient is hospitalized and the rate of death. As Figure 2.1 indicates, the relationship between the original two

Figure 2.1. Spurious Causal Interpretations

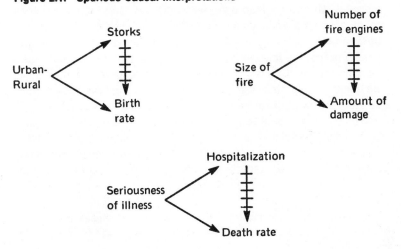

variables is an artifact of the relationship between each of the variables and some antecedent variable.

The data in Table 2.18 showed that there was a relationship between the number of storks and the birth rate. In compiling Table 2.19, we controlled for whether the area was rural or urban and found that within each category of the test factor, the relationship between the original independent and dependent variable was no longer present. It may appear that, insofar as drawing conclusions from data is concerned, Table 2.19 is like Table 2.16 (from which we found the relationship between religion and attitude toward impeachment "disappeared" when we controlled for liberalism). In both cases, the three-variable tables look similar. Should we then conclude that saying religion causes attitude toward impeachment is a spurious interpretation? To answer this, we must ask if the relationship meets the three conditions of causality. Religion is associated with attitude toward impeachment and religion precedes this attitude in time. Thus, the relationship meets the first two conditions. Is there any third variable that antecedes in time the independent variable and that, when held constant, will make the relationship between the independent and dependent variables disappear? Liberalism does *not* antecede religion in time. Religion influences liberalism, not vice versa. Thus, the relationship between religion and attitude toward impeachment *does* meet the three criteria of causality. Of course, if some other variable is found that antecedes religion in time and, when controlled, eliminates the relationship between religion and attitude toward impeachment, then we would conclude that the interpretation of this relationship as causal would be spurious. But very few variables antecede religion and in all cases we usually assume a relationship is causal until we find a third variable that will make the causal interpretation spurious.

The difference between the two examples under discussion is the time order of the test factor. In the first example, the test factor *intervenes* in time between the independent and dependent variables. In the second example, the test factor *precedes* the independent variable:

religion ⟶ liberalism ⟶ attitude toward impeachment
urban-rural ⟶ storks ⟶ babies

Elaborating Two-Variable Relationships   Causal analysis, in its simplest form, is based on three-variable tables. An understanding of causal analysis depends on the ability to interpret three-variable tables. Three-variable tables may be analyzed by following a systematic procedure. As an example, let us analyze, step by step, Table 2.16 (see p. 44). The first step is to identify the variables. The dependent variable in Table 2.16 is attitude toward impeachment. The independent variable is religion. Political orientation is the test factor. (Political orientation can also be viewed as another independent variable. However, the variable that comes first in time can be referred to as the original independent variable and the intervening variable, as the test factor.)

The purpose of analyzing a three-variable table is to understand the relationship between the independent and dependent variables. After we have identified the variables, the second step is to determine the percentage point difference of the original two-variable relationship, or, in this case, the difference between the proportion of Jews favoring impeachment and the proportion of Christians favoring impeachment. Table 2.16 shows the proportion of Jews and Christians, according to political orientation, favoring impeachment. We want to know what proportion of Jews and Christians in the entire sample favored impeachment, regardless of political orientation. We need to construct a two-variable table. Any three-variable table, like Table 2.16, can easily be converted into three separate two-variable tables by a process known as "collapsing." Thus, if we want to know the relationship between religion and attitude toward impeachment, we must compute from Table 2.16 the percentage of Jews who favored impeachment and the percentage of Christians who favored impeachment. First, we will compute the percentage of Jews who favored impeachment. There were 400 Jews who were liberals and 100 Jews who were conservatives, or a total of 500 Jews. Of the 400 Jews who were liberals, 80 percent favored impeachment. Eighty percent of 400 is 320. Of the 100 Jews who were conservative, 30 percent, or 30 Jews, favored impeachment. Thus, a total of 350 (320 plus 30 is 350) Jews favored impeachment. Three hundred and fifty divided by 500 is 70 percent. So we now know that 70 percent of all the Jews included in the sample favored impeachment. We must now do the same computation for Christians. There was a total of

500 Christians. Of the 200 Christians who were liberal, 80 percent, or 160 Christians, favored impeachment. Of the 300 Christians who were conservative, 30 percent favored impeachment. Thirty percent of 300 is 90. Thus, a total of 250 Christians, or 50 percent, favored impeachment. The original relationship is summarized in Table 2.5 (see p. 38). We would say that in the three-variable table, Table 2.16, there was an original relationship of 20 percentage points between the original independent and dependent variables. Thus, religion influences attitude toward impeachment.

The next step in analyzing three-variable tables is to examine what has happened to the original relationship in each category of the test factor. The relationship between the original independent variable and the dependent variable in each category of the test factor is termed a *partial* because it represents part of the original relationship. If all the partials are lumped together, we will get the original relationship. In Table 2.16 there are two partials. In the first partial is the relationship between religion and attitude toward impeachment only for liberals. Eighty percent of liberal Jews and 80 percent of liberal Christians favored impeachment. Thus, in the first partial, the percentage difference is zero. We then examine the original relationship in the second category of the test factor (the second partial). Thirty percent of conservative Jews and 30 percent of conservative Christians favored impeachment. Thus, in the second partial, the percentage difference is also zero. The original relationship has been reduced from 20 percentage points to zero in both partials. Is the original relationship causal? This depends completely on whether the test factor comes before or after the independent variable. Since political orientation comes after religion, we conclude that religion does have a causal influence on attitude toward impeachment and that the mechanism through which religion works is political orientation.

Interpretation and Explanation There are two basic reasons for using a three-variable table to establish the relationship between variables. First, if we want to know if a relationship is causal, we examine test factors that are antecedent to the independent variable and see if the original relationship is maintained or reduced in the partials. If it is maintained, we conclude it is a causal relationship; if it is substantially reduced, then it is not a causal relationship. This is how we discovered that the presence of storks does not influence the birth rate. The second reason to use a three-variable table is to find out in what way the independent variable influences the dependent variable. In this case, we look for test factors that intervene between the two original variables. If, when controlled, the intervening test factor brings about a reduction in the original relationship in the partials—in the ideal case, reducing it to zero—then the test factor is the reason why the independent variable influences the dependent variable. For example, we found out that political orientation is a reason why religion influences attitude toward impeachment. In both cases, it is necessary to see what happens to the original relationship in each category of the test factor.

The process of examining a two-variable relationship in different categories of a third variable is termed *elaboration*. There are basically three different types of elaboration, and we have already discussed the first two. The first type is *explanation* and occurs when an original relationship is reduced in the partials of an antecedent test factor. If this happens, we say an interpretation of the original relationship as being causal is spurious. The second type of elaboration is *interpretation* and occurs when an original relationship is reduced in the partials of an intervening test factor. If this happens, we say the test factor interprets why the independent variable influences the dependent variable. Before going on to look at the third type of elaboration, we will analyze the first two types further.

There is no mathematical difference between explanation and interpretation. In both cases, the three-variable tables look the same. The only way to determine whether an elaboration is explanation or interpretation is to know the causal order of the variables. In both cases, an original relationship disappears in the partials. When this happens, it is because both the original independent and dependent variables are associated with the test factor. These associations are termed *marginals* because they are found in the margins of three-variable tables.

Let us return to Table 2.16 (see p. 44) to demonstrate that the test factor is in fact related to both the original independent and dependent variables. To do this, we must again collapse Table 2.16 to get the necessary two-variable tables. We use basically the same procedure as when we computed the original relationship between religion and attitude toward impeachment. First, we want to know the relationship between religion and political orientation. Since religion normally precedes political orientation in time, for purposes of percentaging the two-variable table correctly, we will designate political orientation as the dependent variable. We want to know the percentage of Jews and the percentage of Christians who were liberals. There was a total of 500 Jews, of which 400 were liberals. Four hundred is 80 percent of 500. There was a total of 500 Christians, of which 200 were liberals. Two hundred is 40 percent of 500. Thus, the relationship between religion and political orientation could be summarized as in Table 2.14 (see p. 43). The two variables are strongly associated. There is a 50-point percentage difference.

In computing the relationship between political orientation and attitude toward impeachment, the latter is clearly the dependent variable. We want to know the percentage of liberals and the percentage of conservatives who favored impeachment. There were 400 liberals who were Jews and 200 liberals who were Christians or a total of 600 liberals. What proportion of the liberals favored impeachment? Since 80 percent of the Jewish liberals and 80 percent of the Christian liberals favored impeachment, it is easy to see that 80 percent of all liberals favored impeachment. Accordingly, 30 percent of all conservatives favored impeachment. However, if the respective percentages were not the same, you could easily compute the proportions as we did in computing the original relationship. The relationship between political orientation and attitude toward impeachment is presented in Table 2.15 (see p. 43). There is a 50-point percentage difference. Tables 2.14 and 2.15 show that both marginal relationships in Table 2.16 are positive.

If the elaboration process, at this point, looks like a mechanical series of tricks in which the sociologist makes relationships disappear, there is no need to become discouraged. Understanding elaboration and the logic of causal analysis is not easy. There is only one real way to master it. You must go over many examples of tables and analyze them in terms of the logic of elaboration. It is also helpful to make up your own tables and then try to prove the point to yourself. The logic of causal analysis cannot be fully taught by either books or teachers; they can only help you learn it by yourself. Yet, whether you are primarily curious about why people behave as they do or are mainly interested in bringing about meaningful social change, you will be aided by knowledge of the logic of causal analysis. Before going on to a discussion of the third type of elaboration, we will present several examples of interpretation and explanation.

An excellent hypothetical example of interpretation is presented by Herbert H. Hyman in his book, *Survey Design and Analysis*.[10] He bases the example on the study of the American soldier we discussed previously. The sociologists doing this study found that soldiers who had graduated from high school were more likely than those with less education to volunteer for the armed services or to feel it was right that they were drafted. Soldiers with less than a high school education were more likely to feel they should have been deferred. Why was education associated with acceptance of military duty? The sociologists reasoned that people were likely to evaluate their own conditions by comparing themselves with their friends and acquaintances. If you had friends who had been deferred, then you were more likely to feel you should be deferred. If you had friends who had been drafted, then it was more likely for you to feel it was legitimate for you to be drafted. During World War II, the men most likely to be deferred were those working in defense industries. These were predominantly men who had not completed high school. Thus, the researchers hypothesized that men who had not completed high school were more likely to feel they should be deferred *because* they were more likely to have friends who were deferred.

It might help in understanding elaboration if in each category we use the number of people rather than a percentage. The researchers began with the relationship between education and acceptance of military duty (see Table 2.20). In percentaging this table, we find that of those men with high education, 88 percent (1,556 divided by 1,761) accepted military duty and 68 percent (1,310 divided by 1,876) of those with low education accepted military duty. Thus, there was an original relationship of 20 percentage points. We want to elaborate this relationship by looking at whether or not the men had

[10]Herbert H. Hyman, *Survey Design and Analysis* (Glencoe, Ill.: The Free Press, 1955), chap. 7.

Table 2.20. Education and Acceptance of Military Duty

	Education		
	High	Low	Total
Acceptance of military duty			
Yes	1,556	1,310	2,866
No	205	566	771
Total	1,761	1,876	3,637

Source: Herbert H. Hyman, *Survey Design and Analysis* (Glencoe, Ill.: The Free Press, 1955), Table XIII, p. 279. Reprinted with permission by Macmillan Publishing Co. Copyright 1955 by The Free Press, a corporation.

friends who were deferred. Does having friends who were deferred come before or after education? This is crucial, because if it comes before we will be testing whether or not the original relationship was causal; if it comes after we will be trying to understand the way in which education influenced acceptance of military duty. Education influences the type of job a man has and the type of job a man has influenced whether or not he was deferred. Thus, education precedes in time having friends who were deferred, and our elaboration will be interpretation.

In Table 2.20 we have classified each man simultaneously on two variables: education and acceptance of military duty. We now want to classify each man simultaneously on three variables (see Table 2.21). On the left-hand side of Table 2.21 is the data from Table 2.20; on the right-hand side is each group of men divided according to whether or not they had friends who were deferred. Thus, of the 1,556 men who had high education and accepted military duty, 210 men had friends deferred and 1,346 men did not have friends who were deferred. Of the 1,310 men who had low education and accepted military duty, 939 had friends who were deferred and 371 did not have friends who were deferred. Each table on the right-hand side is a partial. By percentaging these tables, we can see if the original relationship is reduced in the partials. The marginal relationships can be found in the margins of Table 2.21 For example, if we were interested in the relationship between the dependent variable (acceptance of military duty) and the test factor (having friends deferred), we would want to know what proportion of those men with friends deferred (1,819) accepted military duty (1,149). At this point,

Table 2.21. Acceptance of Military Duty by Education and Having Friends Deferred

	Total sample Education				Friends deferred Education				Friends not deferred Education		
	High	Low	Total		High	Low	Total		High	Low	Total
Acceptance of military duty											
Yes	1,556	1,310	2,866	=	210	939	1,149	+	1,346	371	1,717
No	205	566	771		125	545	670		80	21	101
Total	1,761	1,876	3,637		335	1,484	1,819		1,426	392	1,818

Source: Hyman, *Survey Design and Analysis*, Table XIII, p. 279. Reprinted with permission of Macmillan Publishing Co. Copyright 1955 by The Free Press, a corporation.

it may prove helpful if you compute the two marginal relationships from Table 2.21.

To understand how Table 2.22 was computed from Table 2.21, it would probably help you to do the arithmetic yourself. The data in Table 2.22 shows that the original relationship has been reduced to zero in both partials. For example, among men who had friends deferred, education had no influence on acceptance of military duty. We would say the original relationship has disappeared in the partials. This happened because of the way in which the cases are distributed on the test factor (see Table 2.21). For example, of the 1,556 men who had high education and accepted military duty, the great bulk (1,346) did *not* have friends deferred. Of the 1,310 men who had low education and accepted military duty, the great bulk (939) *did* have friends deferred.[11]

But even though most people with high education did not have friends deferred, a minority did; just as although most men with low education did have friends who were deferred, a minority did not. If we did not have this statistically deviant minority in each group of men, we could never test our theory, since we would then have all men with high education not having friends deferred and all men with low education having friends deferred. As you can see, then, without the minority we would be unable to test our theory, since we want to know whether or not men with different educational backgrounds, when *alike* on the test factor, will also be alike on the dependent variable.

Table 2.22. Percent Accepting Military Duty by Education and Having Friends Deferred

	Friends deferred			
	Yes		No	
Education				
High	63%	(335)	95%	(1,426)
Low	63%	(1,484)	95%	(392)

Source: Hyman, *Survey Design and Analysis,* Table XIV, p. 280. Reprinted with permission of Macmillan Publishing Co. Copyright 1955 by The Free Press, a corporation.

[11]To really understand this, it may prove helpful to refer to Table 2.20 and distribute the cases on the test factor to make up a three-variable table in which the original relationship would not disappear.

If, when having friends deferred is controlled, education has no influence on acceptance of military duty, then why does it make sense to consider education a cause of attitude toward military duty? The answer is that the three variables are related in a causal chain. Education influenced whether or not each man had friends who were deferred. To prove this to yourself, compute the two-variable relationship:

education ⟶ friends deferred

Having friends deferred influenced the acceptance of military duty. Compute the two-variable relationship:

friends deferred ⟶ acceptance of military duty

Thus, the three variables are linked together in the following way:

education ⟶ friends deferred ⟶ acceptance of military duty

Both education and having friends deferred were part of the social processes that influenced a man's attitude toward military duty. Education is a cause of acceptance of military duty because education influenced the type of friends one had and the type of friends directly influenced acceptance of military duty.

What would have happened if the researchers had begun their analysis with the relationship between friends deferred and acceptance of military duty? Then, controlling for education, which antecedes in time friends deferred, might show the relationship between friends deferred and acceptance of military duty to be noncausal or spurious. If this were true, then it would make a great deal of difference which independent variable we used as the original independent variable. Using the data in Table 2.21 and friends deferred as the original independent variable and acceptance of military duty as the dependent variable, we would construct Table 2.23. We would have an original relationship of 32 percentage points. What would happen if we controlled for education, an antecedent variable? Since acceptance of military duty is still the dependent variable and the other two variables are friends deferred

Table 2.23. Percent Accepting Military Duty by Having Friends Deferred

	Percent accepting military duty	
Friends deferred		
Yes	63%	(1,819)
No	95%	(1,818)

and education, the three-variable table would be *exactly* the same as Table 2.22. However, whereas before we compared men with different education in each category of friends deferred to compute the partials, here we compare men who had friends deferred with those who did not in each category of education. In other words, instead of computing the partials in the columns of Table 2.22, we compute the partials in the rows of Table 2.22. The result is that in each category of education, friends deferred still influences acceptance of military duty. In each partial, there is a percentage difference of 32 points; the original relationship is not reduced at all. Thus, even if we began our analysis with the relationship between friends deferred and acceptance of military duty, we would reach the same conclusion as we did before: Both education and having friends deferred were part of the social processes that influenced a man's attitude toward military duty.

It does not matter which of two independent variables is used in the original relationship and which is used as the test factor. In both cases, the three-variable tables constructed will be the same and, thus, yield the same results. This means if we start with an independent variable that antecedes the test factor, and the test factor reduces the original relationship, it is then impossible to start with the test factor, control for the antecedent variable, and reduce the relationship between the test factor and the dependent variable. It would be a good idea to see for yourself that this is an impossibility by trying to construct a numerically consistent example in which an intervening test factor reduces the original relationship and in which the original independent variable reduces the relationship between the test factor and the dependent variable.

Hyman uses another interesting example of interpretation that he takes from a study, conducted by Robert K. Merton, of an interracial

Table. 2.24. Percent Having White-
Collar Jobs by Race

	Percent white-collar jobs	
Race		
White	38%	(287)
Black	10%	(318)

Source: Adapted from Hyman, *Survey Design and Analysis*, Table XIX, p. 292. Reprinted with permission of Macmillan Publishing Co. Copyright 1955 by The Free Press, a corporation.

housing community. Merton found a relationship between race and the type of job held. Whites were much more likely than blacks to have higher paying and prestigious white-collar jobs. Blacks were more likely to have lower paying and less prestigious blue-collar jobs. The original relationship is reported in Table 2.24. The original relationship is 28 percentage points. The researchers were interested in why race influenced the type of job held. Two theories are plausible; both involve discrimination. One theory is that because of discrimination, blacks have unequal educational opportunities and, thus, are less skilled and less qualified to hold white-collar jobs. The other theory holds that even blacks who are qualified are discriminated against, and, therefore, they cannot get white-collar jobs:

Theory 1. race ⟶ discrimination ⟶ education ⟶ occupation

Theory 2. race ⟶ discrimination ⟶ occupation

The difference between these two theories has to do with the point at which discrimination affects people. The first theory says that although discrimination leads to unequal educational opportunities, there is no discrimination in hiring. The reason blacks are not hired is because they are less qualified for the jobs. The second theory says that there is discrimination in the hiring process; even blacks who are qualified will not be hired. Which theory is correct? A three-variable table can help us answer this question. If the first theory is correct, then, when education is controlled, race should not influence occupation. If the second theory is correct, then differences in education will not interpret the relationship between race and occupation (see Chart 2.1).

Chart 2.1. Two Theories of the Reason Race Influenced the Type of Job Held

Theory 1. Percent White Collar

	Education			
	High		Low	
Race				
White	High	(High)	Low	(Low)
Black	High	(Low)	Low	(High)

Theory 2. Percent White Collar

	Education			
	High		Low	
Race				
White	High	(High)	High	(Low)
Black	Low	(Low)	Low	(High)

Both theories accept that whites are more likely than blacks to have high education. The first theory says differences in education account for differences in occupation; the second theory says they do not. The actual data are presented in Table 2.25, which is slightly different from the other three-variable tables we have examined. Instead of having two categories in the test factor, it has three. Thus, this table has three partials.

You should now be able to tell whether the first theory or the second theory is correct. The original relationship was 28 percentage points. In the first partial, it is 27 percentage points (31 minus 4 is

Table 2.25. Percent Having White-Collar Jobs by Race and Education

	Education					
	Grade school		Some high school		Completed high school	
Race						
White	31%	(124)	37%	(78)	49%	(85)
Black	4%	(146)	10%	(113)	24%	(59)

Source: Adapted from Hyman, *Survey Design and Analysis,* Table XX, p. 293. Reprinted with permission of Macmillan Publishing Co. Copyright 1955 by The Free Press, a corporation.

27); in the second, 27 percentage points; and in the third, 25 percentage points. Thus, controlling for education does not significantly reduce the influence of race on occupation. The second theory is correct; blacks having the same educational background as whites are still less likely to have white-collar jobs. This suggests there might be discrimination in hiring.

What kind of elaboration is shown in Table 2.25? The test factor, education, intervenes between race and occupation. Thus, Table 2.25. was an attempt at interpreting the original relationship. However, since the percentage point difference in the partials was basically the same as in the original relationship, the interpretation was not successful. Education is *not* the reason why race influences occupation. Some other intervening variable, possibly discrimination in hiring, must exist that will interpret this relationship.

A great deal of sociological research is like this last example. Researchers must often try many test factors before they find the ones that will reduce the original relationship in the partials. Theory and our substantive knowledge of human behavior act as guides in picking which test factors to use. Sometimes, however, researchers cannot find the right test factor no matter how hard they work. We assume there is a reason for everything: for every original relationship there is some intervening test factor that will interpret it. However, because there is still a great deal to be learned about human behavior and the methods of studying it, our current knowledge is often insufficient to find the right test factor.

Sometimes researchers are unsuccessful in finding the reason why one variable influences another. And sometimes even excellent researchers think they have discovered the reason when they actually have not. One of the most exciting empirical studies ever done in sociology was a study of the printers' union by Seymour Martin Lipset, Martin Trow, and James S. Coleman.[12] They try to explain in their book, *Union Democracy*, why the printers' union has been able to maintain a democratic political system when most unions have not. The book is really a study of the social conditions that enable democracy to persist. As part of this study, the researchers were interested in what conditions led to high levels of political participa-

---

[12]Seymour Martin Lipset, Martin Trow, and James S. Coleman, *Union Democracy* (Garden City, N.Y.: Anchor Books, 1962), chap. 8.

tion. They found that printers working in large shops were more likely to be active in union politics than those working in small shops (see Table 2.26). The original relationship was 19 percentage points.

Table 2.26. Percent Active in Union Politics by Shop Size

	Percent active in union politics
Shop size	
30 or under	24% (165)
More than 30	43% (265)

Source: Adapted from Seymour Martin Lipset, Martin A. Trow, and James S. Coleman, *Union Democracy* (Garden City, N.Y.: Anchor Books, 1962), Figure 28, p. 173. Reprinted with permission of Macmillan Publishing Co. Copyright 1956 by The Free Press, a corporation.

The researchers had several theories to explain this finding. First, they reasoned that workers in small shops would be more management oriented and, thus, less likely to participate in union politics. Management orientation was measured by whether or not the printers wanted to own their own shops, become foremen, or become union officers. Men who wanted to have their own shops or become foremen were considered to be management orientated. Indeed, the researchers found the test factor, management orientation, related to both the independent variable (shop size) and the dependent variable (activity in union politics). To test their theory they constructed a three-variable table (see Table 2.27). Does this table support the researchers' theory? To answer this question we must look at the partials. Whereas the original percentage difference was 19 points, in the three partials of Table 2.27, we get percentage differences of 27 points, 22 points, and one point. The only partial

Table 2.27. Percent Active in Union Politics by Shop Size and Management Orientation

	Management orientation		
	Would rather be union officer	Would rather be foreman	Would like to be neither
Shop size			
30 or less	32% (41)	15% (81)	36% (33)
More than 30	59% (91)	37% (78)	37% (84)

Source: Adapted from Lipset, Trow, and Coleman, *Union Democracy*, Figure 29, p. 176. Reprinted with permission of Macmillan Publishing Co. Copyright 1956 by The Free Press, a corporation.

that is reduced is the one in which the printers expressed no desire to become either foremen or union officers. Yet, on the basis of Table 2.27 the researchers concluded that "the variable of shop size affects the level of printers' union involvement *in part* through the greater tendency of small shops to contain men with pro-management aspirations and orientations.[13] And later they refer to "an additional answer to the question, Why are men in large shops more active in union politics than men in small shops" as if the data of Table 2.27 provided a first answer.

The "additional" answer is that in small shops, printers are less likely to have friends who they can talk with about union politics. In big shops, a man was more likely to have friends who agreed with and would support his political position. In order to preserve consensus in small shops, men avoided becoming active in politics. The researchers reason that in big shops, printers would have more social relations with other printers and, therefore, would be more active in union politics. They present Table 2.28 and Table 2.29 to

Table 2.28. Percent Active in Union Politics by Shop Size and Social Relations

	Social relations			
	High		Low	
Shop size				
30 or less	22%	(82)	18%	(74)
More than 30	51%	(151)	33%	(100)

Source: Adapted from Lipset, Trow, and Coleman, *Union Democracy,* Figure 33, p. 187. Reprinted with permission of Macmillan Publishing Co. Copyright 1956 by The Free Press, a corporation.

test this theory. Do these data support the theory? Again, we must look at the partials to see if the original relationship is reduced. In Table 2.28 we get partials of 29 percentage points and 15 percentage points. Since the original relationship was 19 points, Table 2.28 does not offer much support for the theory. In Table 2.29 we get partials of 12 percentage points and 8 percentage points. This table would seem to offer some support for their theory, except for one fact. Instead of using percent active in union politics as the indicator of the dependent variable in Table 2.29, they have used percent

[13]Lipset, Trow, and Coleman, *Union Democracy,* p. 75.

Table 2.29. Percent "Extremely" Interested in Union Politics by Shop Size and Social Relations

	Social relations			
	High		Low	
Shop size				
30 or less	29%	(82)	23%	(74)
More than 30	41%	(151)	31%	(100)

Source: Adapted from Lipset, Trow, and Coleman, *Union Democracy,* Figure 34, p. 188. Reprinted with permission of Macmillan Publishing Co. Copyright 1956 by The Free Press, a corporation.

"extremely" interested in union politics as the indicator of the dependent variable. When we introduce a third variable to test a hypothesis, we should not change the indicators. In this case, since a new indicator of the dependent variable is used, we must know the relationship between this indicator and shop size (the independent variable). Computing this relationship from Table 2.29, we find that 26 percent of printers in small shops and 37 percent of those in large shops were extremely interested in union politics. The new original relationship is 11 percentage points, about the same as the partials of 12 percentage points and 8 percentage points. Thus, Table 2.29 does not offer support for the researchers' theory. In fact, throughout the chapter they present no table in which they are able to show why printers in big shops were more active in union politics than printers in small shops. Any student who understands the logic of elaboration would be able to read Chapter 8 in *Union Democracy* and see that the authors never really answer the question they set out to.

You have probably noticed that all the examples we have analyzed have been interpretation or attempts at interpretation; that is, the test factor intervening between the independent and dependent variables. We have not analyzed any examples of explanation—that is, the test factor antecedent to the independent variable—because the emphasis in explanatory research is generally on interpretation. Most researchers will not spend much time analyzing relationships they know to be noncausal.

Specification It was stated previously that there are three basic types of elaboration. The first two kinds are explanation and interpretation. The third type of elaboration is termed *specification.* In specification the analyst is not interested in reducing the original relationship but rather is concerned with specifying the conditions under which the relationship is stronger or weaker. To do this, the analyst compares the partials with one another.

A good example of specification is found in a study of voting behavior done by Paul F. Lazarsfeld, Bernard Berelson, and Hazel Gaudet.[14] In their book, *The People's Choice*, they present a two-variable table like Table 2.30. Men are more likely than women to express intention to vote. The percentage difference is 16 points.

Table 2.30. Percent Intending To Vote by Sex

	Percent intending to vote
Sex	
Men	98% (1,294)
Women	82% (1,418)

Source: Adapted from Paul F. Lazarsfeld, Bernard Berelson, and Hazel Gaudet, *The People's Choice*, 2nd ed. New York: Columbia University Press, 1948), Chart 16, p. 48. Reprinted with permission.

Under certain conditions, however, this difference might be greater or lesser. The test factor used by the researchers was level of political interest (see Table 2.31). Table 2.31 shows that the percentage point differences are not the same in each partial. In the first partial, there is a one percentage point difference; in the second, 11 percentage point difference; and the third partial, a 39 percentage point difference. Women who have a great interest in politics are just as likely to vote as men who have a great interest in politics. But

Table 2.31. Percent Intending To Vote by Sex and Political Interest

	Level of interest		
	Great	*Moderate*	*No interest*
Sex			
Men	99% (449)	98% (789)	83% (56)
Women	98% (328)	87% (852)	44% (238)

Source: Adapted from Lazarsfeld, Berelson, and Gaudet, *People's Choice*, Chart 16, p. 48. Reprinted with permission.

[14]Paul F. Lazarsfeld, Bernard Berelson, and Hazel Gaudet, *The People's Choice*, 2nd ed. (New York: Columbia University Press, 1948).

whereas women who are not interested in politics do not intend to vote, most men who are not interested in politics intend to vote anyway.

This type of specification is a half-way step toward interpretation. In Table 2.31, the test factor, level of interest, is related to both the independent variable, sex, and the dependent variable, intention to vote. But we have only reduced the original relationship in two of the partials. There must then be a fourth variable that would reduce the relationship further in the second partial and also reduce it in the third partial. Why would men who have no interest in politics vote anyway? Possibly men may define voting as a social obligation, whereas women would be less likely to do so. Perhaps if we had a measure of this fourth variable and controlled simultaneously for level of interest and whether or not voting was perceived as a social obligation, we might eliminate entirely the difference in intention to vote between men and women.

In a "pure" type of specification, the test factor is not related to one or both of the original two variables. If the test factor is not related to one or both of the original variables, then it is impossible for the original relationship to disappear in all the partials, and the elaboration cannot be interpretation or explanation.

An example of a "pure" specification from another voting study is reported by Hyman. The researchers found that the way in which people vote is strongly influenced by the way in which their fathers voted. The study showed that 87 percent of people with fathers who voted Republican and 51 percent of those with fathers who voted Democratic planned to vote Republican. This strong association indicates a kind of traditionalism among the voters. The analysts were interested in discovering the conditions under which such traditionalism might be broken down. Since Elmira, the town in which the research was conducted, was heavily Republican, the researchers hypothesized that the length of time the person had lived in Elmira would be an important factor in upholding or breaking traditionalism. The political context would reinforce the tendency of people whose fathers had voted Republican to maintain this tradition, whereas it would discourage people whose fathers had voted Democratic from maintaining the family tradition. The data are presented in Table 2.32. The association between the way in which people planned to vote and how their fathers voted is stronger

Table 2.32. Percent Planning To Vote Republican by Father's Vote and Length of Residence

	Length of residence			
	Old timer		Newcomer	
Father's vote				
Republican	87%	(284)	85%	(47)
Democrat	53%	(189)	37%	(27)

Source: Hyman, *Survey Design and Analysis*, Table XXXIX, p. 307. Reprinted with permission of Macmillan Publishing Co. Copyright 1955 by The Free Press, a corporation.

among newcomers. Thus, among newcomers the father's vote makes for a 48 percentage point difference in an individual's vote intention; but among old timers, the father's vote makes for a 34 percentage point difference in an individual's vote intention. The longer children of fathers who voted Democratic have been in Elmira, the more time there has been for the Republican environment to break down their traditionalism.

To understand what is meant by a "pure" specification, let us analyze Table 2.32, using the logic of elaboration. The dependent variable is vote intention, the independent variable is the father's vote, and the test factor is length of residence. We reported that there was a 36 percentage point difference in the original relationship (87 minus 51 is 36). The test factor is related to the dependent variable, but it is not related to the original independent variable. Length of residence in Elmira is not associated with the father's vote. Since the test factor is not related to one of the original variables, the elaboration cannot be either interpretation or explanation. Next we look at the partials and see that the test factor does specify the original relationship, which is larger in one of the partials than the other. Table 2.32 does not show why father's vote influences a person's vote, but it does specify the conditions under which it will have a stronger or weaker influence.

Review of Elaboration In practice, sociologists consider a relationship between two variables to be causal if it meets three conditions:

1. The two variables must be associated.
2. The independent variable must precede the dependent variable in time.

3. There must be no antecedent test factor that, when controlled, will make the relationship between the original two variables disappear.

Sociologists doing explanatory research are interested in finding causal relationships. In addition, they want to know why and under what conditions the independent variable influences the dependent variable. They use the process of elaboration—starting with two-variable relationships and introducing additional variables—to test their hypotheses. There are three basic types of elaboration:[15]

1. *Explanation.* We suspect that a two-variable relationship is not causal. We find a third variable, antecedent in time to the original independent variable, that is associated with both of the original variables. If, when the third variable is controlled, the relationship between the original variables disappear, we conclude that the interpretation of the original relationship as causal would be spurious. If the original relationship is maintained, it is considered to be a causal one (until perhaps another independent variable that precedes the original independent variable is found to eliminate the original relationship).

2. *Interpretation.* We want to know why the independent variable influences the dependent variable. Theory and substantive knowledge suggest that a particular test factor may be the answer. The test factor intervenes in time between the original two variables and is associated with both of them. If, when we control for the test factor, the original relationship disappears, we know our theory is correct. If the original relationship is maintained in the partials, the theory is wrong and we must look for another theory.

3. *Specification.* We want to know the conditions under which a two-variable relationship will be strong or weak. Theory and substantive knowledge suggest that a particular variable may be important. We construct a three-variable table to see if the size of the original relationship varies in the different partials. In a "pure" type of specification, the test factor will not be associated with at least one of the original variables.

[15]For a more detailed discussion of elaboration, in addition to the excellent books by Travis Hirschi and Hanan C. Selvin as well as by Herbert H. Hyman, see Morris Rosenberg, *The Logic of Survey Analysis* (New York: Basic Books, 1968).

EXERCISES

1. Make a list of five sociological dependent variables. For each dependent variable, list at least one possible independent variable and one test factor.

2. The students in a sociology class wanted to determine whether the age of scientists is related to the importance of their discoveries. They collected the data given below. Since 60 percent of the important discoveries are made by scientists under the age of forty, they concluded that older scientists are less creative than younger ones. Are they right? Explain your answer.

	Number making important discoveries	Number making unimportant discoveries	Total
Age of scientist			
60 or older	10	90	100
50–59	20	180	200
40–49	30	270	300
30–39	40	360	400
29 or younger	50	450	500
Total	150	1,350	1,500

3. Percentage the following table.

	Attends religious services	Does not attend religious services
Religion		
Protestant	100	300
Catholic	200	100
Jew	35	65

4. Examine each of the following tables and determine whether it has been percentaged properly. If it has not been percentaged correctly, repercentage it.

a.

	Percent juvenile delinquents	
Type of family		
Lives with both parents	6%	(1,000)
Lives with one parent	20%	(200)
Lives with neither parent	25%	(50)

b.

	Percent working class	
Voted for:		
Democrats	60%	(1,000)
Republicans	40%	(800)

c.

	Percent girls	
Drug use		
Smoked marijuana at least once	40%	(600)
Never smoked marijuana	40%	(600)

5. In a freshman class of 2,410 students, there were 1,125 girls, 1,195 students who had traveled outside the United States, and 733 boys who had not traveled outside the United States. How many girls had traveled outside the United States?

6.

	Support for abortion legislation	
	Yes	No
Political affiliation		
Democrat	200	300
Republican	400	100

a. How many people are in this study?

b. How many are Democrats?

c. How many Republicans support the legislation?

d. How many Democrats support the legislation?

e. What is the dependent variable?

f. What is the independent variable?

g. What percentage of Democrats support the legislation?

h. What percentage of Republicans support the legislation?

7. Examine the following tables and statements. If the data support the statement, put a check at the right of the table. If the data do

not support the statement, change as few numbers as you can to make the table support the statement.

a. Jews were more likely than members of other religious groups to support George McGovern for president.

	Percent supporting McGovern	
Religion		
Catholic	45%	(1,000)
Protestant	40%	(2,000)
Jew	45%	(300)

b. Women study harder than men.

	Percent studying ten hours a week or more	
Sex		
Women	65%	(4,000)
Men	40%	(4,000)

c. Black people are more likely than white people to commit crimes because black people are poorer, and poor people are more likely to commit crimes.

	Percent who have comitted a crime			
	Blacks		Whites	
Income of family				
$7,500 or more	3%	(200)	3%	(2,000)
Less than $7,500	12%	(400)	12%	(300)

d. Male teachers are more likely than female teachers to support a strike because male teachers are more dissatisfied with their jobs, and dissatisfied teachers are more likely to strike.

	Percent supporting strike			
	Dissatisfaction			
	High		Low	
Sex				
Male	70%	(200)	70%	(100)
Female	35%	(100)	35%	(200)

8. In each of the following cases, decide whether or not the table supports the statement and give the reason for your decision.

   a. Women are more likely than men to get high grades in college.

	Percent students with average of B+ or better	
Sex		
Women	30%	(1,000)
Men	30%	(1,000)

   b. Male students are more likely than female students to major in science or mathematics.

	Percent majoring in science or mathematics	
Sex		
Women	10%	(1,000)
Men	30%	(1,000)

   c. Elementary school teachers are less likely than secondary school teachers to support a strike because most elementary school teachers are women, and women are less likely than men to support a strike.

	Percent teachers supporting strike			
	Men		Women	
Type of school				
Elementary	30%	(100)	30%	(900)
Secondary	60%	(400)	60%	(400)

   d. Elementary school teachers are less likely than secondary school teachers to support a strike because they are more likely to fear reprisals, and teachers who fear reprisals are less likely to strike.

	Percent teachers supporting strike			
	Fear reprisals		Do not fear reprisals	
Type of school				
Elementary	25%	(800)	70%	(200)
Secondary	25%	(300)	70%	(500)

9. Is each one of the following sets of statements right or wrong and why?

   a. There is a relationship between authoritarianism and the use of strict child-rearing techniques. When education is controlled, the original relationship disappears. Authoritarianism is not a cause of child-rearing techniques.

   b. There is a relationship between race and family instability. When social class is controlled, the original relationship disappears. Race is not a cause of family instability.

   c. There is a relationship between family instability and juvenile delinquency. When social class is controlled, the original relationship disappears. Family instability is not a cause of juvenile delinquency.

   d. There is a relationship between social class and juvenile delinquency. When family instability is controlled, the original relationship disappears. Family instability is a cause of juvenile delinquency.

10. Study the table below to answer the following questions.

   a. What proportion of teachers coming from lower-class families went out on strike?

   b. What proportion of teachers coming from middle-class families went out on strike?

   c. Is class of origin correlated with attitudes toward unions?

   d. Is the interpretation that class of origin is a cause of striking spurious? Why?

   e. Is the interpretation that attitudes toward unions are a cause of striking spurious? Why?

	Percent teachers striking			
	Attitudes toward unions			
	Favorable		Unfavorable	
Class of origin				
Lower	70%	(70)	30%	(40)
Middle	70%	(60)	30%	(120)

11. Study the table below to answer the following questions.

    a. Are middle-class people more likely than working-class people to smoke marijuana once a week or more?

    b. Are people who attend college more likely than those who do not attend college to smoke marijuana once a week or more?

    c. Who are more likely to attend college—people from middle-class families or those from working-class families?

    d. Does class of origin have a causal influence on smoking marijuana? Why?

    e. Does college attendance have a causal influence on smoking marijuana? Why?

    f. Does smoking marijuana have a causal influence on class of origin? Why?

	Percent smoking marijuana once a week or more	
	Attend college	Do not attend college
Class of origin		
Middle class	50% (600)	20% (300)
Working class	50% (300)	20% (700)

12. Make up tables illustrating the following statements.

    a. Education influences attitude toward socialized medicine.

    b. College graduates are more likely than those who did not graduate from college to favor socialized medicine because college graduates are more liberal.

    c. When we control for class of origin, level of education still influences attitude toward socialized medicine.

    d. People from middle-class families are more likely than those from working-class families to favor socialized medicine because people from middle-class families are more likely to go to college.

Chapter 3 Quantitative Methods: Types of Data

In this chapter we shall review the different types of data collected by sociologists who do quantitative research. In quantitative research the sociologist collects data that either is numerical to begin with (for example, income) or can be converted into numbers. For example, one variable in a quantitative study might be political affiliation; all those who are Republicans could be coded as 1, Democrats as 2, members of other parties as 3, and independents as 4. All quantitative research involves the application of various statistical techniques that are used to arrange and analyze the data so that researchers may answer the questions they set out to investigate. In the next chapter we shall discuss several ways in which quantitative data are analyzed.

SURVEYS Many of the studies discussed in this book use data from social surveys. The study on attitude toward impeachment that we discussed in Chapter 2 employed survey data. There are two basic ways in which survey data are collected. In the first method, interviewers talk directly to people; they read questions to them from a prepared questionnaire. Sometimes interviews are conducted over the telephone. The major disadvantage of telephone interviews is that they must usually be limited to no more than twenty minutes. In the second method, a questionnaire is mailed to the respondent, who fills it out and returns it by mail. The personal interview method is very expensive; but there are fewer refusals to answer the questionnaire, more personal questions can be asked, and the interviewer can explain a question that the respondent does not understand. The only reason for mailing questionnaires is to save money.

There are some groups that could not be studied by a mail questionnaire. An example would be welfare recipients in New York City. Many of them have not been to high school and have difficulty reading. Even if they could read the questionnaire, many would misinterpret some of the questions. Generally, only highly educated groups can be studied by using mail questionnaires.

When sociologists decide to conduct a survey, how do they know whom to interview? Can sociologists rely on data received from the first 300 people they find? Such surveys would generally be of little value, since usually the researchers are interested in finding out something about a particular group of people. If survey results are to be meaningful, then, they must be obtained from a carefully selected group of people. Usually it is impossible to interview all the members of the group being studied. The technique that the sociologist uses to determine whom to interview is termed *sampling*.

Sampling When a sociologist wants to study a group of people, it is usually not necessary or possible to collect data on every member of the group. If we want to study doctors, we would not need to collect data on the approximately 350,000 physicians in the United States. If we wanted to study the attitudes of college students toward drugs, we would not have to interview every college student. In the study of the attitudes of Long Island residents toward impeachment, it was impossible to interview every Long Island resident. What is possible and necessary is to have a properly selected sample of the group.

The group we want to study is termed the *population*, and the group we actually have data on is the *sample*.

One type of sample is a *simple random sample*, one in which every member of the population has an equal chance of being selected. If we wanted to choose a simple random sample of 10 students in a particular sociology class, we could write the name of every student on a different card, put all the cards in a hat, mix them up, and then pull 10 cards out. Each student in the class would have an equal chance of ending up in the sample if the cards were thoroughly mixed.

If a sample is actually randomly selected, we can use information obtained from the sample to make statements about the population. Statisticians have figured out the relationship between the size of the sample and the chance of making an incorrect statement.

In a recent study of patterns of social mobility in the United States, Peter Blau and Otis Dudley Duncan used data collected by the Bureau of the Census on about 20,000 Americans.[1] This sample was so large that it was almost impossible for the researchers to draw conclusions from the data that would not be correct for the population. Although it is usually preferable to have large samples, sometimes relatively small samples can be surprisingly useful. Thus, the people who study the viewing audience of television shows, by monitoring about 1,000 randomly chosen television sets, can make a very accurate estimate of how many Americans watched any particular television show. Political pollsters, who interview as few as 1,500 Americans, are able to come up with pretty close estimates of how people will vote in a presidential election. What is important is *not* the proportion of the population included in the sample, but the absolute size of the sample and how variable the population is.

The more variation there is in the population being studied, the larger the sample required to adequately reflect the population. As a limiting case, let us consider populations in which there is no variance on a variable (for example, a population in which every person is white). In order to know the racial composition of a population with no racial variance we would only need a sample of

[1]Peter Blau and Otis Dudley Duncan, *The American Occupational Structure* (New York: John Wiley, 1967).

one. Now let us consider a slightly more complex case. We are trying to determine the mean IQ of a population of students. If there is a lot of variance in IQ, there will be a relatively large number of students with either unusually high or low IQs. If we only pick a small sample, the chances of getting one of these cases in the sample will be relatively high. On the other hand, if we have a population of students in which there is relatively little variance on IQ, there will be relatively few extreme cases. In this instance a small sample will be less likely to include extreme cases.

Let us suppose that one of the questions we are concerned with in a survey is the religious affiliation of the respondent. In the population we are studying, 50 percent of the people are Catholics.[2] If the sample were to perfectly reflect the population, then 50 percent of the respondents in the sample would be Catholic. But, in fact, the sample proportion may vary slightly from the population proportion. Let us see what happens when we draw samples of different sizes from the same population. In the first case, if we were to draw 100 different random samples from the same population, we would find that the largest number of samples would show 50 percent of the respondents as Catholics. But some samples would show greater than 50 percent as Catholics and some fewer than 50 percent as Catholics. This is shown in A of Figure 3.1. This bar graph shows the hypothetical distribution of 100 samples of 1,000 people. The numbers along the bottom represent the proportions of Catholics obtained in the samples. In each bar we show the number of samples containing this proportion of Catholics. Thus, in A of Figure 3.1, 25 of the 100 samples had 50 percent Catholics (the exact population proportion). One of the 100 samples had 54 percent Catholics, and one had 46 percent. No sample had either more than 54 percent or less than 46 percent Catholics.

In B of Figure 3.1, we show the second case, the distribution of 100 samples of 5,000 people. Here we see that 52 of the 100 samples had 50 percent Catholics; only 2 samples had 48 percent Catholics, and 2 had 52 percent. No sample had less than 48 percent or more than 52 percent Catholics. Thus, we know that if we have a random

---

[2]Generally, we do not know the exact distribution of a variable in the population. However, even if we did know the distribution, we would still have to collect the data in order to determine the relationships among the variables.

Figure 3.1. Distributions of Samples of Three Different Sizes

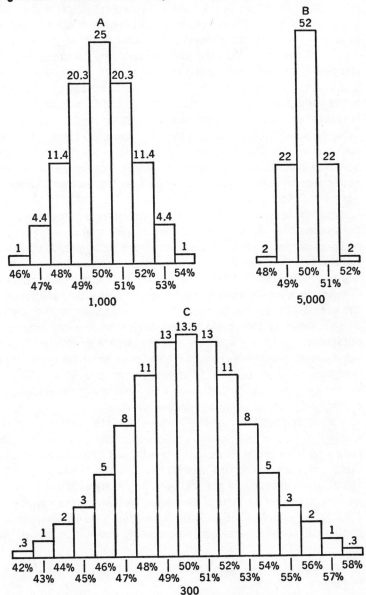

sample of 5,000 cases, our sample proportion will not differ from the population proportion by more than 2 percentage points and usually it will be closer than that. In fact, in the majority of cases it will be exactly the same as the population proportion.

In C of Figure 3.1, the third case, we show the distribution of 100 samples of 300 people. We notice how this distribution of a relatively small sample of the population is much more spread out than those of the larger samples of population. Only 13.5 of the samples have 50 percent Catholics.[3] Some samples show 58 percent Catholics and some 42 percent Catholics. In a sample of only 300 cases, it is quite possible to get considerable discrepancy from the population proportion. However, even with samples of this relatively small size, we notice that most of the samples are concentrated within 3 percentage points of the population proportion.

What these figures show us is that the larger a random sample, the less the chance that the sample results will differ greatly from the real population. Thus, if we are interested in getting results that are accurate within a few percentage points, we should try to have as large a sample as is feasible. In studies that require highly accurate description, such as political polls that will be used to predict who will win an election, it is important to have larger random samples. In studies aimed at showing the relationships among variables, it is possible to use smaller samples. In these explanatory studies it does not make so much difference if the sample proportion differs from the population proportion by a few percentage points. This is because our primary purpose would be to discover the relationship among variables, not the population proportion.

It should be remembered that the precision of a random sample is a result of its size and *not* the proportion of the population represented by the sample. Thus, 1,000 will be just about as accurate a sample of a population of 10,000,000 as it will be of a population of 10,000. If we are doing a political poll in a county of 200,000 people we will need just as large a sample as we would in a country of 200,000,000 people. This would not be true if the variance in the population of the county was considerably lower than that of the

[3]This is a hypothetical number; we would have, of course, either 13 or 14 samples having 50 percent Catholics.

country. Since we usually do not know the variance prior to doing the study, we must assume that it may be large and use a large sample.

One of the problems in taking social surveys is making sure we get a representative sample of the people we want to study. We must pick our sample in such a way that every member of the population actually has an equal chance to fall into the sample. For example, if we wanted to study the students in a particular school, what would be wrong with interviewing every tenth student to enter the library? This would not be a random sample because not all students use the library and the students who do not use it would have no chance to be represented. Our sample would overrepresent students who use the library. A good way to choose a random sample would be to get a list of all students and pick every tenth student on the list. This would be termed a *systematic sample*, and if we interviewed all the students chosen in this way, our results could be generalized to all students at the school. However, what if 30 percent of the students chosen to be interviewed could not be found or refused to be interviewed? We would never know if the students we were able to interview were different from the students we could not interview. This is a very serious problem in using mail questionnaires or telephone surveys. Researchers who use these techniques rarely complete interviews with more than 70 percent of their sample. They never really know if the people who did not return the questionnaire or refused to be interviewed were different from those who did.

There are rough ways to check the accuracy of samples. We do this by comparing characteristics of the sample with known characteristics of the population. If we sent a questionnaire to a sample of students at a particular school, we might compare the proportion of upperclassmen in our sample with the proportion in the school. However, even if the sample is similar to the population on all variables that are known for the population, there would be no guarantee that the sample would be similar to the population on variables that are unknown for the population. For example, if we were using a mail questionnaire to study drug use by students at the school, we would first compare the characteristics of the achieved sample (those who returned the questionnaire) with characteristics of the known population. However, even if the sample perfectly matched the population on known characteristics, it would still be possible that people who returned the questionnaire differed in important ways from those who did not. In a study on drug use, for example, it would be possible that heavy drug users would be less likely to return the questionnaire because they may fear that doing so might give away their identity and result in repercussions. It is important, therefore, to be wary of accepting generalizations made from nonrandom samples and applied to populations.

Measurement After sociologists decide what problem to study and who will be in the sample, they must determine what indicators they will use. In some cases this is quite unproblematic. If one of the variables is sex, it would be measured by one question on the questionnaire. The same would be true for variables such as religion, age, and political party preference. However, as variables become more abstract they also become more difficult to measure. Whereas religion can be measured by one straightforward question, how would you measure religiousness, or how religious a person was? What would be wrong with asking this question: "Do you consider yourself to be very religious, moderately religious, or not too religious?" One problem would be that different people hold different meanings of the term *religious*. To one person it might mean having faith in God; to another it might mean being a kind and charitable person; and to still another it might mean going to church every Sunday. When people answered this kind of question, we would not know what they were thinking of, and, therefore, the answers could not be meaningfully compared. Another problem with the question would be that even if everybody held the same meaning for the term, you would not know the frame of reference each respondent used in deciding how religious he or she was. We know that people do not make judgments about themselves in a social vacuum; they compare themselves with others. If you grew up in a very devout family and someone asks you how religious you are, you might say that you are not too religious. Indeed, perhaps you were not religious in comparison with other members of your family.

A well-known example of the importance of frame of reference in answering questions comes from a study of two housing communities: Crafttown and Hilltown.[4] Interviewers asked people living in these two communities how interested they were in politics. The sociologists doing the study were surprised when the people in Hilltown said that they were more interested in politics than were the people living in Crafttown. This was exactly the opposite of what the sociologists had actually observed. Crafttown seemed to be a very active political community in which the residents took part in a wide variety of political activities; Hilltown was, to the eyes of the observers, much less politically active. Were the impressions of the observers mistaken? Eventually, the sociologists discovered that the answers to the questions could be explained by entirely different frames of reference employed by the people in the two communities. Practically everyone in Crafttown, the politically buzzing community, knew someone who was more active in politics than he or she was. Therefore, when the respondents answered the question, they compared themselves with others in their environment and said that they were not very active. If individuals in Hilltown were politically active at all, they probably were more active than others they knew and therefore thought of themselves as being very active.

Because of these problems in using respondents' self-assessments, the social researcher has to use less direct ways of measuring an abstract variable, such as religiousness. The first step in formulating questions to measure abstract variables is to think of their component parts. If we were doing a study of the attitudes of students toward the different courses they had in college, we might be interested in knowing how relevant the students found each course. We could, of course, directly ask: "Was the course very relevant, somewhat relevant, not too relevant, or totally irrelevant?" But this question would present the same problems as did the one on religiousness. We would be much better off if we broke relevance down into its component parts and then asked a question on each part. Ask yourself, What do I mean by relevance? A relevant course might be one that deals with topics of current interest, one that provides knowledge useful in a future career, one that provides knowledge useful in other areas of life, or one that is merely

[4]This study by Robert K. Merton is still unpublished.

interesting. Instead of asking how relevant the students thought a course was, we could ask the following questions:

1. How interested were you in the subject matter of the course—very interested, interested, or not too interested?
2. Do you think that the material presented in the course will be useful in your future career—definitely yes, probably yes, probably not, or definitely not?
3. Do you think that the material presented in the course will be useful in the future in areas of your life other than career—definitely yes, probably yes, probably not, or definitely not?
4. Compared with other courses that you have taken, was the course—among the most interesting, above average in interest, below average in interest, or among the least interesting?

We might also ask the general question on relevance, and then, by separately cross-tabulating the answers to the general question with the answers to each of the above questions, we could see what the students we interviewed were thinking when they answered the general question.

How do we know if the way we have decided to measure a variable is a good one? Measures can be validated both logically and empirically. If we are measuring religiousness, we might justify using a question on belief in God by referring to traditional definitions of religiousness.

Empirically, measures can be validated by showing that the measure in question is correlated with a less problematic measure. As an example, let us consider how we might measure the quality of research papers published by various professors. All of us have heard that professors today have to publish or perish. Supposedly, professors who publish a long string of trivial papers will be more heavily rewarded than those who publish only a few high-quality pieces. Is this really true? Which is the more important influence on the success of a professor—the quality or the quantity of his or her publications?

To do this study we need measures of success (the dependent variable) and the quantity and quality of publications (the independent variables). Success might be measured by the prestige of the department in which the professor teaches. The American Council on Education does a periodic survey of the prestige of academic departments, so we would not have to measure this ourselves. We can easily find the quantity of publications by referring to a journal of abstracts, which contains short summaries of articles published in many different journals. (For example, most articles published by psychologists are summarized in *Psychological Abstracts*.)

Once we have found the quantity of papers, how would we measure the quality? If we were expert in all academic fields, we could read all the papers and assess them. This would not be practical, however, because it would take forever and, besides, few if any sociologists would be competent to evaluate work done in other disciplines. Another way to measure the quality of a professor's work would be to ask a panel of judges, each of whom would be an expert in the field under consideration, to evaluate the work of the professor. We could do this by sending professors questionnaires in which we asked them to rate the work of the professor in relation to the work of others in the same field. This would be a good way to measure quality if we defined high-quality work as that which is currently valued by one's colleagues. The problem with this measure is that it involves sending out questionnaires to large numbers of people. We can do this if we have the time and money. But if we were to reason that a high-quality paper is one that many other researchers find useful and cite in their own works, we might be able to use the number of citations to a professor's work as a measure of quality. Here we are in luck, because we can look up citations in the *Science Citation Index* or the *Social Science Citation Index*, both of which, taken together, list all references made each year in over 3,000 scholarly journals.

How do we prove that the number of citations a professor has received is a valid way to measure quality of work? We do this by showing that the number of citations is correlated with other measures of quality. We might go to several professors of physics and ask them to name the five physicists who have contributed the most to the field in the last two decades. We would then refer to the *Science Citation Index* and see how many citations their works have received. If they have received many more citations than the average physicist, this is evidence that citations are indeed a good way to measure quality. Another way to validate the measure would be to look up the number of citations received by scientists who have won the Nobel prize. Certainly Nobel laureates have done high-quality work. If citations are a valid measure of quality, then Nobel prize winners should have many more citations to their works than the average scientist. Indeed, this is exactly what happens. In 1965 the mean number of citations to all scientists appearing in the *Science Citation Index* was six. The mean number of citations received by Nobel laureates was 153.[5]

At this point in our discussion, it might be useful to return to one of the studies we analyzed in Chapter 1. The question that Bradburn and Caplovitz used to measure happiness presented some of the same problems as the examples we have been discussing here. People may have used different frames of reference to answer the question: "Taking all things together, how would you say things are these days—would you say you are very happy, pretty happy, or not too happy?" Thus, how do we know that respondents who said that they were very happy were in fact happier than other people who said that they were pretty happy? Also, how do we know exactly what people were thinking about when they answered this question? In order to validate the question, Bradburn and Caplovitz showed that how people answered the happiness question was correlated with how they answered other questions designed to measure positive feelings toward life. Thus, people who were pleased about having accomplished something, proud because someone complimented them on something they had done, particularly excited or interested in something, and "on top of the world" were more likely to say they were very happy. The happiness question was a particularly difficult one to validate, and some sociologists would probably still be skeptical about its validity. Yet despite the fact that the use of this question may have caused the researchers to misclassify some respondents, it was still possible for the study to yield roughly valid results.

Sometimes sociological measurements can yield fairly accurate results even though some people will be misclassified. It is important to remember that sociologists are not so much interested in correct-

[5]Jonathan R. Cole and Stephen Cole, "Measuring the Quality of Sociological Research," *The American Sociologist* 6 (February 1971): 23–29.

ly classifying individuals as they are in finding the relations among variables or in finding out why groups of people act as they do. Today many college students want to become doctors. At the school in which I teach, about 50 percent of the entering students in one freshman class were pre-medical students. Suppose we wanted to know what the effect of social class background is on the decision to become a pre-med. Are students from working-class backgrounds more or less likely to become pre-meds than students from middle-class backgrounds? We might hypothesize that students from working-class backgrounds will be more interested in social mobility than are those from middle-class backgrounds. Since becoming a physician (the most highly paid and prestigious occupation in the United States) depends more on the ability of the student than family connections, it is a good channel of upward mobility.

If we were administering a short questionnaire on occupational choice, the dependent variable for this study might be measured by a simple straightforward question: "At the present time, what occupation do you think you will enter?" One of the choices would be "doctor." Now let us suppose that we have two questions measuring class of origin (the independent variable). In the first question, we ask the students whether or not their fathers graduated from college. Those whose fathers are college graduates will be considered middle class; those whose fathers are not college graduates will be considered working class. In the second question we ask the students how much money their fathers make. Those whose fathers earn $15,000 a year or more will be considered middle class; those whose fathers earn less than $15,000 will be considered working class. Although the answers to these questions are associated, they are not perfectly correlated. If you cross-tabulated the answers to the two measures of class of origin, you might get the data in Table 3.1. Using either measure the 400 cases in cell 1 would be classified as middle class, and the 700 cases in cell 4 would be classified as

Table 3.1.

	Income of the father	
	$15,000 or more	Less than $15,000
Education of the father		
College graduate	400	100
Not college graduate	300	700

working class. But using each measure, the cases in cells 2 and 3 would be classified differently. This would be serious if it led to different substantive conclusions. Such discrepancies in classification, however, do not often lead to different substantive results. Consider the two-variable tables we might obtain using the two different measures of class of origin (see Table 3.2.) Although not all

Table 3.2. Two Measures of Class of Origin by Decision To Become Pre-Med Students

	Percent saying they were pre-meds	
Education of the father		
College graduate	60%	(500)
Not college graduate	45%	(1,000)
Income of the father		
$10,000 or more	60%	(700)
Less than $10,000	41%	(800)

the same students would be classified as middle class or working class in the first and second parts of Table 3.2, both measures yield quite similar substantive conclusions; that is, students coming from middle-class backgrounds are more likely to be pre-meds than students coming from working-class backgrounds. The data in Table 3.2 would lead us to reject our hypothesis. If we use both social class indicators as independent variables in a three-variable table, we can get a better idea of why the two indicators yield similar substantive results (see Table 3.3.) In cells 2 and 3 of Table 3.3, the cases that are misclassified in either part of Table 3.2 have a roughly equal proportion wanting to become doctors. The point is that when sociologists study a fairly large group of people, they can make

Table 3.3. Education and Income of the Father by Decision To Become Pre-Med Students

	Percent saying they were pre-meds			
	Income of the father			
	$15,000 or more		Less than $15,000	
Education of the father				
College graduate	62%	(400)	50%	(100)
Not college graduate	57%	(300)	40%	(700)

"errors" in classifying some of these people that will not greatly affect the substantive conclusions of the study.

Indexes Although we should not be overly concerned with the possibility of misclassifying individuals on a particular variable, we obviously would like to make as few mistakes as possible. One way to cut down the number of mistakes is to combine several indicators of the same variable into an index. We might make a mistake in classifying a particular individual on one of the indicators, but we are unlikely to misclassify the *same* individual on all the indicators. When we use several indicators to measure a particular variable, we construct an *index*. For example, if we wanted to find out whether or not people were liberal or conservative, we might ask them the following questions:

1. Do you favor the nationalization of oil companies and other power-producing industries?
   (a) Yes
   (b) No
2. Do you favor the legalization of marijuana?
   (a) Yes
   (b) No
3. Are you in favor of allowing any person over eighteen to see films containing explicit sex scenes?
   (a) Yes
   (b) No
4. Are you in favor of socialized medicine?
   (a) Yes
   (b) No

We can divide the answers into two categories: those indicating a liberal orientation toward some major issues and those indicating a more conservative orientation. In all four questions in this example, answer (a) indicates a liberal attitude and answer (b) a conservative attitude. For the simplest type of index, we would add up the number of liberal responses. If a respondent gave answer (a) to all four questions, he or she would be given a score of 4; if a respondent gave answer (a) to three out of the four, he or she would be given a score of 3, and so on. The lowest score on the index would be zero.

The higher the respondent's score on the index, the more likely that he or she would have liberal attitudes. In order to ensure that all items in the index actually measure the same concept, each item should be positively correlated with every other item. Thus, people who favor socialized medicine should be more likely to favor the legalization of marijuana than people who oppose socialized medicine. If one of the items is not correlated with the others, the question is either a poor question or one that measures some different concept and should be left out of the index.

After we have given each person a score on the index, we might decide to divide the scores into three groups—liberals, moderates, and conservatives. For example, people who scored 4 and 3 might be classified as liberals; people who scored 2, as moderates; and those who scored 1 and zero, as conservatives. The cutting points are arbitrary because the index would only measure *relative* degrees of liberalness. Usually, we put the cutting points at the places that will give a roughly equal number of cases in each category. Thus, if we wanted to divide the scores into liberals and conservatives, and out of 1,000 cases, 500 people scored 4 and the other 500 were distributed between 3 and zero, we might classify only those who scored 4 as liberals and classify those who scored zero, 1, 2, or 3 as conservatives. When classifying people whom we study, we usually do so relative to the other people in the sample. Occasionally, however, we are interested in a more "absolute" classification and must determine before the data are collected how we will classify the people.

Thus far, we have discussed only the simplest type of index, one in which the number of positive responses are added. Researchers sometimes use more complicated indexes. One of these types is the *Guttman scale*. In the simple index, it is not necessary to note which questions receive positive answers, but this is not the case in a Guttman scale. Although in a Guttman scale, like in the simple index, the scores assigned to respondents are equivalent to the sum of the positive responses, the Guttman scale is based on the premise that there should be an order among the questions if a group of questions is a good indicator of one variable. For example, if we wanted to measure mathematical ability, we might ask the following three questions:

1. Can you add and subtract?
2. Can you do long division?
3. Can you solve equations with one unknown?

What are the possible combinations of answers to these questions? In Table 3.4 a plus indicates a positive answer; and a minus, a negative answer. There are eight possible combinations of answers to the set of three questions. However, some of these combinations are rather unlikely to appear. How likely would it be for response pattern 7 to appear? Very few people who cannot add, subtract, or do long division can solve equations. In fact because the questions are ordered in terms of difficulty, we would expect almost all the responses to fall into patterns 1, 2, 4, and 8. Anyone who can do the hardest problems can do the easier ones, but the opposite is not necessarily true. If many responses fall into patterns 3, 5, 6, and 7, the questions are not very good.

Table 3.4.

	Question 1 (add and subtract)	Question 2 (long division)	Question 3 (simple equations)
1.	+	+	+
2.	+	+	−
3.	+	−	+
4.	+	−	−
5.	−	+	+
6.	−	+	−
7.	−	−	+
8.	−	−	−

An excellent model of a Guttman scale can be found in a study of the attitudes of college students.[6] The researchers wanted to measure how religious the students were. In Table 3.5 we present the five questions asked and the proportion of students who gave a "religious" response. The sociologists found that if they left out the fourth item, the one on attendance at religious services, the other four items met the criteria for a Guttman scale. The other four items

---

[6]Rose Goldsen et al., *What College Students Think* (Princeton: Van Nostrand, 1960), chap. 7.

Table 3.5.

	Students giving "religious" response
Questions	
1. Need for religious faith	80%
2. "I believe in a Divine God. . . ."	48%
3. Church or religion "has its own personality"	38%
4. Attend religious services once a week or more	27%
5. Religion is expected to be a major source of satisfaction in life	17%
Total number of students = 2,975	

Source: Rose Goldsen et al., *What College Students Think* (Princeton: Van Nostrand, 1960), p. 159. Reprinted with permission of Van Nostrand Rheinhold Co. © 1960 by Litton Educational Publishing, Inc.

measure religious philosophy as opposed to religious behavior. Just like the mathematics example we used above, the four items on religious philosophy are ordered. Practically everyone who said that religion is expected to be a major source of satisfaction in their lives also said that he or she had a need for religious faith, but many people who had a need for religious faith did not expect religion to be a major source of satisfaction in their lives.

Indirect Indicators When conducting a survey it is not always possible to think of all the variables that will turn out to be important in the analysis. Frequently research analysts will have to use their ingenuity to improvise indicators of variables that were either left out of the questionnaire or were not adequately measured.[7]

An example is provided by a survey I recently conducted on the determinants of political participation. We wanted to find out why some people were registered to vote and others were not. We interviewed by telephone a random sample of 648 Long Island residents. On one question we asked them: "Were you registered to vote in November of 1974?" Since we knew that many people who are not registered say that they are, we went to the Board of Election

---

[7]This improvisation is even more important when doing "secondary analysis." In secondary analysis the researcher analyzes a body of data collected by someone else, frequently for a problem different than the one the researcher is interested in. Since the data available may not contain direct measures of some important variables, the researcher must try to use indirect measures.

records and looked to see if the people we had interviewed were actually registered and had voted. It turned out that although 87 percent of the people we interviewed said they were registered, only 65 percent were in fact registered.

As an aside, this discrepancy points up a very important problem in survey research: getting respondents to tell the truth. There are two types of questions on which you can expect a significant amount of lying. The first type question is related to topics for which strong norms exist. People in the United States are expected to register and vote. In fact, 96 percent of the people we interviewed agreed with the statement: "Every citizen has a moral obligation to vote." Those people who are not registered may feel guilty about this and lie. Although lying on this type of question can be minimized by using certain techniques,[8] it can almost never be completely eliminated. The other type of question on which people are likely to lie are those about deviant forms of behavior, such as cheating, deviant sex practices, or criminal behavior. The respondents are afraid that if they tell the truth there may be repercussions. Again, although lying on the second type of question can be dealt with in various ways, it will not be completely eliminated. Researchers asking these kinds of questions must realize that their results will be distorted and should not treat them as accurate descriptions.

To return to the example of indirect indicators, I mentioned that I used the Board of Elections data as a measure of the dependent variable (being registered to vote). On doing so, I found that middle-class people were more likely than working-class people to be registered. Why? I had two hypotheses. The first was that middle-class people, through their education and jobs, acquired greater interest in politics. By controlling for indicators of political interest I produced three-variable tables showing a reduction in the effect of social class on registration when interest is held constant.

The other hypothesis was that norms (social expectations) concerning political participation vary from class to class and that the norms regarding political participation would be stronger for

---

[8]For example, on our survey, before we asked people whether or not they were registered, we asked them the names of the candidates. We hoped that people who couldn't tell us who the candidates were wouldn't lie about being registered. As it turned out, many of them lied anyway.

middle-class people than they would be for working-class people. I had no good direct measure of these norms. Since 96 percent of the sample had agreed that voting was a moral obligation, I could not use this indicator. It occurred to me that the discrepancy between the number of people who said they were registered on the survey and the number of people who were actually registered (Board of Election statistics) might be a good indirect indicator of the norms regarding political participation. The greater this discrepancy, the stronger the norms. Therefore, I took all those people in each social class who were in fact not registered and computed the proportion who incorrectly had said they were registered. The results are presented in Table 3.6.

Table 3.6. Proportion of People Who Are Not Registered Who Said that They Were Registered

	Percent saying they were registered	Number of people
Education		
Some high school	54	35
High school graduate	57	81
Some college	72	57
College graduate	78	45
Income		
Under $15,000	57	65
$15,000–$25,000	56	80
Over $25,000	79	33

The data confirm my hypothesis that the norms regarding political participation are stronger in the middle class. People with more education and higher income are more likely to lie about being registered than are people with relatively little education and income.

Problems in Measuring Variables In concluding our discussion of measurement, it should be pointed out that the choice of adequate indicators for variables cannot be done by some mechanized process; it is dependent on the intuitive judgment of the researcher. Sensitive researchers will use clever and valid indicators of the variables; insensitive researchers may measure variables inadequately even though they possess great technical skill. As an example of some of the problems that occur in the choice of indicators, let us consider the use of IQ tests to measure intelligence.

Are standardized IQ tests, such as the Otis or Stanford-Binet tests, a good measure of intelligence? Reliance on IQ tests as an indicator of intelligence can lead to error for at least three reasons. First, some people may be frightened by examinations and not perform well in a test situation. Second, the tests may be unfair to members of ethnic minorities because the material in the test presupposes familiarity with the dominant culture. Third, the tests may measure only one facet of intelligence, and other facets may be ignored. On the other hand, those in favor of using IQ tests as a measure of intelligence could argue that test scores are highly correlated with any other measure of intelligence we would like to use and are excellent predictors of ability to perform tasks for which intelligence is generally considered a prerequisite.

We do not intend here to resolve this debate over the adequacy of IQ tests. We do want to point out, however, that the same problems found in the use of IQ tests are found in the measurement of other variables; the very same measure might be a good indicator of a variable in one situation and a poor measure in another. Take the problem of the test situation. The same problem exists in the administration of questionnaires—the answers may be influenced by the setting. To use an extreme example, if someone were being interviewed about the relationship with his or her spouse, and if the spouse were present, the person being interviewed might be expected to give answers that would be different from those given if the spouse were not present. Thus, a careful researcher will try to ensure that the interviews are conducted in a setting that will not distort the answers.

Consider next the problem of questions on IQ tests being "culture bound." This problem is far more serious in attitude surveys. Even the most carefully planned and worded questions do not mean the same thing to all people. The problem is especially acute when middle-class sociologists are making up questions to ask lower-class members of ethnic minorities. For example, the following question was recently asked of a sample of mothers on welfare:

> Is each of the following statements true almost all of the
> time, more often true than false, more often false than
> true, almost always false? Whether or not you have ever
> worked, answer as if you had worked. If by chance
> somebody left me enough money to live comfortably
> without working, I think I would not work.

This question is confusing to answer, even for well-educated people. It is impossible to expect poorly educated people to give a meaningful answer to such a complex question. The respondent has to first imagine that she has worked in the past, then imagine that someone has left her a lot of money, and then decide whether it is almost always true, more often true than false, more often false than true, or almost always false that she would not want to work. This is an extreme example of a poor question. But the point is that even simple attitude questions, such as "Luck is more important than hard work in getting ahead—would you agree or disagree?" may be interpreted in different ways by members of different cultural groups. For example, what does "getting ahead" mean? To a middle-class respondent it might mean earning $50,000 a year; to a welfare mother it might mean finding a man who will marry her and support her so that she can get off welfare. The researcher must be able to assess when the answers to such questions are meaningful and when they are not.

Finally, consider that IQ tests measure only one facet of intelligence. This is certainly a problem faced in all measurement. Some indicators will be adequate measures of a variable defined in one way and inadequate indicators of the same variable defined in another way. This is because abstract concepts like liberalism, intelligence, and religiousness usually have several different components. For example, liberalism has at least two important components. A liberal may be someone who favors progressive social programs, such as socialized medicine, or he may be someone who strongly supports civil liberties, such as the right to free speech. If we were interested in researching the latter type of liberalism, we would not ask: "Do you favor socialized medicine?" This question, however, would be a perfectly adequate indicator of the first type of liberalism. Because of this problem, the researcher must always give clear definitions of all the variables and show that the particular indicator chosen is a sensible way to measure the variable as it is defined.

PRECOLLECTED DATA   Although many of the examples in this book deal with data collected through surveys, you should know that sociologists frequently collect data by other means. Generally, the logic of interpreting data, no matter how they are collected, is similar.

Often sociologists try to make use of data that had been previously collected. The sociologist can get useful data from literally thousands of sources. One of the most important of these is the information from the Bureau of the Census. In its main questionnaire, the Census Bureau collects data on the basic demographic characteristics of the population, such as occupation, education, race, sex, and age. The bureau also reports information collected on special topics; for example, the census of 1960 contained a lot of information on professionals. One limitation of census data and all other precollected data sources is that these sources often lack information on important variables. For example, census data do not contain information on religion.

To illustrate, as an example, the type of research that sociologists do using census data, let us consider the problem of occupational discrimination against blacks. Suppose you were interested in whether or not all the recent protest movements and governmental programs have had any effect on occupational segregation of blacks and whites. If there were no racial discrimination, then the distribution of whites and blacks among occupational groups would be the same. Thus, if one percent of whites were in a particular occupational group, then one percent of blacks would also be in that group.[9] If we now want to see if occupational segregation of blacks and whites has decreased, we would make separate computations for each

---

[9]By subtracting and summing the difference in the percentage of whites and blacks in each occupational group, we can get a measure of occupational segregation. (In fact, the computations are slightly more complicated. You must actually take the sum of one-half of the absolute value of the differences in the two percentages.) The closer the summed differences are to one, the more segregation exists. This measure was developed by Julius Jahn, Calvin F. Schmid, and Clarence Schrage. "The Measurement of Ecological Segregation," *American Sociological Review* 12 (June 1947): 293–303.

census year from 1940 through 1970. Each census contains a summary table listing the proportion of whites and blacks in about 150 occupational groups.

Using precollected data from government sources other than the census, William M. Mason and Robert W. Hodge compared the median incomes and occupations of blacks and whites from 1947 to 1972. Data from their study are presented in Table 3.7.

Table 3.7. Income and Occupational Differences Between Blacks and Whites, 1947-1972

Year	Ratio of nonwhite median family income to white median family income	Index of occupational dissimilarity
1947	.51	*
1948	.53	40.3
1949	.51	*
1950	.54	41.0
1951	.53	41.6
1952	.57	*
1953	.56	*
1954	.56	40.0
1955	.55	40.0
1956	.53	41.0
1957	.54	41.2
1958	.51	41.2
1959	.52	40.6
1960	.55	39.4
1961	.53	39.8
1962	.53	39.8
1963	.53	38.2
1964	.56	36.8
1965	.55	36.7
1966	.60	35.1
1967	.62	33.6
1968	.63	32.4
1969	.63	30.2
1970	.64	29.6
1971	.63	28.6
1972	.62	27.0

Source: These data were compiled from various government publications by William M. Mason and Robert W. Hodge. The table is used with their permission.
*Data unavailable.

In the second column of the table, the ratio of the median black-families' incomes to the median white families' incomes is presented. The lower this ratio, the greater the income difference between blacks and whites; if black income equalled white income, the ratio would be 1.0. In 1947 black families earned only about one-half as much as white families.[10] This ratio remained fairly constant until the late sixties, at which time the gap between the incomes of blacks and whites began to narrow. In 1972 black families earned 62 percent of what white families earned.

The index of occupational dissimilarity (the third column of Table 3.7) shows us the extent to which blacks and whites are in the same occupations. If there were no occupational segregation of blacks and whites, the index would be zero. The lower the index score, the greater is the similarity of the occupational distribution of blacks and whites and the lower the amount of occupational segregation. From 1947 to 1962 the index score remained close to 40. In 1963 it began to drop rather dramatically, and in 1972 the score was 27.0. This decline in occupational segregation is undoubtedly the primary reason for the reduction in the income gap between black and white families in the late sixties. We know this because we know that a person's occupation is the primary social determinant of income.

Using census data, Edward Gross did a study of the occupational distribution of men and women from 1900 to 1960.[11] This study showed that there has been no change in the integration of women into the occupational structure. Recent data collected from government reports by William M. Mason and Robert W. Hodge show no change in occupational sex segregation through the early 1970s.[12]

In the United States there is a substantial income gap between men and women. In 1966 the mean income of men was $7,444, and the mean income of women was $2,875. This amounts to a huge difference of $4,569. Larry E. Suter and Herman P. Miller, using data collected by the Bureau of the Census, tried to explain this differ-

---

[10]These figures include data only on employed people. Throughout the period, the unemployment rates for blacks were higher than those for whites.

[11]Edward Gross, "Plus Ça Change . . . ? The Sexual Structure of Occupations over Time," *Social Problems* 16 (Fall 1968): 198–208.

[12]Personal communication.

Table 3.8. Determinants of Male-Female Income Differences

Variable	Dollars (1966 income)
Education	$55
Occupational status	$124
Full-time or part-time work	$961
Lifetime work experience	$601
Subtotal	$1,741
"Discrimination"	$2,828
Total	$4,569

Source: Adapted from Larry E. Suter and Herman P. Miller, "Income Differences Between Men and Career Women," *American Journal of Sociology* 78 (January 1973): Table 3, p. 970. Reprinted with permission of University of Chicago Press.

ence.[13] Does it result from the different occupational distributions of men and women? The results of their analysis are shown in Table 3.8.

In their analysis Suter and Miller wanted to control for other variables on which men and women might differ and then compare the income difference. In Table 3.8 we see that education accounts for only $55 of the $4,569 difference in income between men and women. This means that if men and women had exactly the same amount of education, there would only be a reduction of $55 in the difference between their incomes. This is not surprising as the education received by men and women in the United States does not differ very much. The data also indicate that if there were no difference in the prestige of occupations held by men and women, the difference in their incomes would be reduced by only $124. Of course, it is possible that although men and women are entering occupations of roughly equal prestige, women, by choice or necessity, may be entering occupations that have equal prestige but pay less than those of men. Further research is needed on this question.

A significant portion of the income difference between men and women is a result of the fact that women are more likely than men to

[13]Larry E. Suter and Herman P. Miller, "Income Differences Between Men and Career Women," *American Journal of Sociology* 78 (January 1973): 962–74.

be part-time workers and to have dropped out of the labor force for a period of time. If women worked as much and for as many years as men, the difference in their incomes would be reduced by $1,562.

Nonetheless, when we control for the relevant variables on which men and women workers differ, we find a very large unexplained difference of $2,828. We might call this the "cost" of being a woman. Although it is possible that some of this difference might be due to differential motivation of men and women, which affects their performance and choice of assignments within jobs, it is possible that a large part of this $2,828 difference is due to sex discrimination against women.

Thus far we have discussed only those studies that have employed census data. There are many other sources of precollected data. Sometimes it is possible to test very interesting theories with a relatively small amount of easily accessible data. As an example, let us look at a study, done by Jack P. Gibbs, in the field of deviance.[14] For well over one hundred years social scientists have been debating whether punishment acts to deter people from committing crimes. In favor of the deterrent theory are those who see deviant acts as being controlled by external constraints. Were it not for fear of punishment, they argue, the natural aggressive instincts of human beings would prevail, and crime would be rampant. Opposed to the deterrent theory are those who see deviant acts as being controlled by internal constraints. It is only because people have been taught to believe that some acts are wrong that they refrain from commiting these acts. The advocates of the internal constraint theory argue that although punishment is not an effective method of deterrence, it does serve to reinforce the belief that a particular act is wrong. When we see a criminal punished, it reinforces our belief that the criminal act committed was wrong.[15]

Using statistics published in the FBI's *Uniform Crime Reports* and in a report issued by the Federal Bureau of Prisons,[16] Gibbs was able to make an interesting test of the deterrent theory. His unit of

[14]Jack P. Gibbs, "Crime, Punishment, and Deterrence," *Southwestern Social Science Quarterly* 48 (March 1968): 515–30.

[15]For a detailed discussion of the deterrent theory of punishment, see Stephen Cole, *The Sociological Orientation* (Chicago: Rand McNally, 1975), pp. 147–52.

[16]*Characteristics of State Prisoners, 1960* (Washington, D.C.: United States Department of Justice, 1960).

analysis was the state. His two independent variables were the severity of punishment for homicide and the certainty of punishment for homicide. He measured severity by the median number of months served on homicide sentences by people who were in prison on December 31, 1960. This number varied from a high of 132 months for North Dakota to a low of 24 months for Nevada. Certainty of punishment was measured by dividing the number of people admitted to state prison on a homicide sentence by the number of reported homicides. This yields an estimate of the proportion of murderers who are apprehended and convicted. This proportion varied from a high of 87 percent for Utah to a low of 21 percent for South Dakota. The dependent variable for the study was the criminal homicide rate per 100,000 people. This varied from a high of 12.9 for Alabama to a low of 0.6 for North Dakota. Gibbs wanted to see if those states in which the probability of getting punished for homicide was high and the punishment was severe would have lower homicide rates than those states in which the probability of getting punished for homicide was relatively low and the punishment was relatively light. He found that this was indeed true. Those states that had the highest certainty of punishment and the most severe punishment had lower homicide rates. Certainty of punishment turned out to be a stronger influence on the homicide rate than severity of punishment.

This ingenious study seems to offer support for the deterrent theory. There are, however, several problems with the study. One potential problem is in the measurement of severity. Gibbs uses the median number of months that people currently in prison on a homicide conviction have served. We do not know how long they will serve before being released or dying. Gibbs's statistics would be an accurate estimate of severity if there were not differential increases in homicide rates in the various states and if the life expectancy of people in prison on homicide convictions were approximately the same. If, for example, the homicide rate in one state has been relatively constant but the homicide rate in another state has risen rapidly, the latter state would have more homicide prisoners who had served relatively few months and therefore appear to have low severity of punishment.

It should be pointed out that this problem and others that Gibbs points out are not the "fault" of the researcher. One of the inherent problems in using precollected data is that we usually cannot find exactly the data we need in order to test a hypothesis or a theory. We must, therefore, use the best available data to make a rough or approximate test. Given the data available, Gibbs conducted an interesting study, which suggests important topics for future research.

In addition to the several technical problems in this study, there is one serious logical problem, which Gibbs himself points out. The research showed a correlation between both severity and certainty of punishment and homicide rates. Under what conditions can we assume causality? In this study the independent variables are associated with the dependent variable, and the independent variable presumably precedes the dependent variable in time.[17] But does the relationship meet the third criteria of causality? Is there some antecedent variable that, when controlled, will eliminate the relationship between the independent and dependent variable? One possibility is the attitudes of the people in the state toward homicide. It is possible that the prohibition to murder is more strongly internalized in some states than others. It could be that in those states in which the norms prohibiting murder are the strongest, the reaction of authorities to murder will be the severest and the probability of committing murder will be the lowest. Only further research can tell us whether or not the relationship found by Gibbs is causal or spurious.

We have discussed several studies using census data and one using government statistics on crime and prisons. Among the other types of precollected data that may be used for research are the recorded congressional roll-call votes. Sociologists studying political behavior often make use of these data. The sociologist might want to find out whether party affiliation or liberal-conservative ideology is more important in determining how legislators vote. For another example, sociologists studying scientists could make use of biographical information published in *American Men and Women of Science*. They might want to find out if the scientists who had

---

[17]We say "presumably" because the measures of the different variables were taken at the same time. Gibbs assumes that severity and certainty have been relatively stable over time.

received the most awards and prizes had worked at the most prestigious universities. Durkheim's study of suicide, discussed in Chapter 1, was based entirely on precollected data.

EXPERIMENTS One of the major problems faced by sociologists doing research is the difficulty of controlling for all the variables that might influence the dependent variable. Suppose that we were interested in studying how well black and white children do in school. There is much data showing that black children generally do not perform as well in school as white children. Some social scientists argue that there may be genetic differences between black and white people that affect their ability to learn.[18] Most social scientists believe that the difference in achievement between black and white children is a result of the different environments in which the children grow up.

One way to examine the environment theory is to compare the achievement of black and white children while holding the environment constant. Shouldn't black children from middle-class families do as well as white children from middle-class families? In many studies in which the researcher tries to control for environment, the results show that there are still differences between black and white children who come from "similar" environments. Middle-class white children perform better than middle-class black children. Should we conclude from these studies that the genetic explanation is correct and the environmental explanation incorrect? This would be unwise because it is difficult, if not impossible, to control for all aspects of environment that might influence the learning ability of children.

Controlling for social class of the parents is at best a rough measure of environment. It does not tell us anything about the neighborhood a child lives in, the kind of friends he or she has, or the way other people treat the child. In short, it is virtually impossible to control for all the ways in which being black in a white society might affect a child.

One way to handle the problem of uncontrolled variables is to do an experiment. In the classic experimental design, subjects are randomly assigned to one of two different groups: the experimental

[18]Arthur R. Jensen, "How Much Can We Boost IQ and Scholastic Achievement?" *Harvard Educational Review* 39 (Winter 1969): 1–123.

group and the control group. If we are studying 100 people, we could write each name on a card, mix them all up, and assign every other name drawn to the experimental group. By randomly assigning subjects to the two groups, we should get groups that are very similar on all the variables which might be important.

For example, suppose we want to find out if viewing an educational film will reduce racial prejudice. We will do the experiment on 100 white students. We randomly assign 50 students to the control group and 50 to the experimental group. Before we conduct the experiment, we give all 100 students a questionnaire aimed at measuring the extent of their racial prejudice. If the students were randomly assigned, there should be little, if any, difference in the attitudes of the two groups. We then show the film to the 50 students in the experimental group. The 50 students in the control group are not shown the film. One month after the film is shown, we again administer to all 100 students a questionnaire measuring extent of racial prejudice. If the film is indeed effective in reducing prejudice, we should see a significant decline in prejudice among the students in the experimental group and no significant change in the attitudes of the students in the control group. Since the process of randomly assigning the students to the two groups effectively controls for all variables other than viewing the film, if the experimental group shows no change in attitude, we can conclude that the film is not effective in reducing prejudice.

Why do we need the control group at all? Why can't we simply administer the questionnaire to all 100 students, show the film to all 100 students, and then a month later administer the follow-up questionnaire to all 100 students? If we did this, we would not be controlling for all the events that might influence prejudice occurring between the showing of the film and the second questionnaire. For example, in the month following the showing of the film, the school basketball team might win the league championship due to the outstanding performance of a black player. This event might serve to reduce prejudice among the 100 students. We would not know if the reduction of prejudice was a result of viewing the film, or the basketball victory, or any other event. If we had the control group, we should then see a significantly greater reduction in prejudice in the experimental group than in the control group.

The classic experimental design should be a very effective method of studying a whole range of sociological problems. However, because sociologists study human beings, it is frequently impossible to perform experiments. Consider the problem with which we began this section—the school achievement of black and white children. Logically, it would be possible to do the following experiment. At birth, we randomly assign 50 white babies and 50 black babies to an experimental group and 50 white babies and 50 black babies to a control group. The control-group babies would be sent home with their parents and brought up as black and white children are normally brought up. The experimental-group babies would be brought up in a school that offered them every cultural advantage. At the end of twelve years, the scholastic achievement of the control group and experimental group would be compared. If scholastic achievement is determined by environment, we should find no difference in achievement between the black and white children in the experimental group and a significant difference between the achievement of the children in the control group and the experimental group. This experiment, of course, could never be conducted, because it would be highly unethical to take children away from their parents and bring them up in a special school even if this school did offer every cultural advantage. This is one of the main reasons why the social sciences have been less successful than the natural sciences in advancing knowledge. Physicists, chemists, and biologists can do experiments to provide data for their most important theoretical problems. Because sociologists study people there are many experiments that can't, and shouldn't, be done.

There are some topics, however, that can be studied experimentally. Sociologists conduct two types of experiments. One type is performed in a laboratory. In laboratory experiments, researchers have a great deal of control over the variables in question; however, they do not know whether people would behave in the real world as they do in the laboratory. Another type of experiment is performed in a real-life setting. These are more difficult to conduct but are generally more valuable, as it is easier to use their results to understand how real people behave in real situations. Many interesting experiments have been done in the laboratory on the determinants of conformity.

There is a great deal of pressure on all of us to conform to the norms of the groups to which we belong. Suppose that the next time you walked into your sociology classroom there were four lines drawn on the blackboard, like the four lines that are illustrated in Figure 3.2.

The instructor asks the class to look at line A and then state which line—1, 2, or 3—is closest in length to line A. The first four students called on all say that line 1 is closest in length to line A. You might think that line 2 looks the closest, but then you think that perhaps what you see is an optical illusion; after all, the other students said that line 1 was the best match.

Figure 3.2.

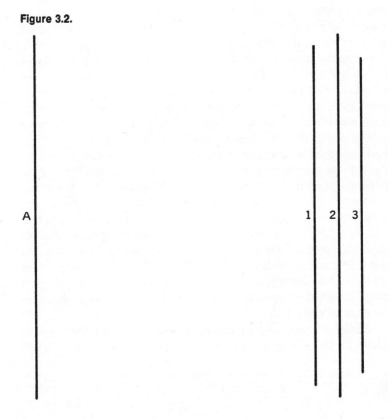

A   1   2   3

The social psychologist Solomon Asch conducted a set of experiments like this one.[19] He had seven actors, or accomplices, in a room. They were all instructed to say that line 1, which was actually shorter than line A, was the best match, even though line 2 was in fact the same length as line A. Subjects were brought into the room one at a time. First the experimenter asked the actors to state which line was closest in length to line A, and then he asked the subject the same question. Most of the subjects said that line 1 was the best match. This experiment illustrates the tremendous pressure on us to conform to the norms of the groups to which we belong.

In everyday life we have to make thousands of decisions for which, unlike the situation in the Asch experiment, there are no "right" or "wrong" answers. For example, if we have to decide which candidate to vote for in an election, whether we should be friendly with a particular person, or what we should think about different drugs, we cannot come up with any right or wrong answers. In the Asch experiment, there was an objective reality; one line was longer than the other. But even in that situation, social pressure was so strong that people denied what their own senses told them in order to conform to the group. If people can be so easily swayed in such a situation, imagine the power of group pressure in the more ambiguous decisions we encounter every day.

Most of us are conformists most of the time. We conform either because we believe what the group does is right or because we do not want to be outcasts. Many people will go along with the group even when they think the group is wrong. But when will people not go along with the group? Asch found that if just one of the actors was instructed to say that line 2 was the best match, then most of the subjects would believe their senses and say that line 2 was closest to line A in size. He concluded that people will maintain an unpopular opinion when there is at least one other person who will support them. We are most likely to stick up for what we believe is right if we have social support.

Conformity may be understandable when it results from intense group pressure as in the Asch experiment. But how can we explain

[19]Solomon Asch, "Effects of Group Pressure upon the Modification and Distortion of Judgments," in *Readings in Social Psychology*, eds. Guy Swanson, Theodore M. Newcomb, and Eugene L. Hartley (New York: Holt, 1952), pp. 2–11.

conformity in situations in which there is little group pressure? Muzafer Sherif conducted a series of experiments that illustrate the propensity to conform even when there is little pressure to do so and when there is virtually nothing to be gained from conformity.[20] Sherif put a subject in a dark room and instructed him to look at a pinpoint of light and describe how many inches the light moved. (In such a situation the light appears to move, even though it is perfectly stationary. This is called the "autokinetic effect.").

Sherif had the individual subjects look at the light many times until each subject had established an individual "norm." After a while, each subject tended to say the light moved about the same distance on every exposure. He then put the subjects together in the room and had them announce aloud their estimates of how far the light had moved. At the beginning of the group session, each subject made estimates consistent with his or her own individual norm. But gradually, as Sherif increased the number of exposures, individuals modified their estimates to make them more consistent with those of the other people in the room. Finally, the group arrived at a collective norm. In this experiment, unlike that of Asch, there were no actors. Conformity emerged naturally.

Experiments on conformity have also been done in field (real-life) settings. Three social psychologists wanted to know how we are influenced by the way other people look.[21] Are we more likely to imitate well-dressed people than poorly dressed people? People were employed to do some acting for the experiment. The first actor was dressed impeccably in a freshly pressed suit, shined shoes, white shirt, tie, and straw hat. He was instructed to walk up to a street corner when the light was red and cross the street during the red light. An observer about one hundred feet away counted the number of people who followed the well-dressed man across the street. The experiment was then repeated with the same man, but this time he was shabbily dressed in well-worn scuffed shoes, soiled, patched trousers, and an unpressed blue denim shirt. The sociologist ob-

[20]Muzafer Sherif, "Group Influences upon the Formation of Norms and Attitudes," *Readings in Social Psychology*, eds. Eleanor E. Maccoby, Theodore M. Newcomb, and Eugene L. Hartley (New York: Holt, Rinehart & Winston, 1958), pp. 219–32.
[21]Monroe Lefkowitz, Robert R. Blake, and Jane S. Moutin, "Status Factors in Pedestrian Violation of Traffic Signals," *Journal of Abnormal and Social Psychology* 51 (November 1955): 704–706.

served that more people followed the well-dressed man across the street than followed the poorly dressed one.

Recently, two social psychologists, Bibb Latané and John M. Darley, have written a book in which they report a series of both laboratory and field experiments on a very interesting topic: Why don't people come to the aid of others who they see in trouble?[22] Their interest in this topic was sparked by a series of highly dramatic and publicized murders. The most infamous case is that of the murder of Kitty Genovese in Queens, New York. Kitty Genovese was attacked by a maniac, who took over half an hour to murder her. During this time, thirty-eight of her neighbors looked out their windows at the gruesome scene. Not one came to her aid by calling the police. Why do people behave like this? Latané and Darley conducted a series of experiments to find out why people fail to act in an emergency to which they are a witness.

Latané and Darley believed that the conditions under which an emergency occurred had a crucial influence on whether bystanders would get involved. They were particularly interested in how the number of observers affected the outcome. Generally, we believe that the more people around, the less likely anything will happen to us. Most of us would feel more secure late at night sitting in a subway car in which there were many people than we would sitting in a subway car in which there was only one other person. Contrary to our expectations, Latané and Darley found that a bystander was much more likely to get involved if he or she were the only observer of an emergency than if he or she were one of several observers of an emergency.[23]

One of the experiments, done in the laboratory, was aimed at finding out under what conditions people would come to the aid of a lady in distress. The following is a description of the experiment:

> We telephoned male Columbia undergraduates and
> asked them, for two dollars, to participate in a survey

[22]Bibb Latané and John M. Darley, *The Unresponsive Bystander: Why Doesn't He Help?* (New York: Appleton-Century-Crofts, 1970).

[23]They do not, however, deal with the probability that an act will be committed under different circumstances. Thus, even though an isolated bystander is more likely to offer aid than a group of bystanders, if an aggressor (for example, a mugger) is less likely to commit an aggressive act in the presence of many bystanders, we still might be safer in crowds than in relative isolation.

being conducted by the Consumer Testing Bureau, a market research organization interested in testing the market appeal of a number of adult games and puzzles. Each subject was asked to find a friend who would also be interested in participating. Only subjects who recommended friends, and the friends that they suggested, were used as subjects. . . .

When the subject arrived for his appointment, he was met by an attractive and vivacious young woman who introduced herself as the "market research representative" and showed him to the testing room. This was a small room, separated by a collapsible cloth folding curtain-wall from the "Consumer Testing Bureau Office" next door. The testing room was furnished with a table and several chairs and a number of adult games were scattered about. A large sign giving preliminary instructions covered most of the one-way window in the room. In the office next door, whose door was open, the subject could see a desk, chairs, and a large rather ramshackle bookcase with stacks of paper and equipment arrayed precariously on the top shelf.

The market research representative briefly explained the purposes of the market research survey, and asked the subjects to fill out several preliminary questionnaires containing items dealing with family background and game-playing preferences. While they worked on these preliminary forms, the representative opened the collapsible curtain and said that she would do one or two things next door in her office but would return in 10 or 15 minutes to show them the games. Each subject thus saw that the curtain was unlocked, easily opened, and that it provided a simple means of entry into the office next door.

The emergency. While they worked on their questionnaires, subjects heard the representative moving around in the next office, shuffling papers, and opening and closing drawers. After about four minutes, if they were listening carefully, they heard her climb up on a chair to get a book from the top shelf. Even if they were not listening carefully, they heard a loud crash and a woman's scream as the chair fell over.

"Oh, my God, my foot . . ." cried the representative. "I . . . I . . . can't move . . . it. Oh, my ankle. I . . . can't . . . can't . . . get . . . this thing off . . . me." She moaned and cried for about a minute longer, getting gradually more subdued and controlled. Finally, she muttered something about getting outside, knocked the chair around as she pulled herself up, and limped out, closing the door behind her.

This whole sequence, of course, was prerecorded on high fidelity stereophonic tape, but the subjects next door had no way of knowing that. In fact, only 6 percent of the subjects later reported that they had had even the slightest suspicion that the episode might have been recorded.[24]

The experimenters were interested in whether or not the subject would come to the aid of the lady and, if so, how many seconds it took from the time the emergency began until they intervened. They ran the experiment under four different conditions: (1) subjects were alone when the emergency occurred; (2) the subject was together with a stooge who was told to do nothing when the emergency occurred; (3) two subjects who did not know each other were together when the emergency occurred; (4) two subjects who were friends were together when the emergency occurred.

In the first condition, subject alone, 70 percent offered to help the victim before she left the room. This contrasts sharply with the second condition, subject and stooge, in which only 7 percent of the subjects offered to help the victim. In only 40 percent of the cases in the third condition, two stranger subjects, did even one of the pair offer to help the victim. If each person acted independently of the other person, we would expect at least one person to have intervened in 91 percent of the cases.[25] In 70 percent of the cases in the

---

[24]Latané and Darley, *Unresponsive Bystander*, pp. 57–58.

[25]This expected percentage is computed by the following formula: $1-(1-P)n$ in which n is the number of observers and P is the probability of a single individual intervening. In this case it would be $1-(1-.70)^2 = 1-(.30)^2 = 1-.09 = .91$.

fourth condition, two friends, at least one person intervened. This was less than 91 percent that would be expected to intervene on the basis of the proportion of single subjects who did intervene. The authors concluded that people are more likely to intervene when there are no other bystanders.

The social psychologists did another field experiment aimed at replicating their results. They proceeded as follows:

> The Nu-Way Beverage Center in Suffern, New York, is a discount beer store. It sells beer and soda by the case, often to New Jerseyans who cross the state line to find both lowered prices and a lowered legal drinking age. During the spring of 1968 it was the scene of a minor crime wave—within one two-week period, it was robbed 96 times.
>
> The robbers, husky young men dressed in T-shirts and chinos, followed much the same modus operandi on each occasion. Singly or in a pair, they would enter the store and ask the cashier at the check-out counter, "What is the most expensive imported beer that you carry?" The cashier, in cahoots with the robbers, would reply, "Lowenbrau. I'll go back and check how much we have." Leaving the robbers in the front of the store, the cashier would disappear into the rear to look for the Lowenbrau.
>
> After waiting for a minute, the robbers would pick up a case of beer near the front of the store, remark to nobody in particular, "They'll never miss this," walk out of the front door, put the beer in their car, and drive off. On 48 occasions, one robber carried off the theft; on 48 occasions, two robbers were present.
>
> The robberies were always staged when there were either one or two people in the store, and the timing was arranged so that one or both customers would be at the check-out counter at the time when the robbers entered. On 48 occasions, one customer was at the check-out counter during the theft; on 48 occasions, two customers were present. Although occasionally the two customers

had come in together, more usually they were strangers. Sixty-one percent of the customers were male; 39 percent female. Since the check-out counter was about 20 feet from the front door, since the theft itself took less than one minute, and since the robbers were both husky young men, nobody tried directly to prevent the theft. There were, however, other courses of intervention available.

When the cashier returned from the rear of the store, he came back to the check-out counter and resumed waiting on the customers there. After a minute, if nobody had spontaneously mentioned the theft, he casually inquired "Hey, what happened to that man (those men) who was (were) in here? Did you see him (them) leave?" At this point, the customer(s) could either report the theft, say merely that he had seen the man or men leave, or disclaim any knowledge of the event whatsoever.[26]

It turned out that when there was a single observer of the "robbery," 65 percent reported the theft. From this figure we would expect that when there were two observers of the robbery, in 87 percent of the cases, at least one of the two would report the robbery.[27] However, in only 56 percent of the cases did one of the two bystanders report the robbery. Again the authors conclude that people are more likely to intervene in an emergency when they are alone than when they are with others.

The authors give several interpretations for this unusual finding. Before an individual will intervene he or she must decide that what is seen is actually an emergency requiring his or her intervention. When an event that might be interpreted as one calling for intervention occurs, people will try to make up their minds what to do; as they try to decide they remain inactive. When other people are present, each individual sees others who are inactive. This reinforces their own inclination to do nothing. In addition, when more than one person is present, responsibility for intervention is diffused. A single person will realize that if something is to be done, it must be

---

[26]Latané and Darley, *Unresponsive Bystander*, pp. 75–76.
[27]Remember the formula $1-(1-.65)^2 = 1-(.35)^2 = .88$.

done by him or her. One of a group may think, "Why doesn't someone else do something? Why should I be the one to get involved?" Also, potential guilt that an individual will feel for not intervening will be diffused if he or she is one of a group. Finally, if there are other observers who the individual knows have seen the event, but the observer does not know what they have done (this was the case in the Genovese murder), the individual observer may believe that somebody else must have done something. Latané and Darley conclude:

> It is possible to look at all of these factors as reductions in the psychological costs of nonintervention. Whether or not they are conceptualized this way, however, they do suggest that even when bystanders to an emergency cannot see or be influenced by each other, the more bystanders who are present, the less likely any one bystander will be to intervene and provide aid.[28]

SUMMARY

1. In quantitative research the sociologist collects data that are either numerical to begin with or can be converted into numbers.

2. Surveys are conducted either in person or by telephone or mail. The latter techniques are less expensive but usually result in lower "completion" rates.

3. When sociologists want to study a group of people, they usually select a sample. A simple random sample is one in which every member of the population has an equal chance of being included in the sample. If we have such a sample it is possible to use the sample to make statements about the population. The larger the sample, the more precise results it will yield.

4. Simple sociological variables, such as sex or religion, can usually be measured by one question. More abstract concepts, like religiousness, require more complex indicators. Because different people use different frames of reference in answering questions, the researcher must sometimes ask very specific questions. Often measurement accuracy is increased by using an index, or set of questions

---

[28]Latané and Darley, *Unresponsive Bystander*, p. 76.

to measure a variable. An index in which the questions are logically ordered is called a Guttman scale.

5. In order to test their hypotheses, sociologists frequently try to use data that have been precollected. The Bureau of the Census and other government agencies are primary sources of precollected data. As examples of studies using precollected data, we discussed studies of racial and sexual discrimination and the determinants of state homicide rates.

6. Sometimes sociologists collect data through experiments. Experiments have the advantage of enabling the researcher to control for all variables that might influence the dependent variable other than the independent variable. Two of the main disadvantages of experiments are that ethical considerations prevent us from doing many important experiments and that experiments done in the artificial setting of the laboratory may not tell us how people actually behave in real life. As examples of experiments, we discussed several studies aimed at examining conformity and a series of experiments aimed at learning why bystanders fail to get involved in emergencies.

EXERCISES

1. In each of the following cases, decide whether or not the sample used is a random sample and give the reasons for your decision.

   a. Population: the voters in a small city
      Sample: every hundredth name listed in the telephone directory

   b. Population: the students at your college
      Sample: all the students in an introductory sociology course

   c. Population: the faculty members at your college
      Sample: every other name listed in the faculty directory

   d. Population: the residents of a large public housing project
      Sample: choosing every third apartment, the first 100 people to answer their doorbell

   e. Population: the students at your college
      Sample: all the students attending classes on the day the teacher evaluation questionnaire is handed out

2. In each of the following sets of samples, which sample is more likely to reflect the population?

	Sample	*Population*
a.	(1) 1,000 residents	Philadelphia
	(2) 2,000 residents	United States
b.	(1) 500 residents	Philadelphia
	(2) 1,000 residents	Philadelphia
c.	(1) 1,000 residents	homogeneous city
	(2) 1,000 residents	heterogeneous city

3. With a random sample of size 1,000 what is the probability that the sample proportion will differ from the population proportion by 4 points or more? What if the sample size is 300?

4. Choose three different concepts. For each concept, construct a five-item index.

5. Make up tables showing how two different and imperfectly correlated indicators of a dependent variable can yield similar results when cross-tabulated with a dependent variable.

6. A researcher wanted to know if increasing the number of police officers who patrolled the streets would reduce crime in the streets. In one precinct the number of police officers patrolling the streets was doubled for two months. During this period the crime rate remained at the same level as it had been before the experiment was begun. The researcher concluded that increasing the number of police officers had no effect on the crime rate. What is wrong with this study? Why might the researcher's conclusion be invalid?

7. A state police commissioner ordered the state police to crack down on violators of the 55-mile-per-hour speed limit. For a three-month period the number of tickets given out for speeding tripled. During this period the number of deaths from traffic accidents declined by 25 percent. The police commissioner claimed that the reduction in traffic fatalities was a result of the

crackdown. What other information would we need to know to decide whether or not the commissioner was right?

8. If a single subject will intervene in an emergency 50 percent of the time, what is the expected proportion of cases in which at least one subject will intervene when there are 2 subjects? What is the probability when there are 3 subjects?

Chapter 4 Quantitative Methods: Types of Analysis

TABULAR ANALYSIS Chapter 2 has provided you with a detailed discussion of the logic of interpreting tables. In this section we shall discuss two types of tabular analysis that are particularly interesting.

Contextual Analysis A basic tenet of sociology is that people are influenced by the groups to which they belong. If the behavior of individuals could be completely explained by characteristics of individuals without reference to the characteristics of the groups in which they interact, then sociology would be unnecessary. Psychologists could explain all human behavior. There is one type of research which clearly shows that we can gain greater understanding of human behavior by knowing something about the groups to which people belong. This is *contextual analysis*. In contextual analysis the sociologist shows how the same kinds of people behave differently when they are in different social settings.

Contextual analysis dates back at least to the time of Emile Durkheim. Let us reconsider a part of Durkheim's *Suicide* that we discussed in Chapter 1. You remember we discussed the fact that single people commit suicide more than married people. This is because marriage creates stability in life. The single person has much more freedom and, consequently, much more instability than the married person. On this level the analysis is not unlike that of a psychologist. However, the next step in Durkheim's analysis would not likely be made by a psychologist. Durkheim observed that the difference in the suicide rates of single and married people was not the same in every country. In some countries there was a much greater difference than in others. Why did marriage act as more of a protection against suicide in some countries than in others? When Durkheim classified countries by the nature of divorce laws, he was able to explain the phenomenon. In those countries that allowed divorce and had a high divorce rate, marriage created less stability than in those countries that did not allow divorce. The type of divorce laws that exist in a country is clearly not an attribute of individuals; it is an attribute of the group in which the person lives.

Today we would call the type of divorce laws in a country a "contextual variable"—a variable that characterizes a group. In contextual analysis we generally show how one individual variable (marital status) affects another individual variable (suicide) differently, depending on the context (type of divorce laws). The idea is to show how people who have the same individual characteristics behave differently when located in different types of groups or societies. Thus, married people in Italy and in the United States behave differently in regard to suicide depending on the context—in this case the type of divorce laws that exist.

As in many other areas Durkheim was considerably ahead of his time in doing contextual analysis. It was not until the 1950s that this became a common mode of analysis. One of the best illustrations of contextual analysis can be found in *Union Democracy*, the study, done by Seymour Martin Lipset, Martin A. Trow, and James S. Coleman, of the printers' union discussed in Chapter 2.[1] In the New York City printers' union, there were two political parties: the

[1]Seymour Martin Lipset, Martin A. Trow, and James S. Coleman, *Union Democracy* (Garden City, N.Y.: Anchor Books), chap. 16.

Progressives and the Independents. The sociologists found that printers who had generally liberal political attitudes were more likely to support the Progressive party than those who had generally conservative political attitudes. The data are presented in Table 4.1.

Whereas 89 percent of the most liberal printers voted for the Progressives, only 15 percent of the most conservative printers voted for the Progressives. Thus far, the analysis has only shown how one variable characterizing individuals (political attitudes) influenced another variable characterizing individuals (vote). We have not yet introduced the contextual variable.

Table 4.1. Percent Supporting the Progressive Party by Political Attitudes, 1951 Election

		Percent printers supporting the progressive party	
Political attitudes			
Liberal	1	89%	(36)
	2	71%	(41)
	3	45%	(98)
	4	29%	(124)
	5	28%	(112)
Conservative	6	15%	(60)

Source: Adapted from Seymour Martin Lipset, Martin A. Trow, and James S. Coleman, *Union Democracy* (New York: Anchor Books, 1962), Figure 51, p. 353. Reprinted with permission of Macmillan Publishing Co. Copyright 1956 by The Free Press, a corporation.

Personal political attitudes created a predisposition to vote for one party or the other. Whether this predisposition was acted on depended on the political atmosphere in the shop in which the printer worked. In some shops there was heavy sentiment for the Progressive party, and in others the majority of printers favored the Independent party. The political atmosphere in the shop was the contextual variable. The sociologists found that printers who had the very same personal political attitudes behaved quite differently, depending on the context in which they worked. Liberal printers who worked in shops in which most of their fellow workers favored the

Progressive party acted in accord with their predisposition, and most of them voted for the Progressive party. But when printers with the very same liberal attitudes worked in shops in which there was little support for the Progressives, they tended to vote against their personal predisposition, and few of them voted Progressive. The effect of the contextual variable is shown in Table 4.2.

Table 4.2. Percent Voting Progressive by Political Attitudes and Shop Context, 1951 Election

	Percent voting progressive			
	Shop context			
	Progressive		Independent	
Political attitudes				
Liberal	68%	(38)	38%	(34)
Conservative	45%	(33)	13%	(55)

Source: Adapted from Lipset, Trow, and Coleman, *Union Democracy*, Table 32, p. 380. Reprinted with permission of Macmillan Publishing Co. Copyright 1956 by The Free Press, a corporation.

If we look across the rows of this three-variable table, we can see that 68 percent of the liberals voted in accord with their predisposition when they worked in a Progressive shop, but only 38 percent voted in accord with their own predisposition when located in an Independent shop. The same phenomenon can be observed in the voting of the conservative printers. To demonstrate the power of the contextual variable, we can combine the cases in cells 1 and 4 and in cells 2 and 3. In cells 1 and 4 the printers were in shops in which the context supported their predisposition. In this situation 80 percent of the printers voted in accord with their predisposition. But when the personal attitudes of the printers were in conflict with the context, only 46 percent voted in accord with their predisposition.[2]

The general point is that knowing something about the context in which a person interacts increases our ability to understand the

[2]The figure 80 percent was arrived at by combining the data in cells 1 and 4 of Table 4.2. The 46 percent represents the combination of data in cells 2 and 3.

person's behavior. Individual characteristics, like political attitudes, and group characteristics, like shop context, influence behavior. We must have information on both.

It is important to note that contextual tables are analyzed differently than the way in which we examined the three-variable tables in Chapter 2. In Table 4.2 the dependent variable is how the printers voted (Progressive or Independent); the independent variable is political attitudes; and the test factor is shop context. In the three-variable tables we analyzed before, we would have compared liberals and conservatives within each category of the test factor (for example, 68 percent of liberals and 45 percent of conservatives voted Progressive in Progressive shops). In contextual analysis we look at all people in a single category of the independent variable and see if they behave differently in the various categories of the test factor. For example, do liberal printers behave differently if they are in a Progressive shop or an Independent shop? The purpose in contextual analysis is not to reduce or eliminate the original relationship but to see if people who have the same individual characteristics behave differently in different social settings.

Perhaps the one area in which sociologists have done the most contextual analysis is the sociology of education. Alan Wilson was one of the first sociologists to use contextual analysis in studying the decisions of high school students as to whether or not they should go to college.[3] What kind of students are most likely to want to go to college? One of the key variables influencing this decision is, of course, academic ability. Students who get high grades in high school are more likely to want to go to college than students who get low grades. Another influential variable is the socioeconomic status of the student's family. Children of professional and white-collar workers are more likely to want to go to college than children of blue-collar workers. Also, children whose parents have been to college will be more likely to want to go to college because they will face a good deal of social pressure from their parents, who generally will place a higher value on education than will working-class parents.

---

[3]Alan B. Wilson, "Residential Segregation of Social Classes and Aspirations of High School Boys," *American Sociological Review* 24 (December 1959): 836–45.

Despite the fact that both academic ability of the student and the socioeconomic status of the family have a strong influence on the decision to go to college, not all the children of middle-class parents intend to go to college, and not all children of working-class parents intend not to go to college. Wilson thought that the decision to go to college might be influenced by the atmosphere in the high school the student attended. As we would expect, the higher the average socioeconomic status of the student body, the higher the proportion of students who intended to go to college and the greater the emphasis the school put on college attendance. Some data from Wilson's contextual tables are presented in Table 4.3.

Table 4.3. Percent Aspiring To Go to College by Personal Characteristics and School Context

	Percent aspiring to go to college					
	School context					
	Upper-middle-class neighborhoods		Middle-class neighborhoods		Working-class neighborhoods	
Father's occupation						
Professional	93%	(92)	77%	(39)	64%	(11)
Manual worker	59%	(39)	44%	(140)	33%	(221)
Father's education						
College graduate	88%	(207)	73%	(109)	73%	(30)
Some high school	63%	(32)	39%	(74)	30%	(109)
Grades in high school						
A	98%	(60)	96%	(24)	78%	(9)
B	90%	(152)	89%	(90)	72%	(46)
C	72%	(145)	55%	(207)	41%	(184)
D	43%	(47)	21%	(120)	25%	(169)

Source: Adapted from Alan B. Wilson, "Residential Segregation of Social Classes and Aspirations of High School Boys," *American Sociological Review* 24 (December 1959): Tables 3, 6, and 11, pp. 836–45. Reprinted with permission.

In looking at the first part of the table, we see that 93 percent of the children of professionals wanted to go to college if they went to school in upper-middle-class neighborhoods, but only 64 percent of children who came from similar families wanted to go to college if they went to school in working-class neighborhoods. Most of the children of manual workers did not want to go to college; but if they went to school in neighborhoods in which most of the families were upper middle class, they were much more likely to want to go to college than if they went to schools in neighborhoods in which most of the families were working class. Again we see that people with the same individual characteristics behave differently in different social contexts.[4]

In addition to influencing our decision to go to college, the environment of the high school also influences how we perform in high school. James S. Coleman, one of the authors of *Union Democracy*, did a study on how the atmosphere in 10 high schools affected the academic performance of the students.[5] He was specifically interested in the correlation between ability and performance. As a measure of performance he used grades, and as a measure of ability he used scores on IQ tests. Despite the fact that there are many problems in the use of IQ scores as a measure of ability, they are suitable as a rough indicator. Coleman wanted to know if the students with the highest abilities got the highest grades. He found that in general they did but that the strength of the association varied sharply from one school to another. In some schools the students with the highest IQs got much higher grades than those with lower IQs. In other schools the grades of the students with the highest IQs were not much higher than the grades of students with lower IQs.

The extent to which one variable characterizing individuals (ability) influenced another variable characterizing individuals (achievement) was dependent on the context in which the individuals interacted (the school). In those schools that valued intellectual achievement, the correlation between ability and achievement was stronger than in those environments that downplayed intellectual achievement. Coleman measured the attitudes toward intellectual achievement in two ways. He asked the students whether they would most like to be remembered as the best student in their class, the best athlete in their class, or the most popular student in their class. The proportion of students saying they would like to be remembered as best student varied considerably from school to school. Coleman

---

[4]A possible flaw in the Wilson study might be that professional families who live in working-class neighborhoods might be significantly different from professional families who live in upper-middle-class neighborhoods.

[5]James S. Coleman, "The Adolescent Subculture and Academic Achievement," *American Journal of Sociology* 65 (January 1960): 337–47.

also asked the students what they had to do to get into the "leading crowd" in their school. Again the proportion saying that good grades were necessary to get into the leading crowd varied from school to school.

Coleman found the highest correlation between IQ and grades in those schools that had relatively high proportions of students saying they would like to be remembered as the best student and that good grades were necessary to get into the leading crowd. Students with equally high IQs performed very differently, depending on the social context. The general conclusion reached by Coleman is that the students with the most intellectual ability are unlikely to fully utilize that ability unless they are in an environment in which intellectual ability is highly valued.

One result of the study that surprised Coleman was the high value placed on athletics in all schools. In virtually all the schools, athletics was considered more important than intellectual pursuits. Coleman hypothesized that one reason for this might be that the athletic teams represent the whole school as well as the individual participants. Having a championship basketball team brings glory to the school and all its students. Intellectual achievement, on the other hand, generally reflects only on the individual achiever. Coleman suggests that one way to alter this situation would be to institute academic fairs in which teams of scholars from one school would compete against teams from other schools. In this way students might begin to take pride in the fact that their school has good students as well as good athletes.

The last contextual study of schools we will discuss had the interesting title, "The Campus as a Frog Pond."[6] This article, by James A. Davis, had as its general conclusion that it is sometimes better to be a big fish in a small pond than a small fish in a big pond. Davis was concerned with how the type of college we go to influences our choice of careers. He started with the interesting observation that the distribution of grades tends to be similar in all colleges; that is, the proportion of students getting *A*'s at schools like Harvard and at small state teachers' colleges is roughly the

---

[6]James A. Davis, "The Campus as a Frog Pond: An Application of the Theory of Relative Deprivation to Career Decisions of College Men," *American Journal of Sociology* 72 (July 1966): 17–31.

same. What does this mean? Consider two students of equal ability. One goes to a highly competitive college in which practically all the students had *A* averages in high school and got 700's on their college boards. The other student goes to a considerably less competitive college in which most of the students had *B* or *C* averages in high school and got 500's on their college boards. We could expect the student going to the competitive school to do less well than the one going to the less competitive school. And this is exactly what Davis found. When you control for intellectual ability, there is a negative association between the quality of the college attended and the student's grade-point average; thus, students of equal ability will get higher grades at "low-quality" schools than at "high-quality" schools. Again we see the great importance of context. Students with the same intellectual abilities get different grades depending on which school they attend.

How does college environment influence career choice? Students who have done well in high school usually start college with what Davis calls "high-performance" career choices, such as medicine, law, and college teaching. These students come to college with strong self-images. After all, they were the best students in their high school class. When they enter college, many of them find that they are no longer the standouts they were in high school. Now they are just one of many bright students, not all of whom can get *A*'s. When indeed they do not get *A*'s, their self-confidence declines. The point is that students generally compare themselves with other students on their own campus rather than with other students across the country. Thus, a bright student who gets *C*'s at a highly competitive college like Harvard might begin to lose confidence and think that he or she was not "good enough" to be a doctor or lawyer. In point of fact the person is probably at least as bright as many students getting *A*'s at less competitive schools. It is for this reason that Davis concludes that it might be better to be a big fish in a small pond than a small fish in a big pond.

Studies of Social Change   Generally we think of the study of social change as being part of macro-sociology dominated by the sweeping historical studies of theorists like Karl Marx and Max Weber. However, empirical researchers frequently study relatively short-term change by doing trend studies and panel studies.

Trend Studies In a trend analysis the sociologist studies the relationship between the same variables at repeated points in time. At each point in time, a new sample is utilized. In order for the trends discovered to be meaningful, the samples at each point in time must be comparable. Otherwise, observed changes might result from differences in the sample. Most trend studies are essentially descriptive; they aim at describing changes in behavior or attitudes.

We have already discussed one example of a trend study—the surveys conducted on the attitudes of Long Island residents toward the impeachment of President Nixon. Table 4.4 presents the data showing the attitudes of Long Island residents toward both the resignation and impeachment of the president. With the exception of June, in which there was a decrease in the percentage of those who favored impeachment, there was a gradual increase in the proportion of those who favored impeachment. In December of 1973, 34 percent wanted Nixon to be impeached, and by July of 1974, fully 54 percent wanted him to be impeached. These figures alone may seem to indicate that more and more people were losing faith in the

Table 4.4. Attitudes Toward Resignation and Impeachment of President Nixon (Residents of Nassau and Suffolk Counties)

	1973	1974				
	Dec.	Jan.	Feb.	April	June	July
Do you think President Nixon should resign?						
Yes	42%	48%	49%	49%	40%	47%
No	45%	41%	41%	44%	50%	46%
Do not know	9%	8%	10%	6%	9%	7%
Refused to answer	4%	2%	1%	1%	1%	1%
Total	100%	99%	101%	100%	100%	101%
Do you think President Nixon should be impeached?						
Yes	34%	39%	39%	47%	39%	54%
No	57%	52%	50%	46%	52%	37%
Do not know	7%	7%	9%	6%	8%	8%
Refused to answer	3%	2%	1%	1%	1%	1%
Total	101%	100%	99%	100%	100%	100%

Source: *Newsday* (August 4, 1974). Reprinted with permission.
Note: The poll was not conducted in the months of March and May.

president. Actually, a closer examination of the data indicated that between April and July, the proportion wanting Nixon out of office either through resignation or impeachment remained about constant. However, in April many people wanted him to resign and not be impeached. In July the opposite was true. When we consider the people who wanted Nixon to resign and/or be impeached, we find that in July 65 percent wanted him out of office (unless there were some people who wanted him impeached to prove his innocence).[7] The corresponding figure for the June poll was 52 percent and for the April poll, 64 percent. If we compare the figure obtained in July with that of April, we can see that there was *not* a substantial increase in the proportion of people who wanted Nixon out of office. But in July more people preferred impeachment to resignation as the means for removing the president from office.

As an additional example of a trend study, we shall use an analysis of changes in the sexual behavior and attitudes of college students. In recent years there has been much discussion of a sexual revolution. Supposedly, there have been marked changes in the sexual behavior of young adults. The mass media paint a picture of a generation of college students who are sexually promiscuous and who engage in much more frequent and varied sexual practices than did their parents. Is this picture accurate, or have the media emphasized sex in order to attract an audience? Some sociologists have claimed that although there is more open discussion of sex today, there has been no real change in sexual behavior. The behavior of our parents was the same as ours, but they just talked about it less. What are the facts on the issue?

Many studies have shown that in the course of the twentieth century, there has been little change in the proportion of college men who have had intercourse. About 60 percent of college males, both at the turn of the century and today, have engaged in sexual intercourse.[8] But what about women? Virtually all studies conducted through the mid-1960s showed that there had been virtually no change in the proportion of college women who had had sexual

[7]This figure was obtained by cross-tabulating the answers to the questions on resignation and impeachment.

[8]Gilbert R. Kaats and Keith E. Davis, "The Dynamics of Sexual Behavior of College Students," in *Intimate Life Styles*, eds. J. S. and J. R. Delora (Pacific Palisades, Calif.: Goodyear, 1972), p. 53.

intercourse—about 20 percent.[9] These studies are, of course, based on reports of behavior, but there is certainly no more reason to believe that college women in today's permissive society would be less likely to report intercourse than were women living in considerably less permissive times.

In the late sixties several studies showed, for the first time, a significant change in the sex behavior of college women. One trend study was conducted first in 1958 at Temple University in Philadelphia and then repeated there in 1968.[10] The authors begin by showing that similar types of women went to Temple in 1958 and 1968. Thus, any differences found in sex behavior would be unlikely to result from changes in the type of student attending the university.

The authors were interested in showing the different proportion of women having intercourse under varying social conditions. For example, in 1958 they found that only 10 percent of the women had intercourse while dating. In 1968, this proportion had risen to 23 percent. In 1958, 15 percent had intercourse while going steady; in 1968, 28 percent had intercourse in the same circumstances. And in 1958, 31 percent had intercourse while engaged, whereas in 1968, 39 percent had intercourse while engaged. The authors concluded that not only has the total proportion of women having sexual intercourse risen but also that it is now more permissible for intercourse to be part of a more casual relationship than ten years ago, when very few college women would have intercourse unless engaged.

Perhaps just as significant as the increase in frequency of intercourse in different social situations was the finding of the authors that there has been a substantial reduction in guilt about sex behavior. Both in 1958 and 1968 the students were asked if they had ever felt that they had gone "too far" in their sex behavior. The results are presented in Table 4.5.

Whereas in 1958 many women who had had intercourse, particularly in casual relationships, felt guilty about it, in 1968 only a minority of women having had intercourse felt guilty about it, even if it had occurred in a relatively casual relationship. This study and

---

[9]Kaats and Davis, "Dynamics of Sexual Behavior," p. 59.
[10]Robert R. Bell and Jay B. Chaskes, "Premarital Sexual Experience Among Coeds, 1958 and 1968," in *Intimate Life Styles*, p. 47.

Table 4.5. Percent of Women Having Had Intercourse Who Felt They Had Gone
Too Far in Different Situations

	Percent of women having had intercourse who felt they had gone too far	
	1958 (N-250)	*1968 (N-205)*
While dating	65%	36%
While going steady	61%	30%
While engaged	41%	20%

Source: Robert R. Bell and Jay B. Chaskes, "Premarital
Sexual Experience Among Coeds, 1958 and 1968,"
Journal of Marriage and the Family 32, no. 1 (February
1970): 83. Reprinted with permission.

several others suggest that since the midsixties, there has indeed
been a significant change in the sex behavior and attitudes of
college women.

Panel Analysis Panel analysis is a technique developed in the late
1930s by Paul F. Lazarsfeld to study change in the behavior and
attitudes of individuals. In panel analysis the researcher interviews
the *same people* at different points in time. This differs from a trend
study in which the researcher studies *different samples of people* at
two or more points in time. A trend study enables us to say what
proportion of people is doing a particular thing at two different
points in time, but it does not enable us to say how many people and
which people have changed. For example, in the trend study
conducted of attitudes toward impeachment, even though the proportion favoring impeachment in January, February, and June is the
same, many people might have changed their minds. One hundred
people favoring impeachment in January might have changed their
opinion by June, and 100 people opposing impeachment in February
might have changed their opinion by June. Since we did not
re-interview the same group of people, we did not know the extent of
stability or instability in this attitude or if the same people who
favored impeachment in January favored it in April.

In order to point out the differences between a trend and panel

Table 4.6.

	Vote intention, Oct. 1940				
	Republican	Democrat	Do not know	Did not expect to vote	Total actual vote
Actual vote Nov. 1940					
Republican	215	7	4	6	232
Democrat	4	144	12	0	160
Did not vote	10	16	6	59	91
Total vote intention	229	167	22	65	483

Source: Paul F. Lazarsfeld, Bernard Berelson, and Hazel Gaudet, *The People's Choice,* 2nd Ed. (New York: Columbia University Press, 1948), p. xi. Reprinted with permission.

analysis, Lazarsfeld gives an example (see Table 4.6) from a study he conducted of the 1940 presidential election.[11]

In October, one month before the election, 167 people, or 42 percent (167 out of 396), of those who intended to vote said they would vote Democratic. In November, 41 percent (160 out of 392 who voted) actually voted Democratic. If we had conducted a trend study, this is all the information we would have had. It would appear as if virtually no one had changed his or her intention. But as the table indicates, within one month prior to the election, many people changed their minds. Four hundred and eighteen people out of 483 did in November what they said they would do in October. Sixty-five people did not do what they said they would.

If our only aim is to know the proportion of people doing a particular thing at different points in time, trend studies are all we need. Lazarsfeld points out that panel studies enable us to answer at least two types of questions that we cannot answer with trend studies. A panel study enables us to find out what kind of people are the most likely to change and under what conditions changes are most likely to occur.

Panel studies have been used extensively in studying the process through which people decide whom to vote for in elections. In 1948 Lazarsfeld and his colleagues conducted a panel study in Elmira,

[11]Paul F. Lazarsfeld, Bernard Berelson, and Hazel Gaudet, *The People's Choice,* 2nd ed. (New York: Columbia University Press, 1948), p. xi.

New York.[12] The repeated interviews with the same people allowed the sociologists to measure the effect of the campaigns, the mass media, and group pressure on an individual's decision. The study showed that as the campaign progressed, the people who were most likely to change their voting intentions were those whose close associates had opinions that differed from their own. In Figure 4.1 we show the effect of the political opinion of one's spouse on change in one's own political opinion.

Figure 4.1. Voting Change Depends upon the Distribution of Family Preferences

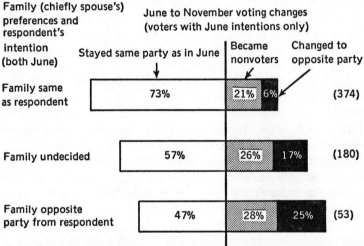

Source: Bernard R. Berelson, Paul F. Lazarsfeld, and William N. McPhee, *Voting* © 1954 by the University of Chicago Press, Chart LVIII, p. 121. All rights reserved. Reprinted with permission.

In those cases in which one's spouse had the same preference as the respondent, very few respondents changed their vote intention. Seventy-three percent voted for the party they intended to vote for in June. However, there was a high probability of changing one's vote intention when one's spouse had a different preference. In this situation, only 47 percent voted for the party they intended to vote

[12]Bernard R. Berelson, Paul F. Lazarsfeld, and William N. McPhee, *Voting* (Chicago: University of Chicago Press, 1954).

for in June. This panel study empirically shows the influence of social pressure on making us change our behavior.

Another area in which many panel studies have been conducted is higher education. One reason for this is undoubtedly because social scientists have easy access to college students, who generally remain in college for a four-year period, during which time considerable change can occur. An interesting recent study of college students was done by Walter L. Wallace.[13] This study, which employed sophisticated quantitative techniques, was conducted at a small, high-quality, liberal-arts college. Freshmen were interviewed in September, then in November, and again in April. When the students arrived on campus, Wallace found that most of them were highly concerned with getting good grades. Amazingly, however, when they were re-interviewed in November, only a few months after they had been in college, the proportion of freshmen interested in getting high grades had fallen sharply.

When the new students entered college, approximately 75 percent of them reported that getting good grades was highly important to them; but by November only 40 percent said this, and by April only 31 percent thought grades were highly important. The attitudes toward grades were significantly related to actual achievement. Those students whose high evaluation of the significance of grades declined actually performed worse in the second semester. Wallace was able to show that a change in attitude preceded a change in performance, rather than poor performance influencing attitudes. What caused the students to change their attitudes toward grades? Wallace found that upperclassmen downgraded the significance of grades and so he hypothesized that the more contact freshmen had with upperclassmen, the more likely it would be that their attitudes would change. The data in Table 4.7 confirm Wallace's hypothesis. Among male freshmen who had heavy association with upperclassmen, there was a drop of 37 percentage points in those having high-grades orientation. Among those male freshmen who did not have heavy association with upperclassmen, there was only an 18-percentage-point drop in high-grades orientation. A similar but weaker result was found for women students.

[13]Walter L. Wallace, *Student Culture* (Chicago: Aldine, 1966).

Table 4.7.   Change in Grade Orientation for Men and
Women Depending upon Their Associates

| | Association with upperclassmen | | | |
| | Men | | Women | |
	Heavy	Light	Heavy	Light
Percent having high-grades orientation				
September	76%	75%	72%	74%
November	39%	57%	29%	41%
Difference	37%	18%	43%	33%

Source: Adapted from Walter L. Wallace, *Student Culture*
(Chicago: Aldine, 1966), Table 2.15, p. 52. Reprinted with permission of Aldine Publishing.

LINEAR REGRESSION ANALYSIS   Thus far in this book we have
been analyzing tables. Today in sociology, however, many researchers do not analyze their data in tabular form but often use a type of
data analysis termed *linear regression analysis.*[14] This type of analysis is more complicated than tabular analysis and requires at least a
minimal knowledge of statistics for its understanding; but the logic
employed in more complex quantitative analysis is generally the
same as that employed in analyzing simple tables. It might be helpful
to discuss some of the ways in which linear regression analysis and
tabular analysis are similar.

In linear regression analysis, the relationship between variables is
generally expressed as a correlation coefficient (r) instead of as a
percentage difference. Thus, if researchers using tabular analysis
were interested in the relationship between social class and income,
they would say, "Seventy-eight percent of middle-class people and
25 percent of lower-class people earned $10,000 a year or more.
Social class makes for a 53 percentage point difference on income."
Researchers using regression analysis might say, "There is a strong
correlation between social class and income; r equals .50." Just like
the percentage point difference, r is a measure of association. The
larger r, the more closely the two variables are related (or the bigger
the percentage difference). Researchers use statistical formulas,

[14] See Hubert M. Blalock, *Social Statistics* (New York: McGraw-Hill, 1960).

usually calculated by a computer, to determine the value of *r*. For the purpose of this book, however, we will discuss *r* conceptually without referring to the formulas.

We have frequently used the term *variable*; now we must introduce the term *variance*. The variance is simply the amount of difference on a particular variable in a particular population. If the variable is prejudice (measured on a scale from 5 [high prejudice] to zero [no prejudice]) and everyone in your class scores 3, then there would be no variance on this variable in your class: Everyone would have the same score. But generally, there is at least some variance. If you made up a scale of prejudice and administered it to your class, you would find some students scoring high and some students scoring low and some in between. The goal of social research is to explain variance in dependent variables; to explain, in this case, why some students are prejudiced and others are not (or in a case we discussed several times before, why some people supported impeachment and others did not.

In order to explain variance, we use independent variables. For this example, we might guess that the educational level of a student's father might influence whether or not the student was prejudiced. We would guess that the higher the education, the less the prejudice. To ask what amount of variance in prejudice can be explained by the father's education is really the same as asking how well can we predict a student's level of prejudice with knowledge of the father's education. If we did not know anything about a particular student and we were going to predict his or her prejudice, what would we predict? The best guess would always be the median prejudice score because that is the score closest on the average to all scores. What we really want to know is how much can we improve our prediction by knowing only the father's education.

If we were using tabular analysis, we would construct a two-variable table; using regression analysis we construct a *scattergram*. A scattergram is simply a two-dimensional graph. In the scattergram depicted in Figure 4.2, the dependent variable, prejudice, is plotted along the vertical axis and the independent variable, the father's education, is plotted along the horizontal axis. We have plotted ten points, which represent ten students. The first student scored 1 on the prejudice index and had a father who had graduated from

Figure 4.2. Scattergram for Prejudice; Education of the Father

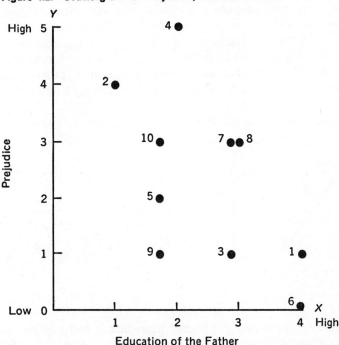

college (scored 4 on the education index). Both the seventh and eighth students scored 3 on the prejudice index and had fathers who had some college (3 on the education index). Now, how do we know if education of the father influences prejudice or explains some of the variance on prejudice? We can see that those students whose fathers had high education generally tended to score low on the prejudice index; those whose fathers had low education tended to score high on the prejudice index.[15] The more closely education of the father is related to prejudice, the better we will be able to predict the latter from the former. In the ideal case, we would be able to perfectly predict prejudice by knowledge of the father's education.

[15]When a high score on one variable (prejudice) is associated with a low score on another variable (education of the father), the correlation is negative. When a high score on Y is associated with a high score on X, then the correlation would be positive.

In order for us to know how good a prediction we can make on the average, we have to draw a line in such a way that the average distance between each point and the line will be minimized. To understand how the location of this line is computed requires an understanding of calculus, but the logic involved is understandable without a knowledge of complex mathematics. If all the points are on the line, as they are in A of Figure 4.3, then knowing X (the father's

Figure 4.3. Three Different Scattergrams for Prejudice; Education of the Father

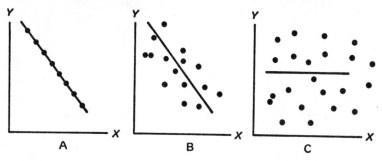

education), we can perfectly predict Y (prejudice), and r will be 1.00, meaning we have explained all the variance on Y with X. If all the points are close to the line, as they are in B of Figure 4.3., then knowing X, we can make a good rough guess as to Y; we have explained some of the variance on Y with X. In this case, r will be higher than zero and less than 1.00. The closer the average case is to the line, the higher will be r, and the more variance we will have explained. If all the points are widely scattered, as in C of Figure 4.3, X is useless in predicting Y; and no matter what X is we would make the same prediction for Y.[16] In this case, r will be zero and we will have explained no variance on Y with X. Computing the best-fitting line is linear regression analysis; r is the measure of how close to the line all the points fall on the average.

---

[16]This prediction would be the median of Y. A median is the number for which half the scores are higher and half the scores are lower. The median is the figure that will be closest on the average to each score.

Figure 4.4 illustrates a scattergram from a recently completed study on the quality of American medical schools.[17] The sociologists sent questionnaires to faculty members at medical schools and asked them to rate the quality of 94 different medical schools. The mean scores ran from a high of 5.71 (out of a possible 6) for Harvard to a low of 2.23. The sociologists wanted to find out what influenced the quality ratings received by the medical schools. They hypothesized that the publication record of the faculty would be important. They, therefore, counted all papers that were published in 1972 by members of the faculties. In Figure 4.4 the relationship between number of papers published by faculty members (the independent variable) and the quality rating received by the medical school (the dependent variable) is presented in a scattergram. The line drawn on the scattergram is positioned so that the average distance from each point to the line is minimized. The equation for this line is generally expressed as $Y = a + bX$; where Y is the predicted value of the dependent variable, a represents the point at which the line crosses the Y axis on the scattergram; b is a constant,[18] and X is the value of the independent variable. The equation for the line in Figure 4.4 is $Y = 2.948 + .002 (X_i)$; Y would be the predicted value of the quality score and X is the number of papers published by a school's faculty. If the correlation between these two variables were perfect ($r = 1.00$), then all the entries on the scattergram would fall directly on the line. If that were the case, knowing X (number of papers published) would enable us to perfectly predict Y (quality score). It is clear, however, that the correlation is not perfect in Figure 4.4. Yet, most of the entries are relatively close to the line. The correlation is $r = .87$. This indicates that most of the variance in Y (quality score) is explained by X (publications of faculty members).

If we have two variables correlated so that r is greater than zero, how do we know if the relationship between the two variables is causal? We use the same three conditions of causality we used before. The two variables must be associated (r would have to be greater than zero), the independent variable must precede in time the dependent variable, and there must be no third variable anteced-

[17]Jonathan R. Cole and James A. Lipton, "The Perceived Quality and Visibility of American Medical Schools," unpublished paper, Columbia University.
[18]The constant b is called the "regression coefficient."

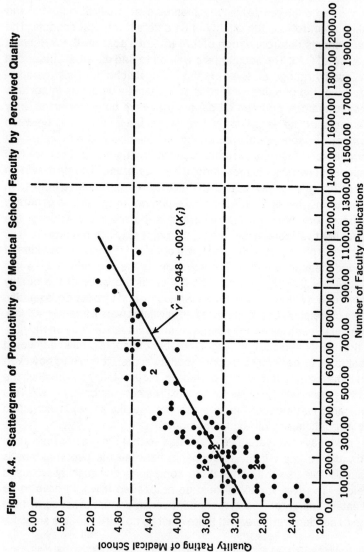

Figure 4.4. Scattergram of Productivity of Medical School Faculty by Perceived Quality

$\hat{Y} = 2.948 + .002 (X_i)$

Number of Faculty Publications

Quality Rating of Medical School

Note: An entry of "2" indicates that two different medical schools fall on the same spot on the scattergram.

ent in time that, when controlled, will reduce the relationship between X and Y.

In regression analysis, we compute *partial correlations* to determine whether or not a relationship is causal. A partial correlation is the relationship between the original independent variable and dependent variable after the variance due to the test factor has been removed (after the test factor has been controlled).[19] (The partial correlation is conceptually equivalent to the average of all the partials in a three-variable table.) If we started with an r of .50 between the number of storks in a county (original independent variable) and birth rate (dependent variable), and then introduced population density as a measure of rural-urban character (test factor), we would expect the partial r to be zero and would conclude that the relationship between storks and babies is noncausal.

What reasons are there to use correlation and regression analysis rather than tabular analysis? In our discussion of tabular analysis, we have considered only two- and three-variable tables. When we discussed the example of sex and voting behavior (pp. 67–68), we suggested the need for computing a four-variable table in which we simultaneously controlled for both level of interest and whether or not voting was perceived as a social obligation. Often human behavior or attitudes have many causes, not just one, two, or three. In tabular analysis, as the number of the independent variables increase so does the complexity of the tables and the number of cases needed in the study. To run a three-variable table, about 300 cases are needed; many more cases are required to run more complex tables. In regression analysis, we can consider the simultaneous influence of many independent variables on the dependent variable without having a large number of cases. For example, with 100 cases we could quite easily consider the *simultaneous* effect of 20 independent variables. In tabular analysis, this would be virtually impossible. Thus, if researchers are interested in seeing what is the maximum amount of variance that can be explained in a dependent variable, multiple regression analysis is probably a superior technique to tabular analysis. Multiple regression analysis yields a

---

[19]In statistical terms, it is not precise to say the test factor is being controlled, but conceptually this is what is happening.

statistic (multiple r) that when squared tells us how much variance has been explained on the dependent variable by all the independent variables. Thus, if we get a multiple of r of .70, we have explained 49 $(.70^2)$ percent of the variance on the dependent variable. The fact that r^2 has a precise meaning makes it more useful as a measure of association than the imprecise percentage point difference.

If regression analysis has these advantages, why should anyone use tabular analysis? Perhaps the most important advantage of tabular analysis is that it is intrinsically easier to understand tables than multiple regression equations. Also, it is difficult to show specification effects in regression analysis, since a partial correlation averages together the partial relationships. Another disadvantage of regression analysis is that it requires us to make certain assumptions about the data. The primary assumption is that the relationships between variables are linear; that is, the relationship can best be described as a straight line (as depicted in Figure 4.4). However, often relationships between variables are not linear. For example, the relationship between the ages of scientists and the number of papers they publish is curvilinear. Very young scientists and very old scientists produce few papers. Scientists between the ages of thirty and fifty produce more papers. Although there are ways to handle most of the problems arising in regression analysis, these techniques make the analysis even more complex. Also, it should be pointed out that generally the substantive conclusions reached by using the more complex analytical techniques are similar to those reached when simple tabular techniques are employed. The method of data analysis rarely affects the conclusions reached.

PATH ANALYSIS In the last ten years an analytical technique called "path analysis" has become very popular in sociology. In path analysis the sociologist develops a causal model that depicts the relationships among the key variables. Then, using multiple regression equations, the researcher can determine the strength of the relationships depicted in the model.

Path analysis has been successfully used by a group of sociologists, led by Otis Dudley Duncan, who has studied social stratification in the United States. One of the basic dependent variables in this research has been income. What determines whether an individual will have a high income or a low income? The four independent variables that have been shown to have the greatest influence on income are the socioeconomic status (SES) of the family an individual grew up in, IQ, education, and the prestige level of a person's occupation. A causal model showing the interrelations of these variables is shown in Figure 4.5. In fact, the model in Figure 4.5 contains seven variables. It has two measures of SES of family of origin—education of the father and occupation of the father. In addition, it contains the number of siblings, which is also known to influence social mobility.

Figure 4.5. Path Model Showing Influences on Income

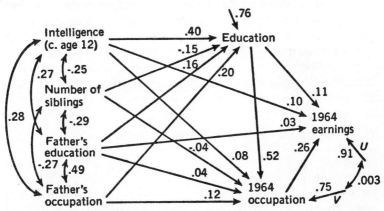

Source: Otis Dudley Duncan, David L. Featherman, and Beverly Duncan, *Socioeconomic Background and Achievement* (New York: Seminar Press, 1972), Figure 5.9B, p. 100. Reprinted with permission.

The number next to each curved arrow is the correlation between the variables connected by the arrow. The number next to each straight arrow is the path coefficient.[20] Each path coefficient tells us the extent to which the variable from which the path is drawn influences the variable to which it is pointing when all the other independent variables are controlled.[21] For example, the path coeffi-

[20]The lines labeled *U* and *V* represent the unexplained variance on 1964 earnings and 1964 occupation.
[21]For didactic purposes, we are oversimplifying the precise meaning of a path coefficient. For most path analyses done in sociology, the path coefficients are computed using regression equations and are equivalent to the standardized regression coefficients.

cient from the father's education to the subject's education is .16. This is the influence of the father's education on the subject's education after controlling for the subject's intelligence, the subject's number of siblings, and the father's occupation.

Figure 4.6 illustrates a simplified version of the path model. To understand a model like this we must know that each variable can have an influence on another variable in two ways: direct and indirect. If we say, for example, that IQ has a direct influence on income, this means that after controlling for all the other variables, IQ would still have an effect on income. In other words, if everyone were alike on all the variables other than IQ, IQ would still influence income. Its influence on income would be independent of the other variables. In Figure 4.6 a solid line from one variable to another indicates the existence of a direct influence. Thus, whereas IQ has a direct influence on income, SES of family of origin does not.

An indirect influence occurs when one variable has its effect through a third one. The best example of this is the influence of SES of family of origin on income. SES of family of origin, as we have

Figure 4.6.   Simple Path Model Showing Influences on Income

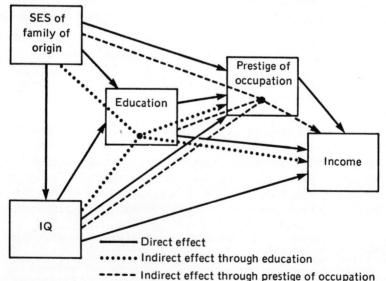

pointed out, has no direct influence on income. Does this mean that SES of family of origin has no effect on income? Not at all. It simply means that its influence is exerted indirectly through its influence on education and on the prestige of a person's occupation. This is exactly analogous to the logic used in constructing the three-variable tables presented in Chapter 2. SES of family of origin is the independent variable; income, the dependent variable; and education, the test factor. A three-variable table with hypothetical figures might look like Table 4.8.

Table 4.8. Indirect Effect of SES of Family of Origin on Income (Hypothetical Figures)

	Percent having high incomes			
	Education			
	High		Low	
SES of family of origin				
High	80%	(1,000)	40%	(600)
Low	80%	(800)	40%	(1,600)

Table 4.8 shows that SES of family of origin influences income because high-SES people are more likely to get more education and people with more education are more likely to earn high incomes. In Figure 4.6, if one variable has an indirect effect through education, this is indicated by a dotted line going from the variable and passing through education. Thus, IQ has an indirect effect on both prestige of occupation and income through education. Indirect effects through occupational prestige are indicated by dashes. Finally, it should be understood that a variable can have both a direct and an indirect effect on another variable. IQ has a direct effect on income and an indirect effect on income through its influence on education.

ANALYSIS OF VARIANCE The analysis of variance is a technique of assessing the effect of one variable on another when the dependent variable is expressed as a mean (or average).[22] Let us begin

---

[22]This section was written in collaboration with Eugene A. Weinstein.

with the simplest case, in which we are comparing two groups.[23] If, for example, we were conducting a study of the scholastic achievement of students in a particular college, grade point average (GPA) might be the indicator of the dependent variable. We might be interested in knowing whether sex status had any influence on GPA. After drawing a random sample of students, we would compute the average GPA separately for men and women students. Suppose we found the average GPA for male students to be 2.90 and the average for female students to be 3.15. Is this difference meaningful? Or is it so small that it could have simply been a result of chance? As we saw in the discussion of sampling (see pp. 77–84), it is possible to find differences among samples drawn from the same population. Sociologists frequently use a set of statistical techniques to determine whether an observed difference is *statistically significant* or should be treated as a probable result of sampling error. To say that a difference between two groups is statistically significant means the difference is so large that we may assume that the samples were drawn from two different populations. The analysis of variance is a way of determining whether or not the difference in means between groups is statistically significant.

We use the analysis of variance to compare group averages on some dependent variable. Typically, it is used in assessing the results of sociological and social psychological experiments. Suppose, for example, that a sociologist wanted to know if viewing specially made films could influence the opinions students held of government officials. First, the researcher would make three versions of a film, one emphasizing dramatic incidents of corruption of public officials, another emphasizing the hard work and dedication of public officials, and the third merely describing organizational ties between several branches of government. The researcher would also draw up a questionnaire containing an index designed to measure the dependent variable—attitudes toward government officials. If 300 subjects were recruited to participate in the experiment, they would be divided randomly into three groups of 100 persons each. Before the films would be shown, the questionnaire would be

[23]Analysis of variance is generally used in cases with three or more groups.

administered to all the subjects (all three groups). Since the subjects were divided randomly, we would expect the average score on the index of attitudes toward government officials to be about the same in each group. Then one group would be shown the film emphasizing corruption of government officials; the second group would be shown the film pointing out the dedication of government officials; and the third group, which could be regarded as a control group, would be shown a film displaying neither positive nor negative attitudes toward government officials. This last group is needed in order to make sure that any change in attitude is not simply a result of film watching per se or uncontrolled events that might have occurred between the showing of the film and the administration of the second questionnaire. After the films would be shown, a second questionnaire would be administered to all 300 subjects. In the second questionnaire we would again measure attitudes toward government officials. The difference between the scores before seeing the films and the scores after seeing the films would be obtained for all the people in the experiment. Table 4.9 shows the hypothetical group averages for the study.

Table 4.9. Film Effects: Average Change in Attitudes Toward Government Officials After Seeing Film (Hypothetical Study)

Film Emphasis		
Corruption	Dedication	Organizational Relationships
−3.5 (100)	+0.7 (100)	+0.5 (100)

Note: A minus sign indicates that attitudes have changed in a negative direction; a plus sign indicates that attitudes have changed in a positive direction.

The data in Table 4.9 show that the attitudes of people who saw the film emphasizing corruption of government officials changed, on the average, more than those of people who saw either of the other two films. On the average, the attitudes of those viewing the film emphasizing corruption of government officials became more unfavorable. The people who saw the film emphasizing dedication of government officials became slightly more favorable, and the people who saw the control film also became slightly more favorable. What can we conclude from these data? Since there was some change in the control group, can we then conclude that seeing a film about intergovernmental organizational relations makes people more disposed to have favorable attitudes toward government officials? Or should we conclude that the change is small and likely to be the result of random factors (such as people in the control group checking a little more or a little less extreme responses on the questionnaire the second time as compared to the first). Would we want to draw the same conclusions about the group who saw the film emphasizing the dedication of government officials? Since their responses changed only slightly, would we assume the change is due to random error? And what about the group seeing the film emphasizing corruption of government officials? Is the change in response too large to be attributed to random error? This group clearly has a larger average difference than the other two groups, but is it sizable enough to justify rejecting the idea of simple chance fluctuation? How does the researcher decide?

It is at this point that the analysis of variance can be used to provide us with a basis for deciding whether the observed differences between group averages are too large to be attributed to mere random fluctuations. It provides us with a statistic (F ratio) that enables us to determine how likely it is that the differences could be due to chance alone. It is possible that the differences could be explained by chance alone, because if we didn't show the films at all but administered the questionnaire on ten different occasions, we would find fluctuations in the average score. If it is unlikely that the differences in group averages could be due to chance, we say that the differences are statistically significant. This means that the differences in the group averages are so large that if they were due only to random fluctuations, we would find differences that big in only five or fewer times out of one hundred.

The analysis of variance works by comparing differences in the averages between the groups with differences among the individuals within each group. If the films were the only cause of attitude change, then each member of the group seeing the film emphasizing corruption should have become 3.5 points less favorable, while each member of the group seeing the film emphasizing dedication should have become .7 points more favorable, and so on. There would be no variation in responses given by the members within the group, since they had all been exposed to the same causal influence (the films). But there would be variation between the groups, since the exposure (type of film) varied from group to group. This would be the ideal case in which the dependent variable was influenced by a single independent variable. In actual experiments, however, we rarely find such ideal cases. Usually, within the groups there exist random factors that could be causing differences in the amount of change from member to member. Some people in the group may be more resistant to change than others; some people may have misunderstood the intent of the films; and still others may have fallen asleep. However, there is no reason to believe that these random forces would be particularly stronger in one group than another. Thus, if the films do in fact influence the dependent variable, they should produce differences in group averages too large to have occurred just by chance.

If the differences between group averages are due solely to chance, statistical theory predicts that the variation between the group averages should be equal to the variation among members within each group. Thus, for example, in the experiment we have been describing, if there were much variation in the change of scores for individuals within each of the three groups—that is, in the same group some individual scores went up sharply and others went down sharply—it would be possible to find the observed differences reported in Table 4.9 simply by chance. The logic here is similar to that used in our discussion on sample size (pp. 79–80). In that section, we pointed out that the more variance there is in a population, the larger the sample will have to be in order to be precise. In the example under discussion, the more variance there is within groups, the larger the difference between the averages will have to be in order to be statistically significant. The larger the variation between the groups becomes, relative to variation of individuals within groups, the closer we come to that ideal condition in which we can predict the score of an individual merely by knowing the average score of his or her group. The F ratio compares variation between groups to variation within groups. The larger the F ratio, the less likely it is that group differences are due to chance and the more statistically significant is the relationship.

Just as is possible with other data analysis techniques, the analysis of variance can be used to examine the effects of several independent variables on a dependent variable. Elaboration (pp. 51–70) enables us to control the influence of one variable while examining the effects of another and, as in the case of specification, to see if there are any effects associated with a particular pattern of independent variables. The following example demonstrates how the analysis of variance can be used to make such an examination.

An experiment was conducted to find out the conditions under which individuals present distorted versions of reality when communicating with other people.[24] The researchers were particularly interested in how the status of the individual spoken to would affect the amount and type of the subject's distortion. Students who had taken an examination were asked to guess their scores on the examination before receiving their actual scores. In one-half of the cases, the estimated scores were reported to the graduate assistant in the course, in the other half, to the professor teaching the course. Forty-eight students in all participated, 24 in each group. The students were divided on the basis of their actual scores on the test. One group consisted of 24 high performers, the other group, 24 low performers. Each group was assigned to both types of "audiences," to whom they related their performance estimates. Since there was an equal number of people at each actual performance level assigned to each audience, and similarly an equal number of each type of audience (professor vs. graduate assistant) for each actual performance group, the influence of each independent variable is controlled while examining the influence of the other. Table 4.10 shows the actual results in terms of average amount of distortion in estimate.

The data in Table 4.10 show that both high and low performers distort their grades. Low performers tend to overestimate while high performers tend to underestimate. This can be seen from the bottom

[24]Adapted from E. Weinstein and L. Beckhouse, "Audience and Personality Factors in Presentation of Self," *Sociological Quarterly* 10 (1969): 527–37.

Table 4.10. Average Amount and Direction of Distortion in Estimating Grade by Performance Level and Status of Audience

	Performance level		
	Low performers	High performers	Group average
Status of audience			
Professor	+9.67	−8.08	+1.59
Assistant	+4.42	−5.17	−0.75
Group average	+7.04	−6.63	

Source: E. Weinstein and L. Beckhouse, "Audience and Personality Factors in Presentation of Self," *Sociological Quarterly* 10 (1969): Table 1, p. 543. Reprinted with permission.

row of the table containing the averages for each performance group, disregarding the status of the audience to which the estimate is made. In the last column of Table 4.10, it can be seen that on the average, grades were overestimated slightly to the professor and underestimated slightly to the assistant. Is the difference between these figures so slight that it can be attributed to random fluctuation? And are the differences between high and low performers so large that they cannot be attributed to mere chance? The researcher used the analysis of variance to determine the answers to these questions (see Table 4.11).

The analysis of variance, as we stated previously, is based on a comparison between a statistical measure of the variation in averages between groups and a statistical measure of the variation among individuals within groups. The first column of Table 4.11 indicates

Table 4.11. Analysis of Variance of Distortion in Grade Estimation

	Mean square	F
Source of variation		
Between performance levels	36.739	10.32**
Between status of audience	6.023	1.72
Interaction	14.774	4.15*
Within groups	3.56	

*$p < .05$
**$p < .01$

what source of variation is being considered. The rows indicate the results for that source. For example, the first row indicates the results of the analysis comparing high and low performers in their grade estimates. The column labeled "Mean Square" represents the statistical measure of variation between groups. To get the F ratio, the measure of variation between groups (mean square, 36.739) is divided by the measure of variation within groups (3.56). The result is an F of 10.32. This result is compared with a table that indicates how likely it is to get an F of 10.32 or larger by chance alone. The two asterisks refer to the key below the table, "$p < .01$," indicating that there is only one chance in a hundred that the difference between performance levels could have occurred by chance. We, therefore, assume that this is a real difference and that performance level is a cause of distortion. The absence of asterisks after the comparison between different status audiences indicates that differences between average distortion could have come about by chance alone.

In the third row we report the amount of variance due to *interaction*. Interaction in the analysis of variance is directly analogous to specification in tabular analysis. It examines whether the relationship between the dependent variable and the independent variable is the same within the categories of another independent variable (or test factor). In other words, interaction deals with the possibility of the existence of effects that are due to the combination of independent variables beyond the effects of each one operating separately. When low performers and high performers are combined, we found that the status of the audience made no difference in distortion. Students reporting to the professor slightly overestimated their grades and those reporting to the assistant slightly underestimated their grades. The analysis of variance found this difference to be statistically insignificant or possibly simply a result of chance. But by averaging the scores of the high and low performers together, we are masking an interesting result. Both low and high performers *are* more likely to distort their grade estimates when reporting to the professor. However, since the direction of their distortion is different, the group averages do not show it. The difference is cancelled out in the averages.

When we look at the amount of variance due to the interaction between the variables, we are essentially examining differences in distortion *within* performance categories (the test factor). It is equivalent in this case to looking at the effect of audience status while controlling for performance level. As the single asterisk next to the *F* score for interaction indicates, the variance due to interaction is so large that it could only occur five or fewer times out of one hundred if it were simply a result of chance. We, therefore, conclude that it represents a real difference. This finding confirmed the main hypothesis of the study that distortion in communication would increase as the status of the audience to whom it is directed increases.

Thus far we have used the analysis of variance as a way to determine simply whether or not an observed difference between two group averages is real or due to chance. The analysis of variance can also be used to determine the strength of an independent variable or the amount of variance in the dependent variable determined by the independent variable. Essentially, the larger the variation between groups is relative to the total variation, the more variance is being explained. There are statistical procedures that sociologists use in the analysis of variance to determine how much variance is being explained by each independent variable and a combination of all the independent variables.

SUMMARY

1. In contextual analysis we construct three-variable tables to see if people who are alike on one variable (the independent variable) behave differently in different social contexts. We used an example from a study of printers that showed liberal printers are more likely to vote for the liberal party if they work in shops in which the majority of their co-workers are liberal. We also used several examples from studies done in the sociology of education.

2. Tabular analysis can be used to study short-term social change. In trend studies we interview different samples at different points in time in order to examine change in the same set of variables. As examples we discussed a study of change in attitude toward impeachment and a study of the change in sexual attitudes and behavior of college women. In a panel study we re-interview the same set of people at different points in time. A panel study enables us to find out what kind of people are the most likely to change and

under what conditions changes are most likely to occur. We discussed examples of a voting study and a study of the change in attitudes of freshmen toward getting good grades.

3. Linear regression analysis is a technique of analyzing quantitative data in which the relationship between two variables is expressed as a correlation coefficient (*r*). In doing regression analysis of two variables the researcher constructs a scattergram. Then using a set of equations a line is drawn so as to minimize the average distance from the line to all the points in the scattergram. The more closely the points are clustered around the line, the higher is *r*. When *r* is high, it is possible to predict the value of the dependent variable from knowledge of the independent variable. Partial correlations are used to examine the effect of one independent variable while controlling for the other independent variables.

4. Path analysis is a technique based on linear regression analysis. The researcher draws a model depicting the hypothesized causal interconnections among the variables. Then using regression equations the path coefficients are determined. The path coefficient tells us what the effect of an independent variable is on a dependent variable while controlling for the other independent variables. In path analysis an independent variable can directly influence a dependent variable or have an indirect effect on an independent variable through some other variable.

5. The analysis of variance is a statistical technique used to analyze data for which the dependent variable is expressed as an average. For example, if we want to know if there is a difference in the IQ of men and women students, we compute the mean IQs of men and women separately. We then use the analysis of variance to determine whether the observed difference in mean IQ is greater or smaller than could be expected by chance. This is done by comparing within-group variance with between-group variance. The analysis of variance enables us to look at the effect of a single independent variable while controlling for others and to look at the effect of combinations of independent variables (interaction).

EXERCISES

1. Liberal teachers are more likely than conservative teachers to support a teacher's strike. Make up a table showing that teachers

are more likely to act in accord with their predisposition when the school context supports that predisposition.

2. Liberals are predisposed to vote Democratic, and conservatives are predisposed to vote Republican. What proportion of people voted in accord with their predisposition when the context supports their predisposition? What proportion voted in accord with their predisposition when the context opposes their predisposition?

	Percent voting Democratic			
	Neighborhood			
	Predominantly Democratic		Predominantly Republican	
Political attitudes				
Liberal	80%	(1,000)	50%	(500)
Conservative	50%	(300)	30%	(900)

3. Make up a table showing that IQ and grades are more strongly associated in high schools in which the students place a high value on academic achievement than in those in which the students place a low value on academic achievement.

4. Make up a table showing that when we control for intellectual ability, there is a negative association between the quality of the college attended and the student's grade point average.

5. Construct a scattergram for each of the following correlations between X and Y:

   a. A high positive correlation

   b. A low positive correlation

   c. A high negative correlation

   d. A low negative correlation

   e. No correlation

6. A sociologist collects two sets of data (I and II) and computes a

correlation coefficient and a regression line for each data set. The formula for the regression line is $Y = a + bX$. In both cases, $a = .46$ and $b = .82$. Is the correlation higher for data set I or data set II?[25]

	I		II	
	X	Y	X	Y
Case 1	1	0	1	0
Case 2	1	1	1	2
Case 3	1	3	1	1
Case 4	2	0	2	2
Case 5	2	2	2	1
Case 6	2	4	2	4
Case 7	3	3	3	2
Case 8	3	3	3	4

7. Read an article from a sociology journal in which the researcher conducts an explanatory analysis using tables. Draw a path model (including hypothesized path coefficients) that would display the causal processes described in the article.

8. Suppose that for the research depicted in Figure 4.6 (see p. 146), the correlation between SES of family of origin and prestige of occupation is $r = .40$; but the path coefficient from SES of family of origin to prestige of occupation is close to zero. Could SES of family of origin be considered to have a causal influence on prestige of occupation? What is the process through which SES of family of origin might influence prestige of occupation?

9. For the data presented in Table 4.9 (see p. 149), what information would you need to determine whether the experimental films had a statistically significant effect?

10. A team of investigators want to test the hypothesis that the political structure of cities affects the incidence of public distur-

---

[25]This exercise is based on one presented by Richard A. Zeller, "On Teaching Correlation and Regression," *Teaching Sociology* 1 (April 1974): 224–41.

bances. They have divided city political structures into four categories: mayor-no council, mayor-strong council, city manager, council president-no mayor. The researchers have data on the number of disturbances for the period 1965–1970 for 25 cities of each type. How would they analyze these data? How would they determine if the political structure had a statistically significant influence on the number of disturbances? Make up a table with hypothesized figures to illustrate your answer.

Chapter 5   Qualitative Research

Since the end of World War II, American sociology has become an increasingly quantitative discipline. Just one indicator of this trend is the proportion of articles utilizing quantitative or numerical data that are published in the major sociology journals. In a recent study of 4 major journals, it was found that between 1895 and 1965, the proportion of articles using quantitative data increased from 14 to 69. When the leading American sociology journal, the *American Sociological Review,* began publication in 1936, 41 percent of the articles were quantitative; in 1956–65, 71 percent were quantitative.[1]

Despite the fact that sociology is becoming more and more quantified, qualitative research still plays an important role in the growth of sociological knowledge. Sociologists doing qualitative

[1]Narsi Patel, "Quantitative and Collaborative Trends in American Sociological Research," *The American Sociologist* 7 (November 1972): 5–6.

research collect data that are not converted into numbers. The two most frequently used types of qualitative research techniques are in-depth interviews and participant observation.

In-depth interviews differ considerably from interviews conducted by survey researchers. In the latter type of interview each subject is asked the same set of questions, and the answers are converted into numerical codes. In in-depth interviews, the interviewers, rather than having a specific set of questions, have a list of topics that they are interested in covering. Using this rough guide, the interviewer engages the subject in a conversation. During the interview the researcher either takes notes or, preferably, tape records the interview.[2] When doing this type of study each interview is different. Since different respondents vary in their knowledge and interest concerning the various aspects of the research topic, some interviews will be more useful than others in learning about the various components of the topic. The data used by sociologists doing this type of research are excerpts from the interviews.

In participant observation, researchers interact with the group of people they are studying for an extensive length of time. Sometimes researchers studying a community will live in that community for several years. During this time they get to know many members of the group they are studying and participate in many group activities. Usually, participant observers tell the people they are studying that they are researchers, although sometimes this information is withheld. The data used in this type of research consist of the extensive field notes taken by the observer. Generally, the field notes are written up from memory when the interviewer is alone immediately after he or she has interacted with the group being studied.

Just as it was not the purpose in the preceding two chapters to teach you how to do quantitative research, it is not the purpose in this chapter to teach you how to do qualitative research. Instead the purposes of this chapter are to discuss the type of problems for which qualitative research is useful, to give you some detailed

---

[2]Some researchers do not like to use tape recorders because they believe that the informant will be inhibited by the machine. This may be true when interviewing criminals, for example. But most informants are not bothered by the recorder, and the machine enables the interviewer to concentrate on what the informant is saying rather than on taking notes.

examples of the type of information that sociologists get from qualitative research, and to discuss briefly some of the problems that arise in doing qualitative research. Probably the only way to learn how to do research, either qualitative or quantitative, is to work on a research project under the guidance of an experienced researcher.

How do sociologists decide what research strategy is appropriate for the problem that they are interested in? First, it should be stated that there are many problems that require several different research strategies. In fact, some of the best empirical work done in sociology has combined several different techniques. Thus, for example, the authors of *Union Democracy* conducted a quantitative survey, carried out a series of in-depth interviews with union leaders, and studied the history of the union by using traditional historical techniques. David Caplovitz's study of the consumer problems faced by poor people effectively combined a survey with a series of in-depth interviews with both merchants and consumers (see Chapter 6).

Most sociological studies, however, rely primarily on one research strategy. Frequently this is because the sociologist has been trained in only one technique or because time and monetary considerations rule out some techniques. For example, survey research generally costs a lot of money, whereas participant observation just requires the time of the researcher.

Qualitative research techniques are generally not suited for determining causality. Let us take as an example the study of attitude toward impeachment discussed in Chapter 2. In-depth interviews or participant observation would not be suitable for determining why some people favored impeachment and others opposed it. In order to test our hypotheses on this question, we would need data on a relatively large representative sample of the population we were studying. If we conducted a series of in-depth interviews, we might be able to develop hypotheses about why people felt as they did about impeachment, but we would not have enough cases or the representative sample that would be needed to test the hypotheses. Participant observation would be an even less suitable technique. The researcher would not be able to observe enough people in enough places to know if the attitudes expressed were representative. Furthermore, since most people spend only a small part of their time in political discussion or activity, observation would be a very inefficient way of collecting data on this topic.

PURPOSES OF USING QUALITATIVE RESEARCH   Qualitative techniques generally are used for three different purposes: description, formulation of hypotheses, and understanding causal processes. The distinctions among the three uses of qualitative research, which we will discuss, are made for analytical reasons. In fact, most qualitative research is to some extent used for all three purposes. The most important one of these, however, is description.

Description   If we know very little about a group of people or a social phenomenon, in-depth interviewing and participant observation are good ways to learn about them. For example, consider a very large group of people about which very little is known—urban slum dwellers. How do these people live? How do they deal with the difficult conditions in their environment? What are their attitudes toward other groups? An excellent way to collect data to answer these questions is participant observation. By living in an urban slum for a period of time and interacting on a daily basis with the residents, sociologists can develop a full and rich description of the behavior and attitudes of the people. For this kind of study, a method like survey research would be inappropriate. Having little knowledge of what we were studying, we would not even know what questions would be relevant. Even if we could make up a questionnaire that would suit our purposes, the relatively uneducated slum residents might not understand the questions or give us those answers they thought we wanted to hear rather than those expressing their real feelings. Also, a questionnaire would not enable us to see how the people really behaved as opposed to how they thought they should behave.

A good example of how expressed attitudes and actual behavior can differ significantly is shown in a study, done by James F. Short, Jr., and Fred L. Strodtbeck, on delinquent gangs in Chicago.[3] When questioned individually about their attitudes toward the kind of family life they wanted to have, the boys expressed traditional

[3]James F. Short, Jr., and Fred L. Strodtbeck, *Group Process and Gang Delinquency* (Chicago: University of Chicago Press, 1965).

attitudes not differing significantly from those typical of the traditional middle-class family. A father should work hard to provide for his family, be faithful to his wife, and be devoted to his children. The observers noted, however, that when in a group, the boys expressed quite different attitudes. One observer reported the following incident: A group of boys belonging to a gang called the "Chiefs" were standing on a corner when a former member walked past with his wife:

> Jackson (the former chief) had the baby in his arms; and such howling, clapping, and carrying on—they were razzing him.
> Q. Razzing him for being a legitimate father?
> A. Legitimate father walking around the street with his baby. Then Billy said, "Let me shut up 'cause I might be out walkin' my baby. You, too, Henry." Henry said, "Not me. I ain't walkin' nobody's baby."[4]

The observers also noted that in practice the boys were highly promiscuous and treated women as sex objects. Observation led the sociologists to conclude that the discrepancy between the boys' privately expressed attitudes on the one hand and their publicly expressed attitudes and behavior on the other resulted from an attempt by the boys to maintain their status in the gang. The gang was the most significant group for these boys, and the gang valued sexual prowess as an indication of masculinity.[5]

Formulation of Hypotheses   A second use of qualitative techniques is the formulation of hypotheses. Frequently, sociologists conduct research on social phenomena of which they have no firsthand experience and have very little knowledge. This is especially true when doing applied research. The study of illness among welfare mothers, reported on in Chapter 1, was part of a large study of the utilization of health facilities by welfare recipients. This study was commissioned by the United States Public Health Service for the purpose of improving the delivery of health care to welfare recipients

---

[4]Short and Strodtbeck, *Group Process*, p. 36.
[5]Short and Strodtbeck, *Group Process*, p. 38.

in large cities. The primary dependent variable was the extent to which the subjects used the facilities available to them. The sociologists conducting the research knew very little about the type of facilities that were available or the health-related behavior of welfare mothers. Thus, although the major part of the study was to be a survey administered to 2,000 welfare mothers, the researchers began by doing some qualitative field work. They visited the various types of health facilities, such as clinics; observed what went on; and spoke informally to the patients who were waiting there. They also conducted about a dozen in-depth interviews with welfare mothers. The qualitative data obtained from the field observation and in-depth interviews provided the information necessary to construct the questionnaire to be used in the quantitative survey.

Understanding Causal Processes A third use of qualitative research is to gain greater insight into the mechanisms through which a known causal process works. For example, many quantitative studies of academic scientists have found that scholarly productivity (the number and quality of papers published) is the most important determinant of academic success. Those professors who publish papers that are highly evaluated by their colleagues are the most successful. But very little is known about why some scientists are able to publish and others are not. Quantitative data indicate that this ability is not a result of measured intelligence. Practically all scientists have relatively high IQs, and there is no relationship between IQ and productivity. In order to gain greater insight into this problem, Leonard Rubin conducted a series of 40 in-depth interviews with scientists who began their careers as assistant professors in departments at prestigious universities.[6] All 40 scientists were initially judged to have high potential. Some of these young scientists, however, were promoted and received tenure while others were denied tenure and had to find jobs at less prestigious schools. What differentiated these two groups? Rubin found that there were indeed significant productivity differences between those who were and were not promoted. His interviews focused on the conditions leading

[6]Leonard Rubin, "The Dynamics of Tenure in Two Academic Disciplines" (Ph.D. diss., State University of New York at Stony Brook, 1975).

some scientists to publish and others not to publish. He found that whether or not scientists were able to publish resulted from a subtle combination of psychological factors, such as degree of commitment to career, and sociological factors, such as the type of training the scientists have received and the type of support they were given by their departments. The kind of detailed understanding of academic careers that emerged from Rubin's qualitative interviews could not have been gained through a quantitative survey.

This third use of qualitative research is the one most concerned with understanding the process of causality. In Rubin's research he was really looking for antecedent variables that influenced productivity. In this sense he was also engaged in developing hypotheses. The data that he collected were insufficient for determining the causes of the ability to publish; but they were useful in developing a set of hypotheses.

TYPES OF QUALITATIVE RESEARCH

Participant Observation of Urban Communities   In order to gain a greater understanding of the type of knowledge that can be gained through qualitative research, let us examine in some detail a set of studies of poor urban residents. All the studies employed the technique of participant observation.

Street Corner Society   One of the first and still the most famous study employing the technique of participant observation is William Foote Whyte's book, *Street Corner Society*.[7] In 1937 while attending graduate school at Harvard University, Whyte began a study of Cornerville, a lower-class Italian neighborhood in Boston. Soon after beginning his study Whyte moved into the neighborhood and lived there for three years with an Italian family. All the data that he used in writing his book came from his field notes, which described the behavior and attitudes of the people whom he came to know.

The first and most interesting part of the book describes the behavior and life-style of two groups of young men with whom Whyte became friendly. He called these two groups "corner boys"

[7]William Foote Whyte, *Street Corner Society* (Chicago: University of Chicago Press, 1943).

and "college boys." All of the young men were poor, but whereas the college boys had their sights focused on upward mobility and leaving the neighborhood for "bigger and better" things, the corner boys had little interest in leaving the neighborhood in which they had grown up.

The corner boys, led by Whyte's friend and chief informant, Doc, were a group of 13 young men in their twenties who hung around on Norton Street. Through his friendship with Doc, to whom he was introduced by a local social worker, Whyte became a member of this group. By participating in most of their activities, he found that there was a very definite status hierarchy among the 13 members of the Norton Street gang (see Figure 5.1). The status that a man occupied in the group determined how he behaved and performed in a wide range of activities. This was most clearly illustrated in an everyday activity in which the men frequently participated—bowling.

Figure 5.1. Status Hierarchy in the Norton Street Gang: Spring and Summer 1937

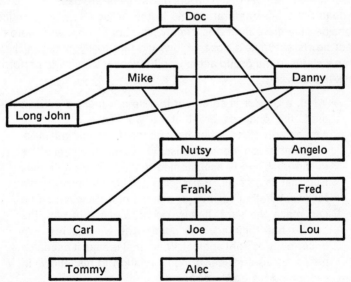

Source: William Foote Whyte, *Street Corner Society* (Chicago: University of Chicago Press, 1943), p. 13. Reprinted with permission.

Note: Positions of boxes indicate relative status; lines indicate influence.

When Whyte first began to bowl with the Nortons on Saturday night, he viewed the activity simply as a form of recreation. After bowling with the men for many months, a revealing event occurred. One night in April all the members of the group who regularly bowled had a competition for ten dollars in prize money to be divided among the three highest scorers. There was much interest in and prior discussion of the match, with the different gang members predicting who would perform the best. It was agreed that Doc, Danny, and Long John would be near the top and that Joe, Alec, Frank, and Carl would be near the bottom. When the contest took place, the men finished in almost the exact places that everyone had predicted. Whyte suddenly realized that the ranking of the bowlers corresponded very closely with their position in the group's status hierarchy. Why should this be?

The correlation between bowling performance and rank in the group could not be explained by natural athletic ability or by amount of practice. For example, Frank, one of the worst bowlers and a low-ranking member of the group, played semi-pro baseball and was probably the best natural athlete in the group. He also practiced considerably more than Doc, Danny, and Long John, who were the best bowlers. Whyte's observations led him to hypothesize that a man's status in the group actually influenced his ability to perform a task like bowling:

> When a bowler is confident that he can make a difficult shot, the chances are that he will make it or come exceedingly close. When he is not confident, he will miss. A bowler is confident because he has made similar shots in the past and is accustomed to making good scores. But that is not all. He is also confident because his fellows, whether for him or against him, believe that he can make the shot. If they do not believe in him, the bowler has their adverse opinion as well as his own uncertainty to fight against. When that is said, it becomes necessary to consider a man's relation to his fellows in examining his bowling record.[8]

[8]Whyte, *Street Corner Society*, p. 17.

Alec, when bowling in a noncompetitive situation, was one of the best bowlers in the group, In the group contest Alec started out strong but soon lost confidence and his game collapsed. Later, Whyte, who actually finished first in the match, talked to Doc and Long John about what had happened.

> Long John: I only wanted to be sure that Alec or Joe Dodge didn't win. That wouldn't have been right.
> Doc: That's right. We didn't want to make it tough for you, because we all liked you, and the other fellows did too. If somebody had tried to make it tough for you, we would have protected you. . . . If Joe Dodge or Alec had been out in front, it would have been different. We would have talked them out of it. We would have made plenty of noise. We would have been really vicious. . . . [9]

Whyte then asked Doc what would have happened if Alec or Joe had won. Doc responded:

> They wouldn't have known how to take it. That's why we were out to beat them. If they had won, there would have been a lot of noise. Plenty of arguments. We would have called it lucky—things like that. We would have tried to get them in another match and then ruin them. We would have to put them in their places.[10]

Whyte then comments on his winning the match:

> Every corner boy expects to be heckled as he bowls, but the heckling can take various forms. While I had moved ahead as early as the end of the second string, I was subjected only to good-natured kidding. The leaders watched me with mingled surprise and amusement; in a very real sense, I was permitted to win.[11]

After winning the match, Whyte wanted to be considered one of the better bowlers in the group. A match was arranged between him and Long John.

[9]Whyte, *Street Corner Society*, p. 21.
[10]Whyte, *Street Corner Society*, p. 21.
[11]Whyte, *Street Corner Society*, pp. 21–22.

> If I won, I should have the right to challenge Doc or Danny. The four of us went to the alleys together. Urged on by Doc and Danny, Long John won a decisive victory. I made no further challenges.[12]

Thus, group status and support was able to influence even the performance of the researcher.

Whyte's hypothesis about the relationship between athletic performance and group status was confirmed by another incident that he observed. The Nortons organized a baseball game between themselves and some of the younger men who gathered on Norton Street. It would have been expected that Frank, the semi-pro baseball player, would have been one of the better players. Yet in the game he performed very poorly. Frank explained his poor performance to Whyte:

> I can't seem to play ball when I'm playing with fellows I know, like that bunch. I do much better when I'm playing for the Stanley A.C. against some team in Dexter, Westland, or out of town.[13]

Whyte comments: "Accustomed to filling an inferior position, Frank was unable to star even in his favorite sport when he was competing against members of his own group."[14]

Later on in the study Whyte observed how a change in a man's status in the group could influence a change in his bowling performance. Long John was a close friend of Doc but had no independent standing in the group. He was, however, included in the inner circle due to his friendship with Doc and several other leaders. Long John was one of the best bowlers in the group, and as long as Doc remained the leader of the Nortons, Long John continued to be a top bowler. At one point, Doc left the Nortons to join a group that hung out at Spongi's, a local gambling house. Long John, without the support of Doc, was no longer included in the inner circle of the Nortons and was not admitted to the inner circle at Spongi's. Now, whenever Long John bowled with the Nortons, he was teased and

---

[12]Whyte, *Street Corner Society*, p. 22.
[13]Whyte, *Street Corner Society*, p. 19.
[14]Whyte, *Street Corner Society*, p. 19.

ridiculed. Having lost his position in the group, he lost his self-confidence and his bowling ability sharply declined. It was only after Doc spoke to Whyte about Long John and after Whyte suggested that Doc try to get Long John included in the inner circle at Spongi's that Long John's self-confidence returned and with it his bowling ability.

Whyte learned an interesting lesson in participant observation from his bowling experience. At first he thought of bowling simply as recreation, not as a part of his research:

> I found myself enjoying the bowling so much that now and then I felt a bit guilty about neglecting my research. I was bowling with the men in order to establish a social position that would enable me to interview them and observe important things . . . only [later] . . . did I suddenly realize that the behavior of the men in the regular bowling-alley sessions was the perfect example of what I should be observing. Instead of bowling in order to be able to observe something else, I should have been bowling in order to observe bowling. I learned then that the day-to-day routine activities of these men constituted the basic data of my study.[15]

The lesson Whyte learned was that a good deal about the social structure of a community can be learned from observing the seemingly most mundane activities. The connection between group status and task performance is the kind of knowledge that would have been very difficult, if not impossible, to obtain through a quantitative survey of the residents of Cornerville. It is only by observing people in their day-to-day lives over an extended period of time that such knowledge can be acquired.

Another part of *Street Corner Society* indicates both the advantages and limitations of qualitative research. When considering the process of social mobility out of Cornerville, Whyte comments on the difference between the corner boys and the college boys. Most of the college boys were becoming successful professionals, business-

---

[15]Whyte, *Street Corner Society*, appendix, p. 320.

men, and politicians, whereas most of the corner boys either were unemployed or had blue-collar jobs. Superficially this difference can be explained by the college boys' possession of a college degree, a necessity for upward mobility. But Whyte goes beyond this. Why do some boys go to college and others do not? To begin with, he ruled out differences in intelligence. It was clear to Whyte that Doc was at least as smart as Chick Morelli, the leader of the college boys.

Whyte points out that the differences between the college boys and corner boys began when they were still in junior high school. They developed different behavior patterns, with their attitudes toward a college education and social mobility simply being the culmination of their respective patterns. What were these differences? The corner boys and college boys had very different attitudes toward money. The college boys were frugal and saved the money they earned. They rarely would treat or lend money to a friend. The corner boys, on the other hand, would spend all their money, freely giving it or lending it to friends who were broke.

> Chick and Doc exemplify the two conflicting attitudes toward money. In his life-story Chick said that he had once been a free spender but had learned his lesson when a friend refused to reciprocate. Doc told me: "Bill, I owe money now, but if I was paid all the money owed me, I would have a gang of money. I never saved. I never had a bank account. . . . If the boys are going to a show and this man can't go because he is batted out, I say to myself, 'Why should he be deprived of that luxury?' And I give him the money. . . . And I never talk about it."
>
> Both Doc and Chick recognized that the free spender does not receive an equal financial return, but they drew different conclusions from that observation. While Doc sometimes wished that he could have back a portion of the money he had spent and lent, he thought of spending in terms of personal relations and not in terms of profits, losses, and savings.[16]

In another part of the book Whyte goes into some detail on the

---

[16]Whyte, *Street Corner Society*, pp. 106–107.

importance of having money and being a free spender in maintaining leadership among the corner boys. When Doc was unemployed for a long period of time and, subsequently, ran out of money, he developed dizzy spells, which disappeared after he became employed again. Whyte posited that the periodic dizzy spells were a psychosomatic symptom brought on by Doc's inability to assume his position of leadership among the Nortons.

Another difference between the two groups is the degree of loyalty displayed toward friends.

> Chick judged men according to their capacity for advancing themselves. Doc judged them according to their loyalty to their friends and their behavior in their personal relations. In discussing the difference between the college boys and the corner boys, Doc had this to say about Chick: "Chick says that self-preservation is the first law of nature. Now that's right to a certain extent. You have to look out for yourself first. But Chick would step on the neck of his best friend if he could get a better job by doing it. . . . We were talking one night on the corner about that, and I was sucking him in. I got him to admit it—that he would turn against his best friend if he could profit by it. . . . I would never do that, Bill. I would never step on Danny even if I could get myself a $50-a-week job by doing it. None of my boys would do that."
>
> Both the college boy and the corner boy want to get ahead. The difference between them is that the college boy either does not tie himself to a group of close friends or else is willing to sacrifice his friendship with those who do not advance as fast as he does. The corner boy is tied to his group by a network of reciprocal obligations from which he is either unwilling or unable to break away.[17]

Whyte ends this section with the following story related to him by Doc:

[17]Whyte, *Street Corner Society*, p. 107. During the depression when Whyte conducted his study, $50 a week was considered to be a lot of money.

> I suppose my boys have kept me from getting ahead. . . .
> But if I were to start over again—if God said to me, "Look
> here, Doc, you're going to start over again, and you can
> pick out your friends in advance," still I would make sure
> that my boys were among them—even if I could pick
> Rockefeller and Carnegie. . . . Many times people in the
> settlement and some of the Sunsets [another club] have
> said to me, "Why do you hang around those fellows?" I
> would tell them, "Why not? They're my friends."
>
> Bill, last night at home my brother-in-law was listen-
> ing to his favorite Italian program when my nephew
> comes in. He wants to listen to something else, so he
> goes up and switches the dial—without asking anybody
> . . . I'm in a tough spot here, Bill. They want to do
> everything for these kids, and if I try to discipline the kids,
> they jump on me. . . . But that was too raw. I got the kid
> aside, and I gave him a lecture. Bill, I was really eloquent.
> But then at the end of it, I said, "But don't change too
> much, kid. Stay the way you are, and you'll get ahead in
> the world."[18]

Does this type of analysis tell us why the college boys were
successful and the corner boys were not? Not really. What it does do
is give us a rich and fascinating description of the difference in their
behavior patterns; but it leaves unanswered the crucial question of
why boys living in the same neighborhood develop such different
behavior patterns. Why do some boys become college boys and
others corner boys? Qualitative research is not well suited for
answering this type of question.

When the second edition of *Street Corner Society* was published
in 1955, Whyte included an appendix, in which he described in some
detail how he had done the research. This account provides a useful
description of some of the problems encountered in doing participant observation. The first problem concerns the formulation of the
research design. Since qualitative research generally aims at describing a social setting or phenomenon of which relatively little is

[18]Whyte, *Street Corner Society*, p. 108.

known, it is frequently difficult to specify beforehand what it is that the researcher is looking for. This was certainly true in Whyte's case. When he first began his research he planned an ambitious study requiring ten co-workers, who would delve into all aspects of Cornerville life and society. After he went to live in Cornerville he gave up his ambitious plans but still had no specific focus for his research. In a real sense what he eventually concentrated on was a matter of chance. Another equally brilliant observer going into the same area at the same time might have concentrated his efforts on different phenomena. When doing participant observation it is usually difficult to specify what you are looking for until you have found it.

One of the most difficult problems encountered by the participant observer is gaining entrance into the field. Whyte made a number of abortive efforts to enter the mainstream of Cornerville before meeting Doc. At first he tried doing a survey of housing conditions in the area. He knocked on doors and spoke to the tenants. But this proved to be of little use in really getting to know the people. Then he tried a technique suggested to him by a friend at Harvard. He entered a bar in a local hotel with the aim of beginning a conversation with a woman. Finding no single women, he approached a man talking to two women and asked if they would mind if he joined them. At this point the man threatened to throw him down the stairs. It was only when a social worker at a local settlement house introduced Whyte to Doc that he was able to become a part of the community. Whyte was extremely fortunate in meeting such a knowledgeable and cooperative guide as Doc. Even though many field workers are not so fortunate, most try to establish close relationships with one or more of the people they are studying and rely on these people to bring them into the action.

Another serious problem that participant observers face is not violating the norms and customs of the people they are studying. This is particularly important when studying people who have a culture different from that of the researchers. Whyte occasionally found himself violating the norms of the Cornerville residents. Once when Whyte visited a gambling joint with Doc, he met a man from another part of the city who was describing in detail how gambling was organized. In the course of the conversation Whyte casually

remarked, "I suppose the cops were all paid off?"[19] The man seemed
to be shocked by the question; he denied that payoffs were made
and quickly dropped his discussion of gambling. Later Doc told
Whyte that he should never ask such specific questions but that if he
just hung around and listened he would eventually find out all he
wanted to know. Whyte found this to be good advice. From then on
he addressed specific questions only to people whom he knew well.
He realized it was usually possible to learn a great deal simply by
observing.

Another time Whyte inadvertently violated one of the norms when
he invited a local girl to a church dance and called for her at her
home. The next day some of the Nortons asked him, "How's your
steady girl?"[20] He had not realized that in Cornerville a man did not
go to a girl's home unless he planned to marry her. After this
incident, he decided that he would never again date a local girl.

Finally, a problem sometimes faced by participant observers is
getting overinvolved in the activities they are studying. When researchers become participants, they may lose the objectivity with
which outsiders can view social behavior. They may also feel
uncomfortable while participating in certain activities. For example,
Whyte felt he was violating his own norms when he studied politics
in Cornerville. In order to conduct this part of the research, he
worked as a volunteer for a candidate running for Congress. On
election day it was expected that the campaign workers would
engage in an activity called "repeating" (voting more than once,
using other people's names). Whyte did this and was almost arrested. Not only did he feel uncomfortable in engaging in this behavior,
which violated his own norms, but also had he actually been arrested
it may have jeopardized his entire study. A participant observer has
to learn when not to be a participant.

The Urban Villagers After Whyte's brilliant study conducted in the
late 1930s, there was very little study of urban communities until the
late 1950s.[21] At that time Herbert Gans conducted a participant

[19]Whyte, *Street Corner Society*, appendix, p. 303.
[20]Whyte, *Street Corner Society*, appendix, p. 299.
[21]For an analysis of urban community studies, see Gerald D. Suttles, "Urban
Ethnography: Situational and Normative Accounts," *Annual Review of Sociology* (to be
published in 1976).

observation study, published as *The Urban Villagers*.[22] Gans's study of another Italian neighborhood in Boston differed in scope from that of Whyte. The picture Gans drew of the West End was broader than Whyte's study of Cornerville. Gans included descriptions of the family, work experience, education, medical care, relationships with social workers, and other aspects of life in the West End. Although he covered a wider range of activities than Whyte did, Gans's observations are not as detailed as those of Whyte.

To me the most interesting part of Gans's analysis is the contrast between the way a neighborhood like the West End would appear to uninformed casual observers and the way it appeared to a well-informed participant observer. The casual observer would probably have seen the neighborhood as a slum. Many of the buildings or tenements were in poor condition; some with broken windows were abandoned. The streets were dirty, noisy, and crowded. The crime rate was high. This is the kind of neighborhood that many liberal-minded people believe should be razed and built anew. In fact, while Gans was living there, a plan for urban renewal of the West End was well under way. And shortly after he completed his study, the area was cleared to become the site for new high-rent, high-rise apartments.

The casual observer may have agreed with the urban renewal plan to rid the city of the blighted area; but Gans points out that its residents had built up a local social structure that satisfied many of their needs and provided them with a form of life that most residents found satisfactory. When Gans first came to the neighborhood he too perceived it in terms of the stereotyped urban slum. But his view soon changed.

> After a few weeks of living in the West End, my observa-
> tions—and my perception of the area—changed drasti-
> cally. The search for an apartment quickly indicated that
> the individual units were usually in much better condition
> than the outside or the hallways of the buildings. Subse-
> quently, in wandering through the West End, and in
> using it as a resident, I developed a kind of selective

[22]Herbert Gans, *The Urban Villagers* (New York: The Free Press, 1962).

perception, in which my eye focused only on those parts of the area that were actually being used by people. Vacant buildings and boarded-up stores were no longer so visible, and the totally deserted alleys or streets were outside the set of paths normally traversed, either by myself or by the West Enders. The dirt and spilled-over garbage remained, but, since they were concentrated in street gutters and empty lots, they were not really harmful to anyone and thus were not as noticeable as during my initial observations.[23]

Although Gans makes a special point not to romanticize the area or to ignore the real problems faced by the people who live there, he concluded that "by and large [it was] a good place to live."[24]

The casual observer's evaluation of areas like the West End as an undesirable slum is based on an ethnocentric world view; that is, people evaluate others in terms of their own values. Because many of us would not enjoy living in a crowded, noisy neighborhood, we believe that no one or only some type of degenerate would. Gans points out that the West Enders felt quite at home in their environment and would have felt uncomfortable in the suburbs, which many middle-class Americans aspire to.

Whereas most West Enders have no objection to the older suburban towns that surround the Boston city limits, they have little use for the newer suburbs.[25] They described these as too quiet for their tastes, lonely—that is, without street life—and occupied by people concerned only with trying to appear better than they are. West Enders avoid "the country," by which they mean not only rural and vacation areas, but also the lower density suburban towns. They do not like its isolation and, even at vacation time, they go to the densely populated resort areas where the crowds and entertain-

[23]Gans, *The Urban Villagers*, p. 12.
[24]Gans, *The Urban Villagers*, p. 16.
[25]"The older towns are suburbs only because they are outside Boston's city limits. They are built up with apartments as well as houses. West Enders liked them because they contain Italian neighborhoods and because they had friends and relatives there. Many West Enders eventually moved to these towns when redevelopment came." Gans, *The Urban Villagers*, p. 22.

ment facilities of the city prevail. . . . The younger children like the country because there is more play space
around single-family houses. As they grow older, however, they play in the city streets as did their parents
before them, and their interest in the country vanishes. I
was told by one social worker of an experiment some
years back to expose West End children to nature by
taking them on a trip to Cape Cod. The experiment failed,
for the young West Enders found no pleasure in the
loneliness of natural surroundings and wanted to get
back to the West End as quickly as possible. They were
incredulous that anyone could live without people
around him.[26]

Within their physically run-down community the West Enders had
built a web of social relationships that made their lives meaningful.
Social life centered around age- and sex-segregated peer groups
and what Gans calls the "family circle."[27] The peer groups for young
men closely resembled the Norton gang described by Whyte. The
family circle consisted of members of an extended family and close
friends, who frequently spent evenings together talking late into the
night. In addition to having their friends and family in the neighborhood, the residents did most of their shopping locally, attended
church locally, and engaged in politics locally. In short, most of the
residents of this community had a meaningful social life within it.
When urban renewal demolished the buildings, it also destroyed the
social structure of the residents and undoubtedly had a permanent
negative impact on the lives of many of the people forced to move. At
the end of his book, Gans concluded that calling the old West End a
"slum" reflects the application of ethnocentric middle-class values
to a subculture that differs from the dominant one.

Clearly participant observation was a very suitable methodology
for distinguishing between the physical appearance of a neighborhood and the social lives of its inhabitants. This would have been
very difficult to do using quantitative techniques. What participant
observation is not able to tell us is the extent to which the patterns

---

[26]Gans, *The Urban Villagers*, pp. 22–23.
[27]Gans borrows this term from Michael Young and Peter Willmott, *Family and
Kinship in East London* (London: Routledge & Kegan Paul, 1957).

described by Gans were typical of the majority of West End residents. Like most participant observers Gans knew well only a small number of people. His major contacts were with the family circle of one of his neighbors. A supporter of urban renewal might argue that Gans had failed to describe the majority of the people, who lived in "rat-infested tenements" and were afraid to venture out of their houses at night. Although most readers of *The Urban Villagers* would probably side with Gans, to fully answer the challenge of the urban renewal supporter, for example, some more systematic study would be required.

It may be interesting to note how researchers, such as Gans or Whyte, go about organizing their observations and writing them up. Gans gives a concise description of how he analyzed his data:

> The actual analysis of the data was quite simple. I recorded my observations and interviews as soon as possible after they had been completed, together with the generalizations they stimulated, and placed them in a field diary. When I came to write the study, I read and reread my diary several times, and then put the generalizations and some supporting observations on index cards. Eventually, I had more than 2000 of these. I then sorted and classified them by a variety of subject headings. The classification was determined in part by my initial research purposes, in part by topics in which I had become interested during the field work, and in part by the observations made spontaneously while in the field. The content of the cards was then further digested into pages of notes listing the major generalizations and other ideas. An initial report was written from these notes in 1959. Before I wrote this book, I reread the diary and took further notes on it.[28]

Most researchers follow a procedure similar to that used by Gans.

The Social Order of the Slum In the last ten years a group of sociologists working at the University of Chicago have conducted

[28]Gans, *The Urban Villagers*, pp. 346–47.

several first-rate qualitative studies of urban communities in Chicago. Perhaps the most important of these is Gerald Suttles's book, *The Social Order of the Slum*.[29] Prior to the publication of this book most studies of urban communities focused on one ethnic or racial group. Many urban communities, however, are ethnically integrated. In addition to engaging in the kind of precise description done by Whyte and Gans, Suttles described the interrelations of the Italians, blacks, Mexicans, and Puerto Ricans who lived in what Suttles called the "Addams area."

The Addams area had at one time been predominantly an Italian neighborhood. But as in many inner-city neighborhoods a process of ethnic succession had brought about change in the ethnic composition. Many Italian families, as they became upwardly mobile, had moved to "better" neighborhoods. Their place had been taken by Mexicans and Puerto Ricans who had recently moved to Chicago and had moved into the Addams area because it provided housing at a price they could afford. The city had torn down some of the old tenements and built public housing projects; practically all the residents of these projects were black.

What are the stereotypes that we hold of poor urban residents? "Outsiders" generally consider them to be shiftless, immoral, and violent. In short they are often viewed as dangerous. This stereotype is supported by the high crime rates found in some inner-city neighborhoods. Suttles points out that the people living in these neighborhoods view their neighbors as fitting these stereotypes— particularly neighbors who differ from them in ethnicity. Most people are afraid to live in these neighborhoods and, if possible, move to "safe" areas of the city or to suburbs where they will not be afraid to walk the streets.[30] But how do people who cannot afford to move out of poor inner-city areas deal with the problem of getting along with neighbors whom they fear?

After living in the Addams area for three years Suttles concluded that residents dealt with this problem through a process he called "ordered segmentation." An individual could overcome fear of

[29]Gerald D. Suttles, *The Social Order of the Slum* (Chicago: University of Chicago Press, 1968).

[30]Note here the different pictures of urban neighborhoods painted by Gans and Suttles. This will be discussed further below.

another person through close personal knowledge of that person's history. This knowledge enables a person to judge if another person represents a threat to his or her safety. But clearly it is impossible to know more than several hundred neighbors. There were more than 20,000 residents in the Addams area. In order to live in the same neighborhood with people whom one feared, a social structure was developed in which residents were seen as belonging to a series of groups based predominantly on ethnicity, territoriality (where they lived), age, and sex. (This contrasts sharply with residents of middle-class communities, who would place others by their occupation, educational attainment, income, and prestige in the community.) In the Addams area, ordered segmentation allowed the relationships formed between groups to take the place of mutual trust among people who did not know each other well. These relationships assured a teenage boy, for example, relative safety as long as he stayed in his "own" area and did not violate any of the informal understandings that the different groups had. Thus, for example, the members of the black gangs who lived in the projects knew that they would be held responsible if any blacks beat up an Italian. (It was for this reason that the blacks in the Addams area were frightened and incensed when blacks from an adjacent neighborhood made trouble at a dance.) Suttles's observations led to the interesting hypothesis that one of the primary social functions served by gangs is the protection of a territory from the aggression of others. He calls these gangs "vigilante peer groups."[31]

The function that was being served by teenage gangs was highlighted when the Chicago Youth Development Project was able to turn the interests of the black gang members to various socially constructive activities. The boys became involved in the civil rights movement and athletic teams. This left the black section of the Addams area unprotected.

> The relative decline of street groups in this section brought with it two other unexpected results. First, the Italian groups to the northwest seem to have taken it as sure evidence that the Negroes were relatively defense-

[31]Suttles extends his analysis of gangs in his book *The Social Construction of Communities* (Chicago: University of Chicago Press, 1972), chap. 8.

less. In due course, they became particularly blatant in the indignities they thought necessary to keep the Negroes "in their place." . . . In turn, their traditional rivals in the "Village," below Roosevelt, [another black gang living in an adjacent neighborhood], took offense and did their best to restore a previous order in which they had somewhat overshadowed the boys in the Jane Addams Projects. Their efforts in this case took two different courses. They first made an unsolicited effort to "horn in" on the peaceful demonstrations being carried out by those in the Addams area. . . . As the summer drew to a close and the civil rights movement relaxed over the winter, the boys from the "Village" tried another alternative. Since the Addams area had been stripped of its protective forces, the Village Boys felt free to sample the pleasures, girls, and "action" available in it. At the same time, they also took the liberty of "starting something" with the local Italians and Mexicans, even when the Negro boys in the Jane Addams Projects stood "to take the rap."[32]

Suttles then describes how the Village Deacons started a fight at a dance held by a group of Italian boys. Suttles concludes:

After the inroads of the Village boys and the melee at the dance, it became clear that the Negro gangs were serving a useful social function for their section. They were its guardians and had excluded a wide variety of people whom all the local Negroes feared. Here, the Negro gangs operate much like those among the Italians and Mexicans.[33]

Even the adults living in the type of communities described by Suttles came to depend on the teenage gangs for psychological, if not actual, protection. Suttles gives an amusing example of this. In 1968, when the Democrats held their presidential convention in Chicago, a newspaper reporter asked a local resident if he were

[32]Suttles, *Social Order*, pp. 133–34.
[33]Suttles, *Social Order*, p. 136.

afraid that the Yippies might come into the area and make trouble. The resident replied, "No . . . the kids around here are pretty tough. They'll keep them out."[34] Suttles comments on this reply: "Several thousand federal and state troops had been brought into the area to protect it, but the residents were still depending on their kids."[35] Although adults may depend on teenage gangs for the protection of their territory, they are not necessarily happy about this solution to the problem of order. However, as long as the police are unable to provide adequate protection, the gangs continue to serve a useful social function.[36]

The insight that Suttles gained into how the Addams residents managed the difficult problem of fear of their neighbors and the functions served by the gangs could never have been gained from quantitative analysis. However, a problem in this type of analysis emerges from a comparison of the images that Whyte, Gans, and Suttles portray. Whyte and Gans describe communities that seemed to have relatively stable social structures and a good deal of mutual trust among the residents. Suttles, on the other hand, describes a community that appears to have a much less stable social structure and very little mutual trust among the residents. We do not know whether this difference is real or a result of the different experiences and perspectives of the observers. If the difference is real, how can it be explained? Is it simply the result of differences in the ethnic homogeneity of the communities or the age of the people studied or some other unknown factor? To some extent the descriptions made by participant observers are subjective. It would be desirable to have several independent researchers simultaneously living in and studying the same community. Also, in order to make generalizations from the knowledge gained from participant observation, it would probably be necessary for groups of researchers to systematically sample and then observe a larger number of communities. Quantitative research based on adequate representative samples does not allow the kind of rich description made by participant observers but its results are more easily generalized.

---

[34]Suttles, *Social Construction*, p. 201.
[35]Suttles, *Social Construction*, p. 201.
[36]Suttles, *Social Construction*, p. 191.

Managed Integration   Another excellent study done of a community in Chicago is Harvey Molotch's book *Managed Integration*.[37] Molotch studied a Chicago community, South Shore, which was gradually changing from a white to a black community. The residents of South Shore had utilized the services of a local civic organization, the South Shore Commission, to prevent their neighborhood from becoming all black. Molotch's research was aimed at gaining a greater understanding of the social processes affecting the racial stability of a community. Although he did not live in South Shore he spent two years studying the community. He used an effective combination of qualitative techniques and also collected much quantitative data.

In order to study the community Molotch wanted to be able to specify its boundaries. In particular, how did the people who lived there define the community? In order to find out whether the residents identified the community as "South Shore" and what its boundaries were, Molotch used the following procedure:

> Within the general region south of Jackson Park, below the community of Woodlawn, but north of the steel mills and in the residential areas adjacent to the Lake, I conducted fifty brief interviews with local people. The method was informal; interviews took place under a variety of conditions: some were on street corners (especially the main business crossing under the sign of the South Shore National Bank); others were in stores or offices; three were at gas stations. I asked various bystanders and service personnel such questions as: "What part of town is this?" "How far does South Shore go?" I considered these and similar probes appropriate to determine the respondent's notion of local neighborhoods and their boundaries. My questions were those of an ordinary person seeking orientation.[38]

The South Shore Commission was determined to keep the South Shore integrated. Since blacks were moving into the area, the aim of

[37]Harvey Luskin Molotch, *Managed Integration: Dilemmas of Doing Good in the City* (Berkeley: University of California Press, 1972).
[38]Molotch, *Managed Integration*, p. 46.

the commission was to convince white residents to remain there and encourage new white residents to occupy vacant apartments and houses. The commission was a very powerful group, having among its residents an editor of a leading Chicago newspaper and other important Chicago citizens. The commission also had good political connections with Mayor Daley and the various city agencies. These connections enabled the South Shore to command more resources than a less well-organized community. The members of the commission put in thousands of hours of time as well as contributed their own money to its operation. In short, it is hard to imagine a community making a more effective effort, short of violence, to remain integrated.

The commission did a lot of public relations for the community, trying to emphasize its desirable characteristics and downplay its undesirable ones, such as a rapidly rising crime rate.[39] But perhaps the most important mechanism used by the commission to maintain integration was the Tenant Referral Service (TRS). The purpose of this organization was to make housing opportunities in the neighborhood known to white people and prevent landlords from renting "too many" apartments to blacks. TRS was able to put pressure on landlords because it had become a major way in which people found housing. If TRS refused to list a landlord's vacancies, it would be harder to fill them. Molotch's observation led him to see that the TRS was in fact violating the Chicago fair housing laws by trying to maintain a quota system in those buildings that still had a substantial number of white people in residence.

> The commission did not refer applicants randomly to the buildings and neighborhoods of South Shore. In the words of one commission official, referrals were made with the goal of "keeping whites moving into integrated buildings. That's where we put our primary efforts. Whites must see other whites moving into the building after Negroes have once moved in. Otherwise they will empty out. We definitely focus on integrated buildings and integrated areas."

[39]Molotch shows that the residents' perception that crime was on the increase was accurate. The crime rate was going up more rapidly in South Shore than in other parts of the city.

When a black applied for an apartment at TRS, it would not have been useful to refer him to a racially mixed building if there was a good chance that a white tenant could be found. Indeed, continued integration of the same building would eventually have led to complete resegregation and the defeat of the key purpose of TRS. Also, the commission was generally inhibited from referring blacks to buildings which were *all white*. To do so would have integrated parts of the community whose residents were opposed to such integration and whose landlords often listed their apartments with the understanding that no blacks would be referred.[40]

In addition to trying to maintain racial quotas by TRS, the commission set up the Fair Housing Center, the purpose of which was to make housing opportunities in white neighborhoods throughout the city known to local black residents. Despite all its efforts the attempt of the commission to prevent South Shore from becoming all black was unsuccessful. Molotch presents statistics showing that the racial composition of the neighborhood was changing rapidly. And after Molotch completed his research the community became almost all black, and many leading commission members moved out with the other exiting white residents.

The most interesting conclusion of this book is the inability of determined people to control their own social environment. The social processes at work were too powerful to be interfered with by even a group as strong as the commission. What were these social processes?

Molotch attempted to find out if there was a rampant panic selling on the part of white property owners. In order to do this it was necessary for Molotch to know how many houses were being sold and whether this number was large or small when compared with the number of house sales in other communities. Molotch selected another community, Rogers Park, which was similar to South Shore, except for the fact that it was all white and not under any threat of racial "invasion." He used records published in a real estate journal to indicate the number of houses sold. These records showed no difference in the proportion of houses being sold in the two commu-

[40]Molotch, *Managed Integration*, p. 116.

nities. But Molotch cleverly points out that these data do not tell us how many people wanted to sell their homes. It was possible that more people in South Shore wanted to sell their homes but could not find buyers. In order to find out how many people wanted to sell their homes, he counted the number of For Sale signs on houses in the two communities. He found no difference in the proportion of houses with For Sale signs in the two communities. But, perhaps, residents of South Shore were less willing to publicly display a For Sale sign for fear of angering their neighbors, who were highly concerned about the racial change the community was undergoing. In order to check this possibility Molotch visited local real estate agents, obtained lists of houses for sale, and then visually inspected the houses to see what proportion had For Sale signs. Again there was no difference between the two communities. Molotch concludes that there was no panic selling in South Shore. Houses were changing hands in South Shore at the same rate as in another similar community.[41]

If South Shore residents were not panic selling, then why was the racial composition of the neighborhood changing? Molotch offers an essentially economic reason for this. In Chicago a dual housing market operated—one for blacks and one for whites. He was able to show that blacks pay more than whites for the same quality house or apartment. There was also less good housing available for blacks than for whites. White people in South Shore were moving out of their houses (and presumably apartments) at the same rate as white people were moving in other neighborhoods. But the people who were moving into South Shore were predominantly black. This is because the housing available in South Shore was more valuable to blacks than to whites. White people could find better housing at lower prices elsewhere; blacks could not. Although the whites moving out of South Shore may have moved in part because of prejudice, Molotch claims that this is not necessary in order to explain the racial transition.

Perhaps the lack of white demand reflected a reluctance on the part of whites to locate or relocate in a bi-racial

[41]One problem with this type of case study is that we do not know whether the findings can be generalized so as to include other communities undergoing racial change.

area. But such factors, based on racial attitudes of mobile whites, are not *necessary* to explain transition; variations in demand due to differentials in population growth and available supplies of substantial housing alone suffice to explain the continuing growth of South Shore's black population.[42]

This argument would be stronger if Molotch had some data on where the exiting whites moved to. If they moved into houses that were no "better" than the ones they left and cost substantially more, then racial prejudice may have played a greater role in the transition.

Tally's Corner   The final study of urban communities that we will discuss is *Tally's Corner* by Elliot Liebow.[43] This book is an account of the lives of a group of black men who hung around on a street corner in Washington, D.C. Liebow's book is so well written and contains such a rich description of the people he studied that it reads more like a novel than a sociological study:

> For those who hang out there, the Carry-out [a restaurant] offers a wide array of sounds, sights, smells, tastes, and tactile experiences which titillate and sometimes assault the five senses. The air is warmed by smells from the coffee urns and grill and thickened with fat from the deep-fry basket. The jukebox offers up a wide variety of frenetic and lazy rhythms. The pinball machine is a standing challenge to one's manipulative skill or ability to will the ball into one or another hole. Flashing lights, bells and buzzers report progress or announce failure. Colorful signs exhort customers to drink Royal Crown Cola and eat Bond Bread. On the wall, above the telephone, a long-legged blonde in shorts and halter smiles a fixed, wet-lipped smile of unutterable delight at her Chesterfield cigarette, her visage unmarred by a mustache or scribbled obscenities. In the background, a sleek ocean liner rides a flat blue sea to an unknown destination.

---

[42]Molotch, *Managed Integration*, p. 171.
[43]Elliot Liebow, *Tally's Corner* (Boston: Little, Brown, 1967).

In this setting, and on the broad corner sidewalk in front of it, some twenty men who live in the area regularly come together for "effortless sociability." They are not, in any strict sense, a group. No more than eight or ten, and usually fewer, are there at any one time. There is nothing to join, no obligations, no one to say whether you belong or do not belong. Some of the men have never spoken to some of the others beyond exchanging a casual greeting. Some are close friends, some do not like others, and still others consider themselves enemies. But each man comes here mainly because he knows others will be here, too. He comes to eat and drink, to enjoy easy talk, to learn what has been going on, to horse around, to look at women and banter with them, to see "what's happening" and to pass the time.[44]

The most significant result of Liebow's study is a deeper understanding of how the social conditions faced by poor urban black people give them a sense of hopelessness that pervades all areas of their lives. Typical is the work experience of the men who hung out in front of the Carry-out. Although some of the men had steady jobs, most were unemployed and seemed to have little desire to work. Why was this? Most of the men had little education. The kind of jobs they could have received were either back-breaking construction jobs, which many of the men were not physically able to handle, or menial jobs which pay so little that the men could not have supported their families even if they did work. Another important factor was the men's lack of self-confidence. Most of them had done so poorly at anything they had tried in the past that they were afraid to tackle any job that is demanding.

The world of the men was dominated by self-fulfilling prophecies.[45] Many employers of the men paid them low wages because they thought the men would steal on the job. Because they were paid low wages the men did steal. Even in the unlikely situation that the men stole enough so that their "take" from the job would have been

[44]Liebow, *Tally's Corner,* pp. 21–23.
[45]See Robert K. Merton, "The Self-Fulfilling Prophecy," *Social Theory and Social Structure* (New York: The Free Press of Glencoe, 1957), pp. 421–36.

equitable, they still were deprived of the satisfaction that people get from earning a legitimate decent living. In completing their self-fulfilling prophecies, if they were caught stealing they were fired.

Even men who had steady jobs knew that the jobs carried with them little prestige in the outside world and so frequently they felt ashamed of their work. Liebow relates this conversation with Tally, one of the men who hung around in front of the Carry-out and Liebow's chief informant.

"You know that boy came in last night? That Black Moozlem? That's what I ought to be doing. I ought to be in his place."

"What do you mean?"

"Dressed nice, going to (night) school, got a good job."

"He's no better off than you, Tally. You make more than he does."

"It's not the money. (pause) It's position, I guess. He's got position. When he finish school he gonna be a supervisor. People respect him. . . . Thinking about people with position and education gives me a feeling right here (pressing his fingers into the pit of his stomach)."

"You're educated, too. You have a skill, a trade. You're a cement finisher. You can make a building, pour a sidewalk."

"That's different. Look, can anybody do what you're doing? Can anybody just come up and do your job? Well, in one week I can teach you cement finishing. You won't be as good as me 'cause you won't have the experience but you'll be a cement finisher. That's what I mean. Anybody can do what I'm doing and that's what gives me this feeling. (Long pause) Suppose I like this girl. I go over to her house and I meet her father. He starts talking about what he done today. He talks about operating on somebody and sewing them up and about surgery. I know he's a doctor 'cause of the way he talks. Then she starts talking about what she did. Maybe she's a boss or a supervisor. Maybe she's a lawyer and her father says to me, 'And what do you do, Mr. Jackson?' (Pause) You remember at the courthouse, Lonny's trial? You and the lawyer was talking in the hall? You remember? I just stood there listening, I didn't say a word. You know why? 'Cause I didn't even know what you was talking about. That's happened to me a lot."

"Hell, you're nothing special. That happens to everybody. Nobody knows everything. One man is a doctor, so he talks about surgery. Another man is a teacher, so he talks about books. But doctors and teachers don't know anything about concrete. You're a cement finisher and that's your specialty."

"Maybe so, but when was the last time you saw anybody standing around talking about concrete?"[46]

The hopelessness of their economic situation made the men very "present" oriented. Since they know well that their futures are not bright, they take what pleasure they can get from life when and where they can get it.

The self-conception of the men as failures was reinforced by their job experiences and carried over into other areas of their lives. The men have pretty much the same idea of what a "good" father *should* be as do white middle-class men. However, because of the poor economic situation they are in and the resultant despair, they cannot live up to their own ideals. Many of the men do not live with the mothers of their children and others never see their children at all. The men feel very guilty about their failure to live up to their own image of what a father should be.

Liebow noticed that men seemed to be more affectionate to children who were not their own than to their own children.

This is even more clearly seen in the man who lives with a woman who has had children by another man. For these men, obligations to the children are minor in comparison with those of fathers living with their children. Where the father lives with his own children, his occasional touch or other tender gesture is dwarfed by his unmet obligations.

[46]Liebow, *Tally's Corner*, pp. 61–62.

No matter how much he does, it is not enough. But where the man lives with children not his own, every gentleness and show of concern and affection redounds to his public and private credit; everything is profit. For him, living with children is not, as it is for the father, charged with failure and guilt. Since his own and others' expectations of him as father are minimal, he is free to enter into a close relationship with the children without fear of failure and uninhibited by guilt. It is as if living with your own children is to live with your failure, but to live with another man's children is, so far as children are concerned, to be in a fail-proof situation: you can win a little or a lot but, however small your effort or weak your performance, you can almost never lose.[47]

This kind of subtle observation is typical of the insight that can be gained through participant observation but would be entirely missed in a quantitative study. The quantitative researcher must trade these insights that broaden our understanding for data that can be used to make generalizations. As Liebow readily points out at the beginning of his book, he only interacted with a small number of people on one street corner in Washington, D.C. He does not know the extent to which his observations would apply to other people in other places. Because each type of research, qualitative and quantitative, gives us something that the other does not, our knowledge will be best enhanced by an intelligent pursuit of both research strategies.

In-Depth Interviewing   As we pointed out at the beginning of this chapter the two most frequently used types of qualitative research are participant observation and in-depth interviewing. The latter technique is particularly well suited for gaining information on a topic about which the researcher knows very little. The major disadvantage of in-depth interviewing is that the people interviewed may distort reality. The subject may give the interviewer answers that he or she believes the interviewer wants to hear, or the subject's perception of "reality" may be severely distorted, or there may be significant discrepancies between the attitudes of the subject and

[47]Liebow, *Tally's Corner*, pp. 87–88.

the subject's behavior. Short and Strodtbeck provided an example of such a discrepancy in their study of delinquent gangs (see pp. 163–64). These problems are not at all insoluble, however. A good interviewer quickly gets a sense of whether or not the subject is "leveling."

Since in-depth interviews are not being quantitatively analyzed, "bad" interviews, those in which the subject is guarded or hedges, can simply be ignored in the analysis. But the primary method of handling the problem of the respondents' subjectivity is called "triangulation." We never just interview one subject. We try to interview as many different subjects who are familiar with a topic or event as we can. For example, in my interviews with the leaders of a teachers' union, which will be described below, I interviewed 25 different union leaders. I knew that each of them had a special point of view. But by asking all of them questions about the same events, I was better able to determine what had actually happened. Interviewing several people who have experienced the same thing enables the researcher to see what elements all those interviewed agree on and what elements there is disagreement on. Then, just like a historian, the researcher must sort out the "testimony" and decide what should be discounted and what should be accepted as valid. There are no standardized and infallible techniques by which this can be done. It is a matter of practice and intuition. Frequently it does not matter what "really" happened; what is interesting is the different perceptions of reality. However, despite all the techniques that can be used to deal with subjectivity of subjects this problem can never be completely overcome.

The major advantage of in-depth interviewing over participant observation is that interviewing takes much less time and requires less commitment from the researcher. Forty in-depth interviews can be completed by one interviewer in a few months. As we have seen, participant observation sometimes takes years of intensive work. Sometimes participant observation would be impossible—in study-ing events that occurred in the past, for example. But as long as participants in the events are alive it is possible to conduct such a study through in-depth interviewing. In some instances, participat-ing in an event or even observing it will so alter the situation that it becomes an impossible technique. Although some researchers might like the idea, participant observation is not a practical way to study the sexual problems of married couples. This topic can be studied by in-depth interviews. Let us now look at some examples of studies that have employed in-depth interviews.

In a recent study two sociologists interviewed 24 mugging victims in order to gain a greater understanding of what actually occurs during a mugging and the effect of the incident on the victim. The study showed that the victims had preconceived stereotypes of what a mugger looked like and were often quite shocked by the reality. One victim said:

> He looked so clean-cut, I would never be afraid— wherever, in the darkest alley—if I met any individual like that who is so clean-cut and so unlike the stereotype that people have in their minds—somebody looks scary or he's, you know, wild looking. He looked so wonderful, so proper and conservative and square and clean. . . . Really it was just as much of a shock as to who was doing it to me as the fact that I was being murdered, I was being killed.[48]

The Unionization of Teachers   In my study of the New York City teachers' union (UFT), 25 in-depth interviews with past and present leaders of the union enabled me to assess the impact that the union movement was having on improving the quality of education.[49] When I began my study I had been favorably disposed toward the union, as my mother had been its ardent supporter and one of the first teachers to go out on strike. However, after conducting the interviews with the union leaders I became convinced that the union was not primarily interested in improving the quality of education and in fact might act as a reactionary force blocking any innovative changes in the school system.

After the formation of the union there was a fight for control between two groups. One group, the "unionists" (the group that won the fight and still controls the union), was made up of professional union organizers and people who were more committed to

---

[48]Robert Lejeune and Nicholas Alex, "On Being Mugged: The Event and Its Aftermath," *Urban Life and Culture* 2 (October 1973):259–87.

[49]Stephen Cole, *The Unionization of Teachers* (New York: Praeger Publishers, 1969).

organized labor than to teachers. The other group, the "teachers," was comprised of militant teachers who cared very little about the affiliation with organized labor.

The "teachers" believed that the "unionists" were constantly sacrificing the goals of teachers in order to achieve the wider goals of organized labor. In the early days of the union organized labor did not want the teachers to strike because they believed that strikes would be a hindrance in organizing other white-collar workers. This opinion was expressed in an interview with one of the leaders of the "teacher" group:

> You see, the one thing the unions do not want is the teachers to strike. Because if the teachers strike, white-collar workers get shook up. They don't go for that at all. They want you to be happy with what you got. The standard practice is this: get into a settlement—cry out what we are going to do. We are going to march around City Hall—march, march, march. Send letters to your congressmen. March all around and then we'll have a strike, but we'll settle it before it starts, and then you come back since the people don't want to go anyhow. You come in with a big settlement, and you say what wonderful things you're getting, and you never really say what it is.
>
> Every teacher believes that Van Arsdale [a leader of organized labor in New York City] double-crossed us during one of the strikes, and he did. He said he would scuttle us, and he'll say it any time when he thinks he can get away with it. He doesn't talk this way now because we are too big. What do you need them for? Remember when the pilots went on strike? They weren't going to picket. They said you fly 'em yourself. I say you teach 'em.[50]

In contract negotiations the unionists were primarily interested in issues that would help the union, such as collective bargaining and dues check-off. The teachers were primarily interested in raising salaries and improving working conditions—prerequisites, they be-

[50]Cole, *Unionization of Teachers*, p. 168.

lieved, to raising the prestige of the profession and attracting qualified recruits.

The unionists were constantly trying to recruit nonteaching school employees into a union. The teachers, on the other hand, did not concern themselves with the other employees of the school system. The teachers wanted the union to control entrance standards to the profession. The unionists opposed this:

> There are some teachers who talk about that—about gaining control of entrance. I am not at all sure about that. I think that doctors are mostly fee-takers and don't work for anybody. . . . I'm not sure that teachers as an organization should get involved in a thing like that, and I rather doubt it. I tend to think that, unlike doctors, teachers work for an employer under salary schedules— that there are basic differences between different types of professions.[51]

It is understandable that the unionists should not have wanted to control entrance to the profession. If this were to have come about, it would have been more difficult for union leaders to make their usual distinction between the employer and the worker. Were the union to have an active hand in hiring, it would, in effect, be part of the employing group. Who then would be the enemy? For the same reason, the unionists opposed giving the union any role in supervising professional work. The union defined itself as the protector of the rights of teachers against infringement by the board of education, but, if the union itself were to apply sanctions, it would have trouble locating the enemy in the labor-management system. As a current UFT leader has said:

> I don't think that the union should be the person or the outfit that goes into the school and says "Now look, buster, you're not doing your job—you haven't been standing out in the hall, and we don't like the way you're making out your plan book—you're fired." I think this is the function of management.[52]

[51]Cole, *Unionization of Teachers*, p. 175.
[52]Cole, *Unionization of Teachers*, p. 176.

This view contrasts sharply with that of the leaders of the teachers, who believed it was the ultimate duty of the union to control entrance to the profession and to police its members, in much the same way the American Medical Association has taken responsibility for the professional behavior of its members:

> My point was that we need an increase in salaries to lure aggressive young intellects into this business who are willing to take it over and run it as it should be run. You say we have a Board of Education. The purpose of the Board of Education is to be a citizens' watch dog—not to run it. Because, if they run it *and* they are the watch dogs, they are going to cover up their faults—obviously. It should be run by the professionals. We, the people in the profession, should select who the teachers are with a system of ethics whereby if you are principal or assistant principal or teacher and you don't follow the system of ethics, you are called in by the organization and asked what are you doing—you're ruining it for us.[53]

The teachers believed the UFT leadership had done little to improve the quality of education in New York, because they had done nothing to recruit highly qualified teachers. They believed that only by successfully competing for talent with other professions and with business could teaching become prestigious. A leader of this group criticized the UFT leaders for failure in this respect: "I accuse Cogen and Shanker [leaders of the unionists] of only one thing: the significant failure to develop the stand-up image of the schoolteacher—to go out and get aggressive intellects."[54]

Some of the unionist leaders idealized "real" workers and displayed contempt for teachers:

> I like the way the TWU [Transit Workers Union] runs a strike. You go on strike, and you stay home, or you picket, and that's it. Teachers got to have meetings, they got to have dialogue—you know, educational campaigns

[53]Cole, *Unionization of Teachers*, p. 176.
[54]Cole, *Unionization of Teachers*, p. 177.

and literature and everything else for something that's very simple. You just stay home.[55]

Asked if his criticism did not really have to do with basic differences in attitudes between teachers and other workers, the same unionist replied:

> Yeah, unfortunately it does! I'm inclined to think that workers are a lot more intelligent basically. They see issues much more clearly than teachers do, I think. They can see clearly who the enemy is. Teachers are not clear—largely, I suspect because of the brainwashing on the college level. . . . They're not sure that the principal is not on their side or that the superintendent of schools isn't on their side.[56]

The unionists were committed to the union as a career, while the teachers enjoyed teaching and never considered becoming full-time union employees. I asked one unionist leader whether he enjoyed working full time for the union or would he like to return to the classroom. He replied:

> I think that, by and large, once you have tasted full-time with the union, the life is a different kind of life than a school, which means punching a clock, meeting forty kids, and meeting another thirty-five kids. It is less exciting. . . . I eat in the lunchroom. It's dull. Here I can go out and eat in a good restaurant. I can also order a martini before my lunch. . . . I don't think that after this I would be tempted to go back to the classroom. Don't say that I enjoyed this more than the other.[57]

I concluded that the unionist leaders of the UFT were not primarily committed to improving education and might act to resist improvements if they believed that innovations would jeopardize the power of the union.

This last quote in particular makes it evident that it is possible in

---

[55]Cole, *Unionization of Teachers*, pp. 177–78.
[56]Cole, *Unionization of Teachers*, p. 178.
[57]Cole, *Unionization of Teachers*, p. 180.

tape-recorded interviews to get at the real feelings and opinions of subjects, even when the subjects themselves realize that their attitudes may not be normative or even may be personally damaging. In-depth interviews offer the researcher an opportunity to learn the attitudes of subjects in much greater detail and honesty than do quantitative surveys. In quantitative surveys, there is a much more formal relationship between the subject and the interviewer. The interviewer reads short questions from a prepared questionnaire, and the subject must answer in one of the categories presented. The social setting of a qualitative interview more closely approaches a natural conversation. The interviewer, by establishing rapport with the respondent at the beginning of the interview, can make the respondent feel at ease to express his or her true feelings. The major disadvantage of qualitative interviews is that we do not know the extent to which we can use the information obtained to make generalizations about people who have not been interviewed. In the study of the teachers union this was not a serious problem, because I interviewed almost all of the union leaders.

Crucible of Identity: The Negro Lower-Class Family   An excellent example of the use of in-depth interviews is provided by an article by Lee Rainwater on lower-class black families.[58] Rainwater begins his article by discussing the research done in the past on race relations. Most of this research has concentrated on showing how white racism is responsible for the suffering of black people. Rainwater suggests that this is an overly simplified statement of the problem:

> As an intellectual shorthand, and even more as a civil rights slogan, this simple model is both justified and essential. But, as a guide to greater understanding of the Negro situation as human adaptation to human situations, the paradigm is totally inadequate because it fails to specify fully enough the *process* by which Negroes adapt to their situations as they do, and the limitations one kind of adaptation places on possibilities for subsequent adaptations. A reassessment of previous social

[58]Lee Rainwater, "Crucible of Identity: The Negro Lower-Class Family," *Daedalus* (Winter 1966): 172–216.

research, combined with examination of current social research on Negro ghetto communities, suggests a more complex, but hopefully more vertical, model:

White cupidity

creates

Structural Conditions Highly Inimical to Basic Social Adaptation (low-income availability, poor education, poor services, stigmatization)

to which Negroes adapt

by

Social and Personal Responses which serve to sustain the individual in his punishing world but also generate aggressiveness toward the self and others

which results in

Suffering directly inflicted by Negroes on themselves and on others.[59]

The major purpose of Rainwater's article was to show how the social conditions of blacks have caused them to develop family patterns in which blacks hurt other blacks.

Because urban blacks have been forced to live in segregated ghettos they have developed their own distinctive subculture. Rainwater describes those aspects of the subculture that affect family values and behavior. Particularly interesting are the attitudes that black wives frequently have toward unemployed husbands. Women tend to feel loyal to their husbands only as long as they are bringing money in.

Many wives feel they owe the husband nothing once he fails to perform his provider role. If the husband is unemployed the wife increasingly refuses to perform her usual duties for him. For example one woman, after mentioning that her husband had cooked four eggs for himself, commented, "I cook for him when he's working but right now he's unemployed; he can cook for himself."[60]

---

[59]Rainwater, "Crucible of Identity," p. 175.
[60]Rainwater, "Crucible of Identity," p. 190.

Rainwater relates the history of one of the families he studied:

> When the worker first came to know them, the Wilsons seemed to be working hard to establish a stable family life. The couple had been married about three years and had a two-year-old son. Their apartment was very sparsely furnished but also very clean. Within six weeks the couple had acquired several rooms of inexpensive furniture and obviously had gone to a great deal of effort to make a liveable home. Husband and wife worked on different shifts so that the husband could take care of the child while the wife worked. They looked forward to saving enough money to move out of the housing project into a more desirable neighborhood. Six weeks later, however, the husband had lost his job. He and his wife were in great conflict. She made him feel unwelcome at home and he strongly suspected her of going out with other men. A short time later they had separated. It is impossible to disentangle the various factors involved in this separation into a sequence of cause and effect, but we can see something of the impact of the total complex.
>
> First Mr. Wilson loses his job: "I went to work one day and the man told me that I would have to work until 1:00. I asked him if there would be any extra pay for working overtime and he said no. I asked him why and he said, 'If you don't like it you can kiss my ass.' He said that to me. I said, 'Why do I have to do all that' He said, 'Because I said so.' I wanted to jam (fight) him but I said to myself I don't want to be that ignorant, I don't want to be as ignorant as he is, so I just cut out and left. Later his father called me (it was a family firm) and asked why I left and I told him. He said, 'If you don't want to go along with my son then you're fired.' I said O.K. They had another Negro man come in to help me part time before they fired me. I think they were trying to have him work full time because he worked for them before. He has seven kids and he takes their shit."
>
> The field worker observed that things were not as

hard as they could be because his wife had a job, to which he replied, "Yeah, I know, that's just where the trouble is. My wife has become independent since she began working. If I don't get a job pretty soon I'll go crazy. We have a lot of little arguments about nothing since she got so independent." He went on to say that his wife had become a completely different person recently; she was hard to talk to because she felt that now that she was working and he was not there was nothing that he could tell her. On her last pay day his wife did not return home for three days; when she did she had only seven cents left from her pay check. He said that he loved his wife very much and had begged her to quit fooling around. He is pretty sure that she is having an affair with the man with whom she rides to work. To make matters worse his wife's sister counsels her that she does not have to stay home with him as long as he is out of work. Finally the wife moved most of their furniture out of the apartment so that he came home to find an empty apartment. He moved back to his parents' home (also in the housing project).[61]

A fight occurring within another family being studied reveals some of the family values that develop in ghettos and that, in turn, lead to self-destructive behavior:

The family involved, the Johnsons, is certainly not the most disorganized one we have studied; in some respects their way of life represents a realistic adaptation to the hard living of a family nineteen years on AFDC with a monthly income of $202 for nine people. The two oldest daughters, Mary Jane (eighteen years old) and Esther (sixteen) are pregnant; Mary Jane has one illegitimate child. The adolescent sons, Bob and Richard, are much involved in the social and sexual activities of their peer group. The three other children, ranging in age from

[61]Rainwater, "Crucible of Identity," p. 193.

twelve to fourteen, are apparently also moving into this kind of peer-group society.

When the argument started Bob and Esther were alone in the apartment with Mary Jane's baby. Esther took exception to Bob's playing with the baby because she had been left in charge; the argument quickly progressed to a fight in which Bob cuffed Esther around, and she tried to cut him with a knife. The police were called and subdued Bob with their nightsticks. At this point the rest of the family and the field worker arrived. As the argument continued, these themes relevant to the analysis which follows appeared:

1) The sisters said that Bob was not their brother (he is a half-brother to Esther, and Mary Jane's full brother). Indeed, they said their mother "didn't have no husband. These kids don't even know who their daddies are." The mother defended herself by saying that she had one legal husband, and one common-law husband, no more.

2) The sisters said that their fathers had never done anything for them, nor had their mother. She retorted that she had raised them "to the age of womanhood" and now would care for their babies.

3) Esther continued to threaten to cut Bob if she got a chance (a month later they fought again, and she did cut Bob, who required twenty-one stitches).

4) The sisters accused their mother of favoring their lazy brothers and asked her to put them out of the house. She retorted that the girls were as lazy, that they made no contribution to maintaining the household, could not get their boy friends to marry them or support their children, that all the support came from her AFDC check. Mary Jane retorted that "the baby has a check of her own."

5) The girls threatened to leave the house if their mother refused to put their brothers out. They said they could force their boy friends to support them by taking them to court, and Esther threatened to cut her boy friend's throat if he did not co-operate.

6) Mrs. Johnson said the girls could leave if they

wished but that she would keep their babies; "I'll not have it, not knowing who's taking care of them."

7) When her thirteen-year-old sister laughed at all of this, Esther told her not to laugh because she, too, would be pregnant within a year.

8) When Bob laughed, Esther attacked him and his brother by saying that both were not man enough to make babies, as she and her sister had been able to do.

9) As the field worker left, Mrs. Johnson sought his sympathy. "You see, Joe, how hard it is for me to bring up a family. . . . They sit around and talk to me like I'm some kind of a dog and not their mother."

10) Finally, it is important to note for the analysis which follows that the following labels—"black-assed," "black bastard," "bitch," and other profane terms—were liberally used by Esther and Mary Jane, and rather less liberally by their mother, to refer to each other, to the girls' boy friends, to Bob, and to the thirteen-year-old daughter.

Several of the themes outlined previously appear forcefully in the course of this argument. In the last year and a half the mother has become a grandmother and expects shortly to add two more grandchildren to her household. She takes it for granted that it is her responsibility to care for the grandchildren and that she has the right to decide what will be done with the children since her own daughters are not fully responsible. She makes this very clear to them when they threaten to move out, a threat which they do not really wish to make good nor could they if they wished to.

However, only as an act of will is Mrs. Johnson able to make this a family. She must constantly cope with the tendency of her adolescent children to disrupt the family group and to deny that they are in fact a family—"He ain't no brother of mine"; "The baby has a check of her own." Though we do not know exactly what processes communicate these facts to the children it is clear that in growing up they have learned to regard themselves as not fully part of a solidary collectivity. During the quarrel this message was reinforced for the twelve-, thirteen-, and fourteen-year-old daughters by the four-way argument among their older sisters, older brother, and their mother.

The argument represents vicious unmasking of the individual members' pretenses to being competent individuals. The efforts of the two girls to present themselves as masters of their own fate are unmasked by the mother. The girls in turn unmask the pretensions of the mother and of their two brothers. When the thirteen-year-old daughter expresses some amusement they turn on her, telling her that it won't be long before she too becomes pregnant. Each member of the family in turn is told that he can expect to be no more than a victim of his world, but that this is somehow inevitably his own fault.

In this argument masculinity is consistently demeaned. Bob has no right to play with his niece, the boys are not really masculine because at fifteen and sixteen years they have yet to father children, their own fathers were no goods who failed to do anything for their family. These notions probably come originally from the mother, who enjoys recounting the story of having her common-law husband imprisoned for nonsupport, but this comes back to haunt her as her daughters accuse her of being no better than they in ability to force support and nurturance from a man. In contrast, the girls came off somewhat better than the boys, although they must accept the label of stupid girls because they have similarly failed and inconveniently become pregnant in the first place. At least they can and have had children and therefore have some meaningful connection with the ongoing substance of life. There is something important and dramatic in which they participate, while the boys, despite their sexual activity, "can't get no babies."

In most societies, as children grow and are formed by their elders into suitable members of the society they gain increasingly a sense of competence and ability to master the behavioral environment their particular world presents. But in Negro slum culture growing up involves an ever-increasing appreciation of one's shortcomings, of the impossibility of finding a self-sufficient and gratifying way of living. It is in the family first and most devastatingly that one learns these lessons. As the child's sense of frustration builds he too can strike out and unmask the pretensions of others. The result is a peculiar strength and a pervasive weakness. The strength involves the ability to tolerate and defend against degrading verbal and physical aggressions from others and not to give up completely. The weakness involves the inability to embark hopefully on any course of action that might make things better, particularly action which involves cooperating and trusting attitudes toward others. Family members become potential enemies to each other, as the frequency of observing the police being called in to settle family quarrels brings home all too dramatically.[62]

The combination of in-depth interviews and field observation used by Rainwater and his research staff yields a detailed description of lower-class black subculture that would be difficult if not impossible to learn from quantitative research. In a quantitative survey the respondents would probably give answers that reflected their ideal values of family life rather than their real values and behavior.

The Poor Pay More In Chapter 6 we shall analyze in some detail a study of the consumer problems faced by poor urban residents. We shall analyze a series of tables that shed light on the consumption habits and accompanying problems of poor people. But this study, done by David Caplovitz, also contained a series of in-depth interviews with consumers.[63] These interviews give us a far richer description of the consumer problems than we can get from the quantitative survey. Of course, the quantitative survey, as we shall see in the next chapter, enables us to answer questions that we

[62]Rainwater, "Crucible of Identity," pp. 201–204.
[63]David Caplovitz, *The Poor Pay More* (New York: The Free Press, 1963).

could not answer with the qualitative interviews alone. Caplovitz uses the quotes from the qualitative interviews to illustrate ways in which lower-class consumers are exploited. One technique is "bait and switch," in which low prices are advertised but then the merchant tries to sell a higher priced item:

> Bait advertising was reported by a 37-year-old Negro mother living on welfare. She had seen a newspaper ad, placed by a 125th Street furniture store, announcing the reupholstering of couches with good material for $49.95:
>
> "I phoned them and they sent out a salesman. I told him I saw the ad and wanted my couch covered for $49.95. I asked him to show me the material. He pulled out some patterns and looked at them and said, 'These aren't so hot. I really want to give customers something they'll be satisfied with.' Then he flipped to the higher-priced patterns–*but I didn't know they were higher-priced then.* I picked out a pattern and asked him how much. He told me $149. *But I only had $49 in cash and wanted to pay only in cash, so I told him that this was too high. He praised the material so much, talking about its quality and durability, that I finally told him that if I could get an account I'd take it. He gave me a contract. I just took a quick look and signed it.* They sent for the couch and returned it two weeks later. The work on the seams of the pillows was awful. . . . Six months later the wire in the spring popped out the side and the other side had a pointed end on it."[64]

Another exploitation technique is the "misrepresentation" of prices:

> The manner in which salesmen lie to families about the cost of goods is revealed by another incident involving a door-to-door salesman selling washing machines:
>
> (Husband and wife, aged 33 and 27, Puerto Rican) "A salesman came to the door about three months ago and showed us a pamphlet with pictures of washing ma-

[64]Caplovitz, *Poor Pay More*, p. 144.

chines. He said it would be simple to buy it on credit. We met him at the furniture company, *where he showed us the machine and said it would not cost more than $290. So we signed the papers and didn't have to pay any cash.* When the machine was installed it didn't work.

"We called the store three times and were promised a mechanic, but he never came. *And we got a credit-payment book in the mail for $462.66,* saying we were supposed to pay $18 a month. *(They also received a sales slip, and on this bill there is a typed statement to the effect that a down-payment of $29.30 was made by Mr. R. Both Mr. and Mrs. R. deny any cash payments.)* A month later we got a statement saying that payments were overdue and we would have to pay 93¢ more. We don't want this machine and they're going to sue us."[65]

Most poor people are forced to make major purchases on credit for which they are charged exorbitant interest rates. What happens when payments are missed is vividly illustrated by the following excerpts from interviews:

We got into trouble with our first set of furniture. It cost $450. We paid $250 and were paying $17 a month. Then we missed two payments and they garnisheed my husband at the hotel. His boss said, "Straighten them out or else you're fired." We went to the store and offered them $75. They said they wanted more—they wanted every cent—and wouldn't take the $75. My husband went to Relief for help and they tried to get the store to take the $75 but the store refused. Then the Relief people told us not to pay them. *So my husband got fired from the hotel. He then went to work at a laundry and was garnisheed. We're still paying for it. We were cheated because we'd already paid $250, but on the garnishee we're paying $490, although the furniture was originally valued at $450."*[66]

[65]Caplovitz, *Poor Pay More*, p. 148.
[66]Caplovitz, *Poor Pay More*, p. 157.

In 1953, before we moved to the project, we had bought a TV and refrigerator for a total of $1600, including service, installation, and interest. We paid $790 on time. We were evicted from our old apartment, so we put the TV and refrigerator in storage. *Then my husband had a heart attack and was out of work. I was sick at the same time*, so we missed three monthly payments, which were about $31 each. We made our payments to a bank which was financing for the store. We went to the store and told them that we had moved and told them where the merchandise was. *Three weeks later a Marshal came to the apartment. He said that he must repossess unless some payment was made, at least $5 or so. I paid the Marshal $10.* A few days later I phoned storage and they didn't know anything. Then the storage house sent a note saying that the TV and refrigerator had been repossessed. *I phoned the Marshal, and he said not to worry "since you paid me $10 it won't be auctioned."* When we paid the Marshal, he said he would be back for another payment in two weeks. *The two weeks went by and then I phoned the store and they said the items were auctioned. I waited for the Marshal to come back, but he never showed up.* Later, I learned from a friend of my daughter, who works in the credit department of a department store, that I was listed as owing $383 to the store."[67]

These interviews give the reader an understanding of the ways in which poor consumers are exploited. The researcher can use the technique of in-depth interviews to emphasize the reality of the problem that is being described.

Community Studies Another type of qualitative research that has been used successfully is the community study. In this type of research a group of sociologists live in a town (generally a relatively small town) and use a combination of qualitative and sometimes quantitative research techniques to describe the social structure of the community. Robert and Helen Lynd wrote two books in which they describe Muncie, Indiana, both before and after the depression

[67]Caplovitz, *Poor Pay More*, pp. 162–63.

of the 1930s.[68] Lloyd Warner and his colleagues wrote a series of books on Newburyport, Massachusetts, which they called "Yankee City."[69] As an example of this type of research we shall describe a study done by August B. Hollingshead of a small town in the Midwest. Hollingshead's book, *Elmtown's Youth,* concentrates on the town's stratification system.[70]

Although we can discuss analytically the stratification system of the United States as an entity, the stratification that has the most effect on our lives may be that which occurs in smaller social units. For those people who live in smaller communities, in which most people know each other, rank in the local stratification system may be the most important factor in determining how other people treat them. *Elmtown's Youth* focused on the stratification system of what was seen as a typical midwestern American community and the way in which location in the stratification system affected youth.

When Hollingshead arrived in Elmtown he found that most of the people he spoke with had a very clear idea of the structure of the stratification system and who was in which strata. Hollingshead interviewed many people who gave him detailed accounts similar to this one:

> I know what the system is, and I'll try to tell you how it operates. I won't be able to tell you all of it, but I'll tell you the main class groups and the main sections in some of these classes, and I'll give you illustrations. We will start out with the top and work down.
>
> The top class is what we call the four hundred or society class. A lot of these people are three-ninety-eights, but they think they're Four Hundred. The society class has a lot of families on the fringe, families who have had money and lost it. This whole business is based on two or three things. First, I'd say money is the most important. In fact, nobody's in this class if he doesn't have money; but it just isn't money alone. You've got to

[68]Robert S. Lynd and Helen M. Lynd, *Middletown* (New York: Harcourt, Brace, 1929); Robert S. Lynd and Helen M. Lynd, *Middletown in Transition* (New York: Harcourt, Brace, 1937).

[69]W. Lloyd Warner and Paul S. Lunt, *The Social Life of a Modern Community* (New Haven, Conn.: Yale University Press, 1941).

[70]August B. Hollingshead, *Elmtown's Youth* (New York: John Wiley, 1949).

have the right family connections, and you've got to behave yourself, or you get popped out. And if you lose your money, you're dropped. If you don't have money, you're just out. There's no use talking about people being in a certain class or a certain portion of a class unless they are accepted by the people in that group as equals. If they're not accepted, they just don't belong in that group. So, acceptance is what I am going to use along with family connections and money. (Many illustrations of the "society class" were given here.)

The next class starts with the fringe and takes in certain other elements. This is what you'd better call the upper middle class. This level is made up mainly of the women who dominate the Country Club, along with some other groups, especially the top and the fringe. The society class dominates the Country Club, but not actively. They really control things from behind the scenes. The women in this class are very active in the social life of the Country Club; they split a gut to do things right. It's amusing the way the women in this crowd work and scheme for a little social favor with the society class. These women work hard to keep the activities going out there, but I'm pretty sure they don't have so much say-so in the Country Club as they think they do. Now here are some illustrations of the type of people you find in this class: (the interviewee used names, but we have substituted the occupations or positions some of the persons named held) the president of the First National Bank; the manager of the Public Service Company; the personnel manager at the Mill; most of the lawyers; several doctors; owners of large, family-operated farms who are interested in social affairs; owners of insurance agencies; the Superintendent of Schools (and persons of this nature). All the active leaders in the large churches in town are in this class, but most of them do not belong to the Country Club. They are just segments of the same class.

The next class down doesn't have any social connections of consequence. I call this the lower middle class.

You won't find this class with any social connections outside of the churches and the lodges. Lots of these people have good jobs with good incomes, and many have good businesses, but they don't have any social life at all. Their activities are wrapped up in the church, the Legion, the lodges, and the little clubs around town. Take Harry Glick, the foreman of the forming room at the Mill. Harry's a pretty good friend of mine; so I can tell you about his social life. It consists entirely, absolutely, and completely in going around to Catholic dinners. He really enjoys that. I guess it's all right if you enjoy that sort of thing, but I don't. There are a lot of people in this class who like that sort of thing. You go over to the Lutheran, the Methodist, or the Baptist Church and you will see them at every church dinner. These people go for church dinners in a big way.

A number of substantial farmers are in this class. They run their farms, pay their debts, send their kids to school, own good cars and machinery, and run their farms in a creditable manner. For instance, take Bill and Frank Emerson, who run the Emerson Implement Company. They're in this class. They have a good sound farm background. They went away to school a couple of years; later their father bought them that business. They started in a small way, but now they are coming along nicely and doing pretty well.

The working class is made up of good solid people who live right but never get any place. They work at the Mill, over in the Factory, and in the mines. They work as clerks in the stores, own little businesses like neighborhood groceries, a few trucks—that type of thing.

There is a really low class here that is a lulu. It is made up of families who are not worth a . . . damn, and they don't give a damn. They're not immoral; they're not unmoral; they're plain amoral. They simply don't have any morals. They have animal urges and they respond to them. They're like a bunch of rats or rabbits. Have you ever heard of the Sopers? They don't have any common decency. They're a tribe like the Jukes and the Kallikaks. They shell out kids like rabbits, and they never go any place in school. They're always getting in jams. The kids have been problems for years. The poor little kids are half-starved and ragged all the time. There are dozens of families like the Sopers in this town. They squat along the canal, and in back of the old tannery and up north of the tracks by the old abandoned coal chutes. A few are scattered in shacks along the river and out in the strip-mine area.[71]

Hollingshead finally decided that there were five "classes" in Elmtown and which class a person belonged to depended on wealth; life-style; participation in community affairs; and prestige, or standing, in the community. These five groups could be identified as (1) the old upper class, (2) the upper middle class, (3) the lower middle class, (4) the respectable working class, and (5) the "disreputable" poor. Hollingshead found that a group of community residents used as informants was able to accurately locate each family in this five-class stratification system.

The heart of Hollingshead's study was the way in which location in the stratification system influenced the teenagers in the community. For example, it was generally agreed on that the best student in the high school graduating class of 1941 was a boy from a working-class family. He wanted to go to college, but his parents could not afford it unless he received a scholarship from the school. But the scholarship was given to the daughter of a prominent middle-class family whose father brought pressure to bear on the superintendent of schools. Talking with one of the researchers, the superintendent said:

Last year, Henry Cross [father of the girl who won the scholarship] put a lot of pressure on me to see that Willa got the things they thought she should have. Henry Cross is a funny fellow, and it's taken me a long time to learn how to get along with him.[72]

[71]Hollingshead, *Elmtown's Youth*, p. 69–71.
[72]Hollingshead, *Elmtown's Youth*, p. 183.

This was not the only way in which the children of the more affluent and prominent families were favored in the high school. The way "detentions" were handled is another example. At Elmtown High School there was a rule that if a student was not in the classroom by the beginning of a period, he or she had to report to the principal's office and receive an entrance pass. If the principal thought the excuse for being late was not valid, the student would receive a one-hour detention after school. Hollingshead, who had a small observation desk in the principal's office, noted that students from the two upper classes and from the upper half of the third class rarely were given detentions. The excuses from students who were from the two lowest classes rarely were accepted. Furthermore, when students from the upper classes were given detentions, they frequently did not show up and no action other than a warning was taken against them.

Another way in which the class system affected the daily lives of teenagers in Elmtown was in the matter of after-school jobs. Most of the students from the lowest three classes had to take after-school and Saturday jobs to help out their families. Personal arrangements between parents and the proprietors of the various business concerns determined what kind of job a teenager could get. The "better" jobs, such as that of clerks in locally owned stores and offices, were mainly given to the children of lower middle-class families. Teenagers from working-class families worked in chain stores and as "mothers' helpers." The pay for this type of work was less than that earned by teenagers of lower middle-class families. The least desirable and lowest paying jobs were held by the children of the poorest families. Their parents could not help them to get jobs by speaking to the local proprietors, and many people did not want to hire them because of their lower-class origins. They worked at such menial jobs as washing cars, waiting on tables, janitorial work, and hauling garbage.

Community studies, such as *Elmtown's Youth*, differ in scope from the participant observation studies of urban communities that we discussed previously. The participant observers are usually only able to describe a small segment of the urban community and only limited aspects of the lives of the people who live there. Usually, for example, the work lives of the residents are ignored.[73] In most instances, the sociologists who do community studies cover all the major social institutions. This research provides us with a comprehensive study of the community. Unfortunately, it is virtually impossible to use such techniques to study large cities. Also, in community studies, as in other qualitative research, there is the problem of not being able to make generalizations from knowledge acquired. How do we know that Elmtown is in fact similar to other small towns?

Qualitative Experiments Sometimes sociologists conduct what might be called "qualitative experiments." These experiments differ sharply from the quantitative experiments described in Chapters 3 and 4. Control groups are not used and data are not analyzed quantitatively. Rather, the experiment serves to demonstrate a theoretical point. For example, sociologists may be interested in demonstrating the validity of the labeling theory. Labeling is a currently popular theory of deviant behavior that focuses on the societal reaction to the violation of social norms.[74] Labeling theorists are not interested in what causes people to violate social norms; rather they study how the reaction of society to such norm violation stabilizes deviant behavior patterns and in a sense creates deviance. Deviance, according to this view, is not an attribute of what a person does but rather of the application by others of rules and the punishment of "offenders." Labeling theorists define a deviant as an individual to whom a deviant label has successfully been applied. Deviant behavior is behavior that people label as deviant.

Labeling theory has been successfully applied to the study of mental illness. Sociologists argue that there are just as many "crazy" people outside of mental hospitals as inside. The factors that lead a person to be labeled as mentally ill and committed to a mental hospital have more to do with the societal reaction to people who violate norms than the characteristics of the norm violators them-

---

[73]An exception is William Kornblum, *Blue Collar Community* (Chicago: University of Chicago Press, 1974). Kornblum worked in a steel mill for six months. In addition to describing the work lives of the people he studied, he discusses in detail union and local politics. This book is unusual in the scope of activities it covers.

[74]For a discussion of this theory, see Stephen Cole, *The Sociological Orientation: An Introduction to Sociology* (Chicago: Rand McNally & Co., 1975) pp. 132–47.

selves. They argue that if mental illness really is a disease and the mentally ill person is significantly different from "normal" people, then doctors should be able to agree in their diagnoses and should be able to distinguish between mentally ill and "normal" people. What would happen if a group of perfectly healthy people were to turn up at a hospital clinic and complain that they felt internal pains and thought that they had cancer? After appropriate diagnostic tests had been taken, the doctors would conclude that the patients did not have cancer and must be hypochondriacs. What do you think would happen if a group of "normal" people went to a mental hospital and complained that they "heard voices"? The psychiatrists should be able to interview the people, perform some psychiatric diagnostic tests, and conclude that the "normal" people are indeed normal and not in need of treatment.

The social psychiatrist D. L. Rosenhan recently conducted just such a study.[75] He asked eight people who had never experienced any psychiatric problems to present themselves for admission at twelve different hospitals. All eight people were told to complain that they had been hearing voices, which said things like "empty," "hollow," "thud." Besides this pseudocomplaint and lying about their occupations (some were psychologists), they answered all other questions honestly. Before presenting themselves for admission, all eight people feared that they would be immediately exposed as frauds. Not one was detected. All were admitted and diagnosed as schizophrenics. After they were admitted, they claimed that their symptoms had gone away, acted normal, and tried to get out. The length of hospitalization ranged from seven to fifty-two days, with an average of nineteen days. They were finally released, with the diagnosis of "schizophrenia in remission." During their stay in the mental hospitals, not one staff member ever suspected that these normal people did not belong there.

When Rosenhan reported his results to doctors at a prestigious university medical center, they attributed the findings to incompetence on the part of the hospital staffs and claimed that such a thing could never happen at their university-run hospital. Rosenhan said

[75]D. L. Rosenhan, "On Being Sane in Insane Places," *Science* 179 (January 19, 1973): 250–58.

that sometime in the ensuing three months, he would send one or more pseudopatients to their hospital. Every staff member was instructed to rate each patient presenting himself or herself for admission on the likelihood that the patient was a phony. Judgments were made on almost 200 newly admitted patients in that period. Forty-one patients were rated as highly likely to be phonies by at least one staff member; 23 were suspected by at least one psychiatrist; and 19 were suspected by at least one psychiatrist and one other staff member. In fact, no pseudopatients were sent in at all. What does this prove? Staff members tend to assume that everyone who comes to a mental hospital is insane, and they treat him as such. When this "mental-set" is disturbed, and staff members are alerted to the possibility that some patients may not be insane, they then recognize that there may not be anything seriously wrong with a substantial minority of the patients.

The results of research done by Rosenhan and many others lead to the conclusion that there are some people in mental hospitals who are no more mentally ill than some people who are outside the institutions. There are undoubtedly a greater number of residual rule breakers outside the mental hospital than within. Erving Goffman, who has also done qualitative studies of mental hospitals, reaches the following conclusion:

> In the degree that the "mentally ill" outside hospitals numerically approach or surpass those inside hospitals, one could say that mental patients distinctively suffer not from mental illness, but from contingencies.[76]

What does Goffman mean by "contingencies"? In this context, contingencies are those conditions that affect the probability of a residual rule breaker being labeled as mentally ill. Thus, if we consider a group of people who exhibit the very same behavior, which individuals are the most likely to be labeled as mentally ill? Goffman details a few such conditions:

> Some of these contingencies in the mental patient's career have been suggested, if not explored, such as socio-economic status, visibility of the offense, proximity

[76]Erving Goffman, *Asylums* (Garden City, N.Y.: Anchor Books, 1961), p. 23.

to a mental hospital, amount of treatment facilities available, community regard for the type of treatment given in available hospitals and so on. For information about other contingencies one must rely on atrocity tales: a psychotic man is tolerated by his wife until she finds herself a boy friend, or by his adult children until they move from a house to an apartment; an alcoholic is sent to a mental hospital because the jail is full, and a drug addict because he declines to avail himself of psychiatric treatment on the outside; a rebellious adolescent daughter can no longer be managed at home because she now threatens to have an open affair with an unsuitable companion, and so on.[77]

The general argument here, as in other labeling explanations of deviance, is that we learn at least as much about deviance by studying the social conditions surrounding the individual as by studying the motivations of the individual.

The experiment conducted by Rosenhan and the qualitative observation work done by Goffman enable us to better understand how people are classified as mentally ill. This kind of understanding could never be gained from reading more impersonal quantitative studies. On the other hand, quantitative studies of mental illness can tell us a good deal about this phenomenon that cannot be learned from qualitative analysis. For example, a famous study done by August B. Hollingshead and Frederick C. Redlich shows that rates of mental illness are much higher among the lower class than among the middle class.[78] And a well known study by Herbert Goldhamer and Andrew Marshall has shown that rates of psychosis do not increase with industrialization. They concluded that rates of psychosis are not so much determined by characteristics of the society or its members as by the number of beds that are available in mental hospitals.[79] Once again, the obvious conclusion is that both types of research, quantitative and qualitative, are necessary to understand human behavior and society.

[77]Goffman, *Asylums*, pp. 134–35.
[78]August B. Hollingshead and Frederick C. Redlich, *Social Class and Mental Illness* (New York: John Wiley, 1958).
[79]Herbert Goldhamer and Andrew Marshall, *Psychosis and Civilization* (Glencoe, Ill.: The Free Press, 1953).

Chapter 6　The Role of the Sociologist and the Uses of Sociology

Scientists throughout history have been called on to justify their activities. Why should the society support the work of scientists? Is science of any use? All sciences, including sociology, have relied on two techniques of justifying their support by society. The first is that knowledge is valuable in its own right—the expansion of knowledge is one of the goals of human beings. The second is that the knowledge attained through science is useful in solving people's problems. Members of the physical and engineering sciences focus society's attention on how these disciplines have contributed to the enhancement of people's material existence. Members of the biological sciences point to the improvement in health and increased longevity as evidence that their work is indeed useful. The social sciences, which have received an increasing amount of support since the end of World War II, are today being called on to demonstrate their utility. Is sociology of any use? Although I believe that knowledge for its own sake is a valid justification for the social support of a science, it is clear that our society is unwilling to accept this as the sole justification for the support of sociology or any other science. Society demands to know whether sociology can be of any use in solving social problems. Before we can attempt to answer this question, we must consider what the role of the sociologist should be.

THE ROLE OF THE SOCIOLOGIST   For many years there has been a heated debate in the sociological community as to what the proper role of the sociologist should be. There are at least two important questions on which sociologists disagree. The first concerns the orientation of researchers toward the subject matter of their studies. Should sociologists be neutral observers and analysts of social events and structures, or should they *morally* evaluate and critique them? Should the sociologist be "value-free" or "value-involved?" There is no right or wrong answer to this question—the side a person takes depends on his or her own values. We should, however, be familiar with the arguments used on both sides.

Value-Free Sociology?   The sociologists who believe that sociology should be value-free argue that if researchers do not attempt to be objective and limit their own biases, then the results they obtain and the conclusions they reach have no legitimacy. For example, suppose the sociologist is interested in studying whether or not discrimination against women is occurring in a particular segment of the society. If sociologists start out with the strong belief that there is discrimination and that this is wrong and must be eliminated, won't they design their studies in such a way as to assure that they actually find evidence of discrimination? If their desire to prove that discrimination exists is greater than their desire to know the truth, then they will have difficulty in designing an objective study. They will also have problems in interpreting the results of their studies. Won't they be tempted to ignore any evidence that contradicts their beliefs and emphasize that which supports their beliefs?

Also, what happens if the evidence strongly contradicts the researchers' beliefs? If sociologists start out to prove that women are being discriminated against in a particular segment of society and they find no evidence of discrimination, should they publish these results? Supporters of value-free sociology answer affirmatively; opponents, more than likely, would answer negatively.

The essential problem involves the credibility of the results of the research. If researchers are not objective, why should anybody believe the results of their research? Sociology could become a crude attempt to justify a set of values or a political ideology rather than a way of discovering knowledge about human behavior. If sociology is not value-free, it could become nothing more than ideology. And if sociology becomes ideology or is used merely to justify a particular ideology, it will have no utility in solving social problems.

The critics of the value-free approach, of course, disagree with the above argument. They claim that leaving aside the question of whether or not value-free sociology is a good thing, it is impossible for the sociologist to be value-free. All of us have our own values, biases, and opinions. It is impossible to suppress them; they will influence the design of the studies and the interpretation of the results. We cannot be objective even if we try, and therefore we might as well make our biases explicit. Any attempt to hide our biases produces nothing more than pseudo-objectivity.

Furthermore, even if it were possible to be objective, it would be immoral for researchers to ignore the political implications of their work. Just as nuclear physicists should have refused to work on the development of nuclear weapons, sociologists should refuse to publish work that may have "undesirable" consequences. For example, even if some sociological research provided some evidence in support of the belief that differences in learning ability have a substantial biological component, the sociologists should refuse to publish this work since it will be used by racists to justify continued discrimination against minority groups. Ridding the society of discrimination is more important than discovering the real reasons why some people find it easier to learn than others.

Sociologist as Technician or Reformer? The second major question that sociologists have been debating is: Should sociologists be "technicians" available to society or should they try to change society to conform more closely to their own values? The people who believe in value-free sociology tend to take the first position; the critics of value-free sociology, the latter.

The people who believe that sociologists should act as technicians argue that how society should be organized is a matter of values and not science. Whether, for example, capitalism is "better" or "worse" than socialism cannot be determined scientifically. In fact, all important social questions facing us involve values. Should we have capital punishment? Should heroin be legalized? Should we have a guaranteed national income? Should we have socialized medicine? The answers we give to these questions depend on our values. Since an answer cannot be scientifically proven to be right or wrong, the sociologist's opinion on what *should* be is worth no more than that of anyone else.

Once a goal is determined, however, the role of the sociologist is to inform the society as to what techniques will be effective or ineffective in attaining it and, perhaps even more importantly, what unexpected consequences a particular course of social action might have. For example, let us consider the problem of urban crime. If society wants to reduce urban crime, some sociologists may suggest that one efficient course of action would be to legalize heroin. Since in some cities like New York City, a high percentage of crimes are committed by heroin addicts who must steal to support their habit, the legalization of heroin would reduce crime. This measure, however, might also have the undesirable consequence of increasing the number of addicts. Which is more important to society—the reduction of crime or the limiting of the number of drug addicts? It is the belief of the advocates of the first position (sociologists should act as technicians) that the question of the legalization of heroin is a political and not a sociological one. Each member of society can individually answer this question and can encourage his or her political representatives to act in the way each individual believes is right. Therefore, the sociologist's opinion on this question is no more valid than that of anyone else.

People who believe that the primary aim of the sociologist should be to change society reject the notion that the sociologist should be merely a technician, or consultant. These people argue that if sociologists are merely technicians, they will become flunkies of the ruling class. Only the rich and powerful have enough money to hire sociologists, and these patrons have a vested interest in maintaining the status quo. It is the moral obligation of sociologists to criticize and try to change society. Although it is true that how society should be organized cannot be scientifically determined, this is all the more reason why sociologists must take an active political role. They must become critics of the establishment and champions of the underdog.

As is typical in most ideological debates, the two positions that we have described are not as contradictory as they appear. And they actually have little effect on how sociologists go about their work. Let us consider the question of whether sociologists should be value-free. With few exceptions, most social researchers, whether they be radical, conservative, or totally apolitical, try to convince their readers that their research has been objective. Even sociologists with very radical views realize that few people will take their work seriously if it is obviously biased and subjective. If sociologists of any political persuasion want their colleagues to consider their studies and conclusions, they must convince them that the work was carried out objectively, even if its purpose was not strictly analytical. Thus, in practice, most sociologists who may argue that it is impossible to be value-free still continue with their studies, while working in an objective a manner as they can. There are, of course, some exceptions, but for the most part, they are ignored by other sociologists and nonsociologists alike.

It is important to understand that although it is probably true that it is impossible to be completely objective and suppress personal values, the extent to which objectivity is attained varies. Some studies will have been more affected by the researchers' values and biases than others. Since sociological research, once it is published, becomes public knowledge, it would be difficult for biases to go undetected. Research is subject to criticism and replication. Sociologists who would publish work that is clearly biased and could not be replicated by other researchers would lose credibility and have their work ignored.

The one area in which values enter sociological work in a potentially dangerous manner is in choice of topics. Conservatives may be more likely to choose to do research on areas of social activity in which the society is functioning well and ignore areas in which there are significant problems. Radicals may do the opposite. But since sociologists have widely differing personal values, this does not turn out to be a serious problem. Whereas the value biases of some sociologists may cause them to ignore a particular subject, the value biases of other sociologists direct them to the very topic ignored by their colleagues.

On the question of whether sociologists should be technicians or critics, it is reasonable to state that there is no need to have all sociologists be one type or the other. Here, as in other areas of human endeavor, division of labor solves the problem. There is probably a need for sociologists as technicians and critics, and indeed there are many sociologists who are one type or the other or both.

Now we can begin to consider the more significant question of whether or not sociology can be of any use in solving our social problems. Because we still have so many serious social problems and because in the past sociology has been of limited use in solving problems, some people argue that sociology offers no potential utility.

THE USES OF SOCIOLOGY In an age in which scientists and engineers can put men on the moon and synthesize life in test tubes, it is difficult to understand why our basic social problems remain unsolved. American society has shown great ambition and ingenuity in solving technical problems. In the last ten years, we have seen major advances in the space program and in medical knowledge. But we still face serious racial problems, poverty, inadequate school systems, and a polluted environment. I concur with the many sociologists who believe that the theories and methods of sociology can be used to solve societal problems. In fact, there is an increasing trend for the government to depend on social research in developing new governmental programs.

There are at least two obstacles to the use of sociological research to improve society. First, the interpretation of research results is rarely unambiguous. Sociologists often disagree about what conclusions should be drawn from a particular study. They also disagree on whether or not the methods used in a study are valid. When research methods were not yet highly developed, anyone disagreeing with the conclusions of a study could claim the researcher had employed faulty methods. However, as research methods become increasingly sophisticated and precise, it becomes more difficult to make such a claim.

A second major obstruction to the utilization of social research in improving society is that the great majority of politicians in decision-making positions ignore research unless a particular study supports a position they already hold. A good example is the pronouncement of Richard Nixon, who, as president, said that he would oppose the legalization of marijuana, regardless of what suggestions were made by a presidential commission he appointed. Another example of this attitude can be seen in the privately expressed view of a leading welfare official that the only purpose of research is to provide data to "prove" what he already knew to be true. He candidly stated that if the research did not support his position, then the research was wrong. As long as people who are in decision-making positions think this way, our social problems will remain unsolved.

What can the educated member of society do about this situation? It is often impossible for someone who is not a professional sociologist to decide whether a particular study is valid or invalid or which of two disagreeing social scientists is right. It is possible, however, for someone knowing a little bit about research methods to read reports or summaries of reports and gain a better understanding of the particular social problem. It is also possible for individuals to demand that their elected representatives take informed positions on key political issues. The more the individual understands and appreciates the value of sociological research, the greater the probability that this research will be utilized to solve social problems.

The primary purpose of this chapter is to show how sociological research can be used to understand current social problems. Before looking at specific cases, we must make a distinction between actual use and potential use. Although it would be possible to look at examples of actual use, the examples we discuss here emphasize the potential utility.[1] This is because up until now society has made

[1] For examples of the uses of sociology, see Paul F. Lazarsfeld et al., *The Uses of Sociology* (New York: Basic Books, 1967).

only minimal use of sociological knowledge. It is the purpose of this chapter to show you that sociological research should be done and that you should know something about it.

Descriptive Research To Determine Facts   As discussed in Chapter 2, descriptive research is necessary to determine what the facts are. If we are to eliminate discrimination against blacks and women, we must know in which areas of society discrimination is strongest. If we are to improve medical care, we must know in which areas of society the breakdowns in delivery of medical services are occurring. If we are to improve education, we must know under what conditions our school system works well and under what conditions it does not. We must discover the facts because sometimes commonly held beliefs are not true. For example, it is commonly believed that elementary school pupils learn more in small classes than they do in large classes. We will see that this belief is not supported by much evidence. In fact, reducing the size of classes will probably not result in students learning more. If this fact were accepted, we would be forced to look for other solutions to improving education. Sociological research can tell us which solutions are likely to work and which are not.

Explanatory Research To Discover Causes   Explanatory research, as shown in Chapter 2, is necessary to discover the causes of social problems. Knowing why a problem exists will be useful in suggesting possible solutions. Why do some young people become heroin addicts while others growing up in similar environments do not? Why do some children learn a lot in school and others learn very little? Why do some mothers on welfare utilize the medical facilities available to them and others do not? Why do poor people pay more for consumer goods than those with more money? Again, the answers to these questions are far from simple. But sociological research can provide at least some tentative answers. Because such research offers us better ways to improve our society, all of us should be able to read and understand reports of research that deal with basic social problems. In this chapter, we will analyze three examples of sociological research that are relevant for social problems. We will look at examples of research that contradict some commonplace beliefs and at one example in which the conclusions of the researcher were not really warranted by his study. We will examine studies that deal with the consumer problems of poor people, education of ghetto children, and social problems faced by black people.

Consumer Practices of Low-Income People The first piece of research we will discuss is a study of consumer practices of low-income people living in public housing projects in New York City. The research, done by David Caplovitz, was published in a book entitled *The Poor Pay More.*[2] The United States is a country in which people have an abundance of material goods. From childhood we are taught to want new cars, color television sets, washing machines, cameras, hi-fi equipment, and the like. Poor people are exposed to the same advertising and promotional campaigns as are wealthy people. How do people who do not have much money deal with their desire for material goods? We might think they would learn to suppress such desires, but Caplovitz found that this does not happen. The people he studied made many purchases of appliances, furniture, and other major consumer goods. In fact, they purchased just about the same amount of goods, such as television sets and appliances, as people with considerably more money. It turned out that even among the relatively poor people Caplovitz studied, the family's annual income was not the most important determinant of how much they purchased. In order to show the relative effects of income and need (as measured by family size) on consumer activity, Caplovitz presented Table 6.1

Table 6.1 is a three-variable table similar to those we analyzed in Chapter 2. The only difference is that in this table, each of the independent variables has three categories—three categories of income and three categories of family size. The dependent variable is consumer activity. This variable is an index based on the number of appliances a family has purchased and their intention to purchase additional appliances in the near future. Families that had purchased several appliances and intended to buy more are considered to be highly active consumers. Which variable has the strongest influence

---

[2]David Caplovitz, *The Poor Pay More* (New York: The Free Press of Glencoe, 1963).

Table 6.1. Income, Family Size, and Consumer Activity
(Percent Highly Active)

	Family size					
	1–3 persons		4 persons		5 or more persons	
Income						
Under $3,000	19%	(79)	41%	(46)	43%	(49)
$3,000–$3,999	26%	(46)	36%	(42)	49%	(53)
$4,000 and over	38%	(24)	49%	(39)	44%	(82)

Source: David Caplovitz, *The Poor Pay More* (New York: The Free Press of
Glencoe, 1963), Table 3.7, p. 147. Reprinted with permission of Macmillan
Publishing Co., Copyright © 1963 by The Free Press of Glencoe, a division of
The Macmillan Co.

on consumer activity: family size or income? To determine this, we
must examine the effect of one of the variables on consumer activity
within each category of the other variable. For example, how does
income affect consumer activity in families with 1–3 persons? We
see that families with high income are more likely to be active
consumers. The difference is 19 percentage points (38 minus 19 is
19). The difference in 4-person families, however, is only 8 percentage points.[3] And for families with 5 or more persons, income makes
no difference at all in consumer activity. If we now want to see the
effect of family size on consumer activity, we look across the rows of
Table 6.1. Among families that have income under $3,000 (the first
row), family size makes for a 24 point percentage difference. The
differences in the next two rows are 23 percentage points and 6
percentage points. Because family size creates larger percentage
differences than income, we may conclude that consumer activity is
more influenced by family size than by income. Large families
purchase the most, whether they earn less than $3,000 or more than
$4,000. Caplovitz concluded that consumer activity is more influ-
enced by need than by income.

Perhaps even more surprising than the small effect of income on
consumer activity was that the poorer the family, the more likely they

[3]When a variable has more than two categories and we are figuring the percentage
difference, we usually compare the two extreme categories, even if there is a greater
difference between one of the middle categories and one of the extreme categories, as
in this case.

were to pay high prices for the goods they purchased. The data showing this are presented in Table 6.2. This is really three separate two-variable tables. In each two-variable table, family income is the independent variable and the percentage who pay a high price for a particular appliance is the dependent variable. The first table shows that 46 percent of families in the low-income category and 37 percent of those in the high-income category paid a high price for their television set. For all three appliances, families in the low-income category are more likely to pay high prices than the families with higher income. Why are the people who have the least money most likely to pay high prices? Do they buy better quality goods? On the contrary, Caplovitz found the goods they pay more for are generally of lower quality. One reason poor people pay more for consumer goods is that they do not know where and how to shop. Instead of shopping downtown in discount houses and department stores, they purchase from local merchants who charge more and who use a whole range of unscrupulous sales tactics to cheat their customers. But perhaps the most important reason for poor people paying more is that they usually do not have enough money to pay cash and are charged high interest rates for credit. Caplovitz does not simply assert this; he has data to prove it.

Table 6.2. Family Income and Cost of Appliances

	Family income			
	Under $3,500		Over $3,500	
Television: percent high price	46%	(141)	37%	(145)
Phonograph: percent over $300	29%	(69)	21%	(71)
Washing machine: percent over $230	49%	(49)	35%	(69)

Source: Caplovitz, *Poor Pay More*, Table 6.2, p. 84. Reprinted with permission of Macmillan Publishing Co., Copyright © 1963 by The Free Press of Glencoe, a division of The Macmillan Co.

In analyzing Table 6.3 we first notice that those families who paid cash for their television sets were considerably less likely to pay a high price than those families who purchased their sets on credit. The next thing we would want to know is whether poor people pay more because they are more likely to use credit. The first row of the table shows that those families in the lower income group who paid cash for their television sets were no more likely to pay a high price

Table 6.3. Family Income, Method of Payment, and Cost of Purchasing Television Set (Percent Paying "High" Price)

	Family income			
	Under $3,500		Over $3,500	
Method of payment				
Cash	17%	(36)	14%	(43)
Credit	56%	(103)	47%	(102)

Source: Caplovitz, *Poor Pay More*, Table 6.8, p. 88. Reprinted with permission of Macmillan Publishing Co., Copyright © 1963 by The Free Press of Glencoe, a division of The Macmillian Co.

than cash-paying families in the higher income group. As we see in the second row of the table, however, poor people who used credit to buy their television sets were still likely to pay more. Caplovitz goes on to show that this is largely a result of where the television set was purchased. Low-income families were more likely to purchase their sets from local merchants, who charged more. Thus, the data substantiate Caplovitz's interpretation: poor people pay more for consumer goods because they have to use credit and because they do not know where to shop to get the best buys.

Even though low-income families buy most of their major consumer goods on credit, they must eventually pay for them. Because many families buy more than they can really afford, they often encounter serious financial difficulty. Caplovitz wanted to discover what types of families would be most likely to run into financial trouble. He developed an index of "insolvency." Those families who had no savings, no insurance, and a high debt in relation to their annual incomes he considered to be insolvent. It turned out that race was related to insolvency. Eleven percent of white families, 35 percent of black families, and 41 percent of Puerto Rican families were insolvent. At first Caplovitz thought this finding might be due to the association between race and family income. If white families earned more money, this could explain their lower rate of insolvency. To find out if income explains the relationship between race and insolvency, we have to look at the data in Table 6.4.

Table 6.4 shows us that racial differences in insolvency cannot be explained by differences in income. In every income category, blacks

Table 6.4.   Race, Family Income, and Insolvency (Percent Insolvent)

	Family income							
	Under *$2,500*		*$2,500–* *$3,499*		*$3,500–* *$4,499*		*$4,500* *and over*	
Race								
Whites	6%	(33)	8%	(24)	27%	(30)	4%	(28)
Blacks	44%	(25)	23%	(39)	36%	(42)	44%	(27)
Puerto Ricans	49%	(43)	44%	(88)	44%	(52)	18%	(33)

Source: Caplovitz, *Poor Pay More*, Table 9.11, p. 125. Reprinted with permission of Macmillan Publishing Co., Copyright © 1963 by The Free Press of Glencoe, a division of The Macmillan Co.

and Puerto Ricans are more likely to be insolvent than whites. An especially interesting fact, shown in Table 6.4, is that blacks in the highest income category are just as likely to be insolvent as blacks in the lowest income category. Caplovitz explained this by the interesting concept of "compensatory consumption." He meant that people who did not really have much of a chance to be upwardly mobile used consumption as the "one sphere in which they can make some progress toward the American dream of success. . . . Appliances, automobiles, and the dream of a home of their own can become compensations for blocked social mobility."[4]

It is possible that black and Puerto Rican families might be more likely to engage in compensatory consumption than white families. Because of discrimination, it is difficult for minority group families to be upwardly mobile. To compensate for blocked mobility, they might buy more goods than they can actually afford. So far all we have done is put forth a hypothesis. If this hypothesis is correct, then we should find the effect of race on insolvency low among families in which the father has a relatively prestigious job and high among families in which the father's job has less prestige. The data are presented in Table 6.5. Whereas the original percentage difference between whites and Puerto Ricans was 30 points, when occupational status is controlled, this difference is reduced.[5] In fact, among the highest status occupations—white-collar and business—race had hardly any effect on insolvency. The lower the prestige of the father's

[4]Caplovitz, *Poor Pay More*, pp. 12–13.
[5]This relationship was reported by Caplovitz. We could also arrive at this relationship by collapsing Table 6.5 (see pp. 51-52).

occupation, the greater the effect of race on insolvency. We know from Table 6.4 that this is not a result of different income levels. The data in Table 6.5 lend support to the theory of compensatory consumption.

Table 6.5. Race, Occupational Status, and Insolvency (Percent Insolvent)

| | Occupational status | | |
	Unskilled	Semi-skilled and skilled	White-collar and business
Race			
Whites	0% (16)	16% (45)	17% (24)
Blacks	42% (53)	29% (42)	25% (16)
Puerto Ricans	51% (81)	36% (73)	20% (15)

Source: Caplovitz, *Poor Pay More,* Table 9.14, p. 128. Reprinted with permission of Macmillan Publishing Co., Copyright © 1963 by The Free Press of Glencoe, a division of The Macmillan Co.

The research done by Caplovitz then, is one example of gathering and analyzing data that are relevant to a current social problem. The research also suggests some possible solutions to the problem. The study found that people generally pay more for goods purchased from local merchants, suggesting that educational campaigns be instituted to teach low-income people where and how to shop. But even if this could be accomplished, there would still be a major problem: credit. Because of their relatively low income, many of the people Caplovitz studied could not get credit at discount houses or department stores. They were considered to be poor credit risks. The local merchants were able to extend credit to these people because the prices and interest rates charged were so high that they could make money even if some of their customers defaulted on debts. A law limiting interest rates will not help solve this problem, because merchants can always raise the sale price of the items they sell. The passage and *enforcement* of laws prohibiting a charge in excess of the manufacturer's list price and in excess of a specified interest rate would probably help low-income consumers.

Another effective program might be a government guarantee on installment loans for purchases of items sold at a specified discount from the manufacturer's list price. This would provide incentive for stores to sell goods at a fair price and to extend credit to low-income families. Such loans would only be available to solvent families. Those families defaulting on debts would lose their credit rating. Laws making it impossible for retailers to extend credit to insolvent families would also probably be beneficial.

The Caplovitz study was important because it clearly indicated what problems were encountered by low-income families in purchasing major goods. With this knowledge, we are better able to predict what programs are likely to help low-income families and what programs are unlikely to work. Without studies like this one we have only speculation about the problems low-income people have in purchasing goods.

Compensatory Education Programs   The United States has always been a society with relatively high rates of social mobility. Children who grow up in lower-class families can become members of the middle class. Yet at any point in time only a minority of lower-class children achieve upward mobility. How are those who succeed different from those who do not? A college degree is virtually a prerequisite for entrance into an occupation granting middle-class status. Success in society at large is dependent, to some extent, on success within the school system. Because education is so important a determinant of occupational and economic success, sociologists have been interested in studying the educational achievement of low-income children in general and racial minorities in particular.

All studies show that black and Puerto Rican children achieve less in school than white children. Minority-group children score lower on reading, arithmetic, and other achievement tests than do white children. In what ways do the schools contribute to the poor performance of minority-group children? Can we change the schools to enable minority-group students to learn more?

Perhaps the largest and most systematic study dealing with how characteristics of schools influence the achievement level of students was done by a group of sociologists under the direction of James S. Coleman. This study is known as the "Coleman Report."[6]

[6]James S. Coleman et al., *Equality of Educational Opportunity*, U.S. Department of Health, Education, and Welfare (Washington, D.C.: U.S. Government Printing Office, 1966); see also the summary in *School Policy and Issues in a Changing Society*, ed. Patricia C. Sexton (Boston: Allyn & Bacon, 1971), pp. 55–79.

The data were collected in 1965 from 4,000 public schools in all areas of the United States. More than 500,000 students were involved in the study. The students participating in the study were given several achievement tests, and on all the tests, Puerto Rican, American Indian, Mexican-American, and black students received, on the average, lower scores than white students. (Oriental-Americans scored just about the same as white students.) Since most minority-group students attended segregated schools, the researchers thought that they could gain a better understanding of the variables influencing scholastic achievement by using the mean achievement test score for an entire school as the dependent variable and studying how this was influenced by characteristics of the student body and characteristics of the school. It might be interesting at this point to think of characteristics that we would expect to influence scholastic achievement of students. Generally, it is believed that children will learn more if they attend schools that have well-paid, highly trained teachers; small class size; and up-to-date textbooks and equipment. In other words, it is expected that students will learn more in schools in which the average cost per student is high than in those schools in which it is low.

The findings of the Coleman Report offered little support for this widely held belief. The basic conclusion of the report was that scholastic achievement was largely dependent on "input" variables: the characteristics of the students and their families. Students from middle-class families scored high no matter what type of school they attended; students from lower-class families scored low no matter what type of school they attended. Social class of students—and variables associated with it, such as a high concern with education on the part of parents—was the most important influence on scholastic achievement. Coleman and his colleagues found that when characteristics of the student body were controlled, school characteristics had only minor effects on scholastic achievement.

> The first finding is that the schools are remarkably similar in the effect they have on the achievement of their pupils when economic background of the students is taken into account. It is known that socioeconomic factors bear a strong relation to academic achievement. When these factors are statistically controlled, however, it appears

that differences between schools account for only a small fraction of differences in pupil achievement.[7]

The Coleman Report concluded, for example, that teacher-pupil ratio had almost no influence on the scholastic achievement of students. Two school characteristics that did have a slight influence on achievement were whether or not the school had science laboratories and the quality of teachers as measured by both the teacher's score on a verbal-skills test and the teacher's educational background. Schools that had teachers who scored high on the test and who had a relatively high level of education seemed to have more influence on achievement than schools in which the quality of the teachers was lower.

The Coleman Report concluded not only that input variables had a greater effect than school characteristics but also that individual achievement is more influenced by the characteristics of the other students in the school than it is by any characteristic of the school itself. If two children come from lower-class families, and one goes to a school in which a majority of children are from lower-class families and the other goes to a school in which a majority of children are from middle-class families, the latter child will perform better. In the same manner, it was found that black children in integrated schools performed better than black children in schools in which all the children were black. The most important policy implication of the Coleman Report was that the government could improve the education of minority-group children by promoting greater school integration. Placing black children in integrated schools will probably do more good than improving the quality of segregated black schools.

The Coleman Report received heavy criticism on methodological grounds. It turned out, however, that virtually all of the major conclusions of the study held up even after extensive reexamination of the data. Both the report and the criticisms are too complicated to be discussed in any detail in this book. Instead, we will examine a simpler study of the effectiveness of a program aimed at improving the education of minority-group students. Such programs are called "compensatory education programs." The program we will be discussing here is the More Effective Schools (MES) program, which

[7]Coleman in Sexton, *School Policy and Issues*, pp. 65–66.

was conducted in about 20 ghetto-area schools in New York City.

The More Effective Schools program was planned by a committee of representatives of the board of education and of the teachers' union, the United Federation of Teachers. The idea behind the program was that education in ghetto-area elementary schools could be substantially improved by vastly increasing the resources available in the schools. This was, in fact, done. In the 1966–67 school year, the average cost per pupil in ME schools was about $900. In ghetto-area schools not associated with the program, the average cost per pupil was about $450. Because the ME schools had considerably more money available, they were able to have small classes, a low teacher-pupil ratio, specialized teaching, and psychological counseling. In addition, more and better equipment and books were available. In 1966 the average class size in ME schools was 20; in other ghetto-area schools the average class size was 27. The teacher-pupil ratio in ME schools was 12; in other ghetto-area schools it was 21.

During the 1966–67 school year, a study was done of the MES program by a group of social scientists and educators under the direction of David J. Fox of the Center for Urban Education.[8] The study compared the ME schools with a sample of non-ME ghetto-area schools and with a sample of non-ME ghetto-area schools from which children were being bussed to achieve racial integration (called "sending" schools). These latter two groups of schools were used as controls. (Subjects in a laboratory experiment are randomly assigned to experimental and control groups, by which the researcher creates two similar groups before the experiment is conducted. In the MES study, however, students were not randomly assigned to schools, but on all variables known to affect academic performance, the students in the two groups of schools were alike.) If the MES program really was more effective than the regular school program, then the researchers would find that students were learning more in ME schools than in the control-group schools. The children in the control schools (regular ghetto-area schools) came from the same type of environment as the children in the ME schools. If the MES students did perform better, it could be attributed to the MES program.

[8]David J. Fox, *Expansion of the More Effective Schools Program* (New York: Center for Urban Education, 1967).

The research team collected a wide range of data. They observed hundreds of classes in both ME and control schools; interviewed teachers, administrators, and students; and collected test scores at several different times during the academic year. The trained observers, who visited both ME and control schools, were highly impressed with what they saw at ME schools. Teachers and administrators seemed to be happier, the buildings were more attractive; in general, the ME schools seemed to provide an atmosphere more conducive to learning. Questionnaires revealed that 100 percent of the principals, 92 percent of the assistant principals, and 85 percent of the teachers at ME schools were either enthusiastic or strongly positive about the MES program. Practically everyone thought the program should be continued or expanded.

The observers were asked to rate the quality of instruction in both ME and control schools on eleven dimensions. On six dimensions, the two groups of schools were alike; on five dimensions, the quality of teaching was rated higher for ME schools. In no case was the quality of teaching rated higher in the control schools. The report concluded that "the observers felt the teaching process was somewhat better in the ME schools."[9] The observers also rated the overall school programs.

> Half of the observers would have felt enthusiastic or strongly positive about sending their child to an ME school, a feeling not one of the observers had about any control school. . . . All observers felt the instruction they had seen in the ME school was worth more than the average school day, whereas the instruction they had seen in the control school was not. Obviously then, all recommended that MES be continued, although most wanted slight or considerable modification.[10]

Although the observers and all the adults involved liked the ME schools better than the control schools, thus far we have not considered the crucial question of whether or not children participating in the MES program actually performed better than those in

---

[9]Fox, *Expansion of the More Effective Schools Program,* p. 70.
[10]Fox, *Expansion of the More Effective Schools Program,* p. 82.

the control schools. We will look at two types of data: ratings by the observers on how well the children performed and scores on objective tests.

The data on the observer ratings of the students' classroom performance are presented in Table 6.6. Although the dimensions on

Table 6.6. Ratings of Children's In-Class Performance in ME and Control Schools

	Type of school		
	ME	Control	Sending
1. Verbal fluency of children who participated in lesson: percent better than average	22%	25%	21%
2. Children's interest and enthusiasm during lesson: percent better than average	51%	44%	47%
3. Overall participation of children in lesson: percent in which more than half the class participated	76%	67%	72%
4. Proportion of children who volunteered in response to teacher questions: percent in which more than half volunteered	40%	43%	32%
5. Number of children who raised spontaneous questions: percent in which half or more did	16%	5%	6%

Source: Adapted from David Fox, *Expansion of the More Effective Schools Program* (New York: Center for Urban Education, 1967), pp. 33-35.

which the children were rated tell us nothing about how much they learned, the data do give us information on the extent to which the children participated in the educational process. The results were discouraging. The difference between performance of children in the ME schools and those in the two groups of control schools was either minimal or nonexistent. In fact, Fox reports that only on the last dimension—the number of children who raised spontaneous questions—was the difference "statistically significant."[11] On the other four dimensions the differences between the ME and control schools were more likely to have occurred by chance.

A better test of whether the MES program was effective is the performance of the children on objective tests. The fact that objec-

[11]A percentage difference is statistically significant if the difference is so large that it would be unlikely to occur by chance (see p. 148).

tive tests are "culture bound" and have many faults is not important in this case, since the MES students are certainly at no more of a disadvantage than those attending the ghetto-area control schools. In fact, as was pointed out above, children in ME and control schools came from very similar backgrounds. Therefore, if the MES program was really working, the students who participated should have performed better than the students in the control schools. The data on reading test-scores are presented as medians in Table 6.7.[12]

Table 6.7. Performance on Reading Tests by ME and Control-School Students

| | | Median reading grade | | |
Grade	Type of school	October 1966	April 1967	Gain
2	ME	1.8	2.6	.8
	Control	1.7	2.3	.6
3	ME	2.4	3.4	1.0
	Control	2.4	3.2	.8
4	ME	3.3	3.9	.6
	Control	3.2	3.7	.5
5	ME	3.7	4.6	.9
	Control	3.8	4.3	.5
6	ME	4.9	5.5	.6
	Control	5.0	5.5	.5

Source: Fox, *Expansion of the More Effective Schools Program,* Table 10, p. 52.

The data indicate that students in ME schools did only slightly better than those in the control schools. For example, MES second graders improved their reading scores an average of .8 of a grade-school year between October and April of the school year; control-school students improved their scores .6 of a grade-school year. After conducting a very detailed analysis of the students' performance on reading and arithmetic tests, Fox concluded:

> The MES program has made no significant difference in the functioning of children, whether this was measured by observers rating what children did in class, and how

[12]A median is a number chosen so that one-half of the observed scores are higher and one-half are lower. This differs from the mean, in which all the scores are added up and divided by the total number of scores. Medians are less influenced by extreme scores than are means.

they do it, or whether it was measured by children's ability in mathematics or reading on standardized tests.[13]

The small measurable difference is even more disappointing when we recall that about twice as much money was spent on a MES student as on a control-group student.

Does this mean we should abandon programs that use funds to create small classes, attractive buildings, and fully equipped schools? Some would argue that even if such programs have virtually no measurable effect on the student's performance, they are worthwhile because they have the psychological benefit of making the students enjoy school more. The data of the MES report enable us to find out if this view is correct. If it is, then we would expect the MES students to have more positive attitudes toward school than the control-group students. The research staff administered question-naires called "My Class" and "My School" to all children in grades four through six in both ME and control schools. Students were asked whether it was true or false that "the teachers in this school want to help you"; "the school building is a pleasant place"; "I wish I didn't have to go to school at all"; and so forth. There were hardly any differences in responses of students to these questions. For example, 67 percent of MES students and 68 percent of control students said it was true that the "school building is a pleasant place." In 13 of the 17 items on the questionnaire, there was less than a 10 point percentage difference between students in the two types of school. We may conclude that the heavy expenditure of funds for the MES program did not even yield the psychological benefit of giving the students a more favorable attitude toward school.

Our discussion of the MES report might lead you to conclude that sociologists are always saying what will not work rather than suggesting what will work. Many studies evaluating social programs do conclude that the programs are ineffective, not because sociolo-gists are pessimistic nay-sayers but because, in fact, most programs do not really do what they are supposed to. If most social-change programs did work, our problems would soon disappear. It is often the case that studies of programs that do not work provide informa-

---

[13]Fox, *Expansion of the More Effective Schools Program*, p. 121.

tion that suggests another solution to the problem. This was true of the MES study.

The data presented in Table 6.7 showed that in grades two through six, the students in the ME schools made progress in their reading ability. They did not make much more progress than students in the control schools, but both groups of students seemed to be learning. We would think, therefore, that the students were attaining expected achievement levels throughout elementary school. The data presented in Table 6.8, however, show this was not the case. The first row of Table 6.8 contains the same data presented in the second column of figures in Table 6.7. These are the median reading test scores that were attained by MES students in April 1967. The figures in the second row of Table 6.8 show what the median test score would be among students making normal progress in reading. At the end of the second grade, the MES students were making fairly normal progress. In each succeeding grade, however, the gap between the achievement of the MES students and the norm grew larger. And by the time they reached the end of the sixth grade, the MES students were more than one year behind in their reading skills.

Table 6.8. Median Reading Scores for MES Students Compared with National Norms

	Grade				
	2	3	4	5	6
MES	2.6	3.4	3.9	4.6	5.5
Norm for date	2.7	3.7	4.7	5.7	6.7
Difference	−.1	−.3	−.8	−1.1	−1.2

Source: Fox, *Expansion of the More Effective Schools Program*, Table 9, p. 50.

How could the students have been making progress every year and yet be falling further and further behind? As Fox cleverly points out, to understand this paradox, we must look at what happened to the students between April and October. To continue to make normal progress, a student must continue to improve reading skills during the summer months. The data presented in Table 6.9 are taken from a considerably more complex table presented by Fox in

Table 6.9.   Median Reading Scores of MES Students Over
Three Years Compared with the Norm

	Expected improvement according to norm	Actual improvement
Third grade—school year	+.7	+.8
Summer between third and fourth grade	+.3	.0
Fourth grade—school year	+.7	+.8
Summer between fourth grade and fifth grade	+.3	−.4
Fifth grade—school year	+.7	+.8

Source: Adapted from Fox, *Expansion of the More Effective Schools Program*, Table 12, p. 56.

the MES report. The expected improvements in reading scores from specified time periods are shown in the first column. Students making normal progress will improve their reading scores .7 of a grade between October and April. During the summer months, students making normal progress will improve their score .3 of a grade. The numbers in the second column indicate that MES students made better than normal progress during each of the three academic years. *During each of the two summer periods, however, the MES students did not continue to learn.* In the first summer, during which normal progress would have been .3 of a grade improvement, the MES students made no improvement. In the second summer, the reading skills of the MES students *declined* by .4 of a grade.

Whereas middle-class children improve their reading skills in all months, ghetto-area children improve their reading skills only when they are in school. If this finding were to be supported by further research, its policy implications would be extremely important. More research may suggest keeping children in school for twelve months and giving them frequent short vacations rather than one long one. This does not mean that school during the summer months would be exactly like school during the regular academic year. A program might be developed in which scholastic activities are mixed with supervised-play activities. The students might study from 8:30 to 10:00 A.M. and from 1:00 to 2:30 P.M. Such a program might prevent the students from falling behind during the summer months and thus enable them to make normal progress in important academic skills.

The MES report offers us a good opportunity to discuss the role of sociological research in solving social problems. The report clearly indicated that the MES program was appreciated by all adults concerned but had little measurable impact on the students. You might think that after this report was published, the MES program would have been drastically altered or replaced with some new program. This did not happen; as of 1976 the MES program was still in existence. When the report was published, it was vigorously attacked by the teacher's union. Unlike the criticisms made of the Coleman Report, there was virtually no substantive basis for the union's attack on the Fox report. The union not only denied the validity of the report but made expansion of the MES a major demand in a strike in the fall of 1967. Why did the union do this? One reason for the union's action was that the MES program was clearly better for teachers. Teachers find their jobs easier when they have small classes and the school has many specialists and a lot of equipment. Also, the union had been very active in initiating the MES program and constantly used it as "proof" that the union was trying to improve the quality of education.

We can see that many social programs have vested interests involved. People who are involved in a program will typically be hesitant to admit it has not worked. Sometimes the curtailment of a program means the loss of jobs, and, therefore, the people involved can be expected to resist such a change. Social researchers can tell us whether or not a program is effective, but they cannot initiate or stop a program. This is the job of politicians and others who are in decision-making positions. A more complete sociological understanding of the reasons for resistance to change would probably help these people in acting on the basis of empirical social research.

There is resistance not only to abandoning programs but also to starting new ones. For example, even if further research were to suggest the value of keeping the schools open for twelve months, such a program would be difficult to institute. It is possible that the parents of children involved may not like the program and may view it as an attempt by the government to take their children away from them. State legislators may not like the program because it would necessitate higher school taxes. We must conclude that research is necessary not only on what types of programs will work but also on how to actually get people to accept new programs and abandon those that have failed.

Black Family Structure   In March 1965 Daniel Patrick Moynihan, then an official in the United States Department of Labor, issued a report that has since become one of the most controversial pieces of social research done in the last fifteen years.[14] The report, entitled "The Negro Family: The Case for National Action," had as its basic hypothesis that many intense social problems of blacks are a result of breakdown in the black family. A substantial minority of black children grow up in families in which no father is present. Such a family situation contributes to the poor scholastic performance and the high delinquency rates of black children. Is Moynihan right? Is family instability really a primary contributor to social problems faced by blacks? Some elementary knowledge of research methods and a careful analysis of the Moynihan report should enable us to answer these questions.

First, we will summarize Moynihan's argument. He begins by arguing that the traditional patriarchal (male-dominated) nuclear family is breaking down in the black community. It is being replaced by a matriarchal (female-dominated) family structure, in which the family has no permanent adult male member. Moynihan uses the absence of a father as one of the indicators of family instability. Other indicators of family instability are the proportion of illegitimate children and the divorce rate. Moynihan presents data, collected by the Bureau of the Census, showing that in 1960, 23 percent of urban black women who have been married as opposed to 8 percent of urban white women who have been married were living without their husbands. He also presents data showing that 24 percent of black children and 3 percent of white children are born to unmarried mothers. In addition, he points out that rates of divorce are higher among blacks than whites. Because of high rates of separation,

[14]Daniel Patrick Moynihan, "The Negro Family: The Case for National Action," in *The Moynihan Report and the Politics of Controversy*, eds. Lee Rainwater and William Yancey (Cambridge: MIT Press, 1967), pp. 39–124.

divorce, desertion, and illegitimacy, a substantial minority of black families are headed by a female, and, at any particular time, roughly 35 percent of black children are living in broken homes.[15]

After establishing that black families are more likely than white families to be headed by women, the report contains a section in which Moynihan tries to analyze some of the causes of black family instability. He traces the problem to the slave period, when black slaves were not allowed to marry and slave owners frequently split up slave families. In such a situation, the children stayed with the mother. During the Reconstruction, southern whites were afraid of black males, and the Jim Crow practices were set up to "keep the black male in his place." These practices made it difficult for black males to maintain their dignity and support their families. In the twentieth century, the process of urbanization further contributed to the breakdown in family stability.[16] In the rural South, families had been held together by social control in the local community. In northern cities, control of this type was absent and rates of desertion were high.

Finally, Moynihan analyzes the effect of unemployment and poverty on the breakdown of the black family structure. Statistics show that unemployment rates are much higher among blacks than whites. A man who is unemployed tends to lose his authority in the family, and such loss may be followed by separation, divorce, or desertion. Moynihan presents a chart showing that the proportion of black women separated from their husbands is closely linked to rates of unemployment.

> The conclusion from these and similar data is difficult to avoid: During times when jobs are reasonably plentiful . . . the Negro family became stronger and more stable. As jobs become more and more difficult to find, the

[15]Some critics of the report said that even if a higher proportion of black than white families are headed by females, it is only a minority of black families that are headed by females. The critics thought it was unfair of Moynihan to characterize the black community as having an unstable family structure, since only about 25 percent of the families were unstable by Moynihan's own definition. It should be pointed out that only a minority of blacks face social problems such as juvenile delinquency, and, in defense of Moynihan, if a high proportion of those blacks who come from unstable families are delinquents, this could be an important contributor to black social problems.

[16]E. Franklin Frazier, *The Negro Family*, cited in Moynihan, "The Negro Family," p. 67.

stability of the family became more and more difficult to maintain.[17]

Why is growing up in a matriarchal family harmful for children? Moynihan does not argue that there is anything intrinsically inferior about a matriarchal family. But he does claim that in a society in which most families are patriarchal, it is harmful for black children to be in a different type of family.

> It is clearly a disadvantage for a minority group to be operating on one principle while the great majority of the population, and the one with the most advantages to begin with, is operating on another.[18]

Moynihan then presents data to show that family instability contributes to the poor scholastic achievement and high delinquency rates of black children as well as high rates of welfare dependency. He cites a study in which it was found that black children growing up in families in which the father was present had a mean IQ of 98, as opposed to a mean IQ of 91 for black children growing up in families in which the father was absent. A study of school enrollment, from the census of 1960, shows that black children are more likely to drop out of school if they come from families in which one or both parents are absent. The same census study showed that black children coming from homes in which one or both parents are absent are more likely to be one or more grades behind in school than children who come from families in which both parents are present. Finally, Moynihan presents data to show how family instability contributes to juvenile delinquency. The full causal chain that Moynihan suggests is depicted in Chart 6.1.

Moynihan is saying several things: blacks have been discriminated against; this discrimination has kept most of them from rising out of poverty; poverty breeds family instability; and family instability is a major but underemphasized contributor to the social problems of blacks. By analyzing various links among the variables in the chain, we can find out whether or not the data support his theory and we can also see why Moynihan's analysis was so controversial.

[17]Moynihan, "The Negro Family," p. 67.
[18]Moynihan, "The Negro Family," p. 75.

Chart 6.1. The Causal Structure of Moynihan's Analysis

race → discrimination	→ poverty	family → instability	social → problems
1. slavery 2. Jim Crow 3. ghettoization 4. job discrimination	1. unemployment 2. low income	1. divorce, separation, desertion 2. illegitimacy 3. matriarchal families	1. poor academic performance 2. delinquency 3. welfare dependency

Note: Below each variable in the chain are the indicators that Moynihan uses in his report.

Moynihan has no data on discrimination, but we can easily accept that discrimination is at least one important reason why black people are poor. If we leave discrimination out of the chain, the first part of the chain would suggest that black people have greater family instability than whites *because* they are poorer than whites, and poverty leads to family instability.

$$\text{race} \longrightarrow \text{poverty} \longrightarrow \text{family instability}$$

Moynihan clearly establishes that rates of family instability were higher among blacks than among whites. Black children were far more likely than white children to grow up in families in which the fathers were absent. Why? Can racial differences in family instability be explained by racial differences in poverty? On the average, black people are poorer than white people. Moynihan himself has data to show that rates of unemployment are higher among blacks than whites. As you will recall the principles in Chapter 2, if the relationship between race and family instability can be interpreted by poverty or social class, then there should be little or no difference in family instability between blacks and whites who are in the lower class and between blacks and whites who are in the middle class. The hypothetical data would appear as in three-variable Table 6.10. This table shows that most black families are lower class and most white families are middle class. But if we compare black and white families from the same social class, there is no difference in the rate of family instability. Thus, 40 percent of both black and white families in the lower class are unstable, and 5 percent of both black and white families in the middle class are unstable.

Table 6.10. Percent Unstable Families by Race and Social Class (Hypothetical Figures)

	Percent unstable families			
	Race			
	Whites		Blacks	
Class				
Lower	40%	(1,000)	40%	(5,000)
Middle	5%	(5,000)	5%	(1,000)

The only data that Moynihan presents similar to that in Table 6.10 is presented in Table 6.11 which is taken from a small study done by Martin Deutsch and Bert Brown.[19] Table 6.11 shows that at every social-class level, black children were more likely than white children to come from families in which the fathers were absent. For example, in the lowest social-class category, 44 percent of black fathers and 15 percent of white fathers were absent from the home.[20] Therefore, on the basis of this table, we can conclude that something other than poverty must be the reason for the association of race with family instability. Moynihan does not present any data to substantiate the first important link in his causal argument.

Table 6.11. Percent Fathers Absent from Home by Race and Social Class

	Percent fathers absent	
	Race	
	Whites	Blacks
Social class		
Lowest	15%	44%
Middle	10%	28%
Highest	0%	14%

Source: Daniel Patrick Moynihan, "The Negro Family: The Case for National Action," in *The Moynihan Report and the Politics of Controversy*, eds. Lee Rainwater and William Yancey, (Cambridge: MIT Press, 1967), p. 82. Reprinted with permission.

Why should a table like Table 6.11 upset black leaders and liberals? If black family instability is not a result of poverty, could it be a result of race itself? Could it be that blacks are more immoral than whites? Moynihan certainly did not say this. In fact, Moynihan did not comment at all on the data in Table 6.11. Given the importance of the relationship among race, poverty, and family instability, we would expect Moynihan to have made some effort to

[19]Martin Deutsch and Bert Brown, "Social Influences in Negro-White Intelligence Differences," *Social Issues* 20 (April 1964): 24-35.
[20]Note that there are no indications in Table 6.11 of how many cases the study is based on.

gather better data than that of the Deutsch and Brown study and further analyze the interrelations among these three variables.

In the absence of data like those presented in the Table 6.10, the implication is that it is not poverty that leads to family instability but rather something inherent in the black subculture. The critics of Moynihan felt that he did not emphasize discrimination as the basic cause of black people's problems. They thought the Moynihan report implicitly suggested that the source of the race problem lay within the black community itself rather than in the white-dominated, prejudice-filled society. If the breakdown of the black family was the source of the race problem, then could it not be argued that entirely eliminating discrimination would not solve the race problem? Critics of the report argued that poverty rather than race was the major cause of family instability and that poor white people would have rates of family instability just as high as those of poor black people.

As we have pointed out, Moynihan had very little data on this point. In the census of 1960, from which much of Moynihan's data are taken, a table which bears directly on this point is presented (see Table 6.12). This table tells us that 21 percent of all black families with children and 6 percent of all white families with children are headed by women. The difference is 15 percentage points. What happens, however, when we divide the families up by income? Forty-seven percent of urban black families with incomes under $3,000 and 38 percent of urban white families in the same income

Table 6.12. Proportion of Female Heads for Families with Children by Race, Income, and Urban-Rural Categories

| | Proportion of female heads for families with children | | |
	Rural	Urban	Total
Negroes			
Under $3,000	18%	47%	21%
$3,000 and over	5%	8%	
Whites			
Under $3,000	12%	38%	6%
$3,000 and over	2%	4%	

Source: U.S. Bureau of the Census, Census of the Population: 1960, PC (1)-1D, U.S. volume, Table 225; state volume, Table 140.

bracket are headed by females. This is a difference of 9 percentage points. When we compare urban black and white families with incomes over $3,000, the difference is 4 percentage points. For rural families we get differences of 6 percentage points for families under $3,000 and of 3 percentage points for families over $3,000. Thus, when we control for income and whether the families live in an urban or rural area, the difference between blacks and whites in the proportion of families headed by females is quite small. We notice that in this respect, Table 6.12 is like Table 6.10, which showed that the association between race and family instability could be explained by blacks being more likely than whites to be poor.

According to the data presented in Table 6.12, income has a greater effect on family instability than race. For example, among urban blacks, income produces a 39 percentage point difference in the proportion of families headed by females. Forty-seven percent of urban black families earning under $3,000 and 8 percent of those earning more than $3,000 are headed by females. Without data such as those presented in Table 6.12, it would be difficult to assess the validity of Moynihan's analysis. With these data, Moynihan would have been able to say that one reason why black families are more unstable than white families is because black people are poorer than white people. A careful analyst, however, would also point out that social class or poverty seems to have a stronger influence on family instability than race. It is also true, contrary to what some of the ideological critics of Moynihan would have us believe, that race or some correlate of race other than poverty has *some* influence on family instability.

The most important part of Moynihan's argument is that the relationship between race and social problems, such as poor scholastic performance and juvenile delinquency, can be explained by the high rates of family instability among blacks.

race ⟶ family instability ⟶ social problems

Moynihan is arguing that one reason black people have greater social problems than white people is because blacks are more likely to have unstable families. How would one prove this? We would have to control for family instability and see if blacks and whites who come from similar families experience similar rates of social problems. The table should look like Table 6.13. The data in this table would show that blacks are more likely than whites to have unstable families (one-third of blacks and one-tenth of whites have unstable families); among stable families, however, there would be no difference between blacks and whites in the proportion experiencing social problems. If the family is stable, the rate of social problems is low (5 percent); if the family is unstable, the rate of social problems is relatively high (30 percent).

Table 6.13. Percent Experiencing Social Problems by Race and Family Instability (Hypothetical Figures)

	Percent experiencing social problems			
	Family stability			
	Stable		*Unstable*	
Race				
Blacks	5%	(1,000)	30%	(2,000)
Whites	5%	(4,000)	30%	(500)

Moynihan has no data similar to that in Table 6.13. The closest he comes are the data presented in Table 6.14. Let us take a critical look at Table 6.14. On the surface, this table seems to have the necessary data to test the heart of Moynihan's hypothesis. It seems to have the three necessary variables: race, family stability, and a social problem (juvenile delinquency). Table 6.14 should look like Table 6.13. We notice, however, that Table 6.14 does not tell us what percent of blacks and whites are delinquent (and it should since delinquency should be the dependent variable); instead it tells us what proportion of delinquents are not living with both parents. Thus, the table treats what should be one of the independent variables (family stability) as

Table 6.14. Juvenile Delinquents—Philadelphia—by Presence of Parents, 1949-1954

	White		*Negro*	
Percent not living with both parents	36%	(20,691)	62%	(22,695)

Source: Moynihan, "The Negro Family." Reprinted with permission.

the dependent variable. The table, therefore, cannot be used to test Moynihan's hypothesis. If anything, the table suggests that Moynihan's hypothesis is not correct. If family instability explains the high rate of black delinquency, why shouldn't black and white delinquents have the same rate of family instability?

In fact, Moynihan presents no data to support his contention that black social problems are in part a result of family instability. He does show that black children who come from broken homes do not do as well in school as those who do not, but he never shows that white children who come from broken homes do just as poorly. Perhaps Moynihan meant to argue that broken homes affect black children much more than white children. However, Moynihan never states this.

The Moynihan analysis of the black family contains many other inconsistencies or errors similar to those we have pointed out here. It is not our purpose, however, to present a comprehensive critique of this piece of research. Rather, we use this case as an example of how some relatively elementary knowledge of sociological research methods enables us to assess the validity of research reports dealing with critical social problems. We must conclude that the data presented by Moynihan do not offer support for his conclusion that family instability is a significant variable contributing to the social problems that are faced by blacks.

SUMMARY

There is disagreement within the sociological community on what the role of the sociologist should be. The first area of disagreement concerns the orientation that sociologists take toward the subject matter they study. Some think that sociologists should be value-free and neutral; others, that they must take a stand and be critical. The second area of disagreement concerns the role of sociologists in bringing about social change. Should sociologists act as technicians and merely tell the society how to achieve goals determined through the political process, or should they take an active role in setting goals? We point out that although both these points raise important ideological issues, they have little effect on the day-to-day activity of sociologists. In practice most sociologists try to be objective in their work no matter what their values are, and there are many sociologists who act as technicians while others act as social critics.

The most important purpose of this chapter has been to demonstrate that social research must be done to help solve social problems and that an elementary understanding of this research is useful. We have examined three detailed examples of social research dealing with three key social problems.

1. *Consumer problems.* In *The Poor Pay More*, Caplovitz showed that poor people face considerable difficulties in purchasing consumer goods. They are charged high prices for shoddy goods. The two main reasons why poor people pay more for goods than other people are lack of knowledge as to how and where to shop and inability to pay cash, necessitating high credit charges. The study suggested several possible programs to help poor consumers.

2. *Education.* The main conclusion of the Coleman Report was that school characteristics have only minimal effects on the achievement of students. David Fox, in a study of the More Effective Schools program in New York City, found that children in the ME schools did not learn any more than children in regular ghetto-area schools. The Fox study did suggest, however, the advisability of keeping schools open all year.

3. *Black family structure.* Daniel P. Moynihan argued that one of the reasons why black people face serious social problems is that they have unstable families. A careful analysis of the data Moynihan presents shows that there is very little evidence to support this argument. Understanding the logic of social research enables us to decide whether or not the conclusions reached are warranted.